THE DESIGN OF RIMBAUD'S POETRY

Yale Romanic Studies, Second Series, 11

THE DESIGN OF

RIMBAUD'S POETRY

John Porter Houston

New Haven and London: Yale University Press, 1963

Paris: Presses Universitaires de France

FOR MONA

Acknowledgments

I am indebted to Yale University for a Morse Fellowship in 1961–62, which made possible the writing of this book. I also owe considerable gratitude to Henri Peyre, who took a most generous interest in the project. Finally, thanks are due Alice-Augusta Miskimin and Thomas C. Witherspoon of the Yale University Press for their editorial work, and Mrs. James McGarrell for help with proof.

J.P.H.

Bloomington, Indiana
May 15, 1963

Contents

1. Introduction

THIS study was conceived in the conviction that
Rimbaud's poetry is in need of critical analysis as a whole
and that only by such analysis can we properly appreciate
his place in the currents of French literature. Rimbaud
has suffered as few poets have from extravagant tributes
and interpretations. The esteem he has for decades enjoyed
in surrealist and similar quarters has tended, at least in
France, to prejudice his position with serious critics; they
have been inclined to accept without question his reputation for utter hermeticism and to inquire no further. As a
result, discussions of his work tend to lack rigor and precision; they become lost in hazy divagations about the
poet's spiritual life and destiny. Nor do the traditional
biographies of Rimbaud discourage this penchant, filled
as they are with accounts of obscure events and unlikely
aspirations. A rather salutary attempt at undoing Rimbaud's bizarre legend and rescuing him from his admirers
was undertaken some years ago in a monumentally negative French thesis: the author maintains that Rimbaud
and his poetry have come to form the nucleus of an un-
wholesome myth of social, political, and religious dimensions, and ferociously demolishes it with the tools of
scholarship and cruel logic.[1] Without feeling precisely

1. R. Etiemble, *Le Mythe de Rimbaud*, I–II (Paris, 1952–54).

menaced by obscurantists and impostors, we can still wel-
come the application of the critical spirit to a subject
which is far from clear. The sobering perspective which
M. Etiemble's strictures provide can only inspire one to
seek out ways to discuss Rimbaud other than those which
have been current and whose validity has now been so
sharply questioned. To this end we must briefly consider
the nature and limitations of previous critical methods.

Since the study of his life has occupied the first place in
the attention of most of those who have written on Rimbaud, it is only natural that biographical interpretations
of his poetry have by and large prevailed. However, in
the case of Rimbaud two particular problems arise which
make biographical interpretations much more difficult
than they usually are. First, much of his work avoids anecdote or evident reference to real persons, places, and hap-
penings. For example, the pronoun *elle,* occurring without
antecedent in one of the *Illuminations,* inspires some to
think the poet alludes to his mother, since he is not known
to have often associated with other women. Yet one must
admit that such a reading is by no means so obvious as
most biographical allusions. Furthermore, the assumption
that by *elle* Rimbaud refers to his mother *because he knew
no other women* is somehow negative and subject to re-
vision should new information be discovered about the
poet's habits. Here we arrive at the second problem in
reading revelations of his life in Rimbaud's poems: his
biography is as yet very imperfectly known, despite much
research on the part of many people, and there is little
hope that we will ever learn a great deal more about it.
A large part of what we "know" about Rimbaud is derived
from the vague memories of contemporaries who were
unaware in the 1870s that they were enjoying the company
of a great French poet. Consequently the stories which
have come down to us are often conflicting and seem
strangely to reflect the intellectual, esthetic, and moral

prejudices of their tellers. This state of things should discourage one from asserting categorically that such and
such a poem records this or that hypothetical event in
Rimbaud's life. A neat illustration of this difficulty came
forth recently: one critic offered an unusual reading of
certain *Illuminations* as recollections of Rimbaud's extensive travels in Northern Europe on his return from Java
in 1876. The account of his voyage which inspired this
interpretation was, however, only one of several versions
of how Rimbaud made his way back to France, and, after
considerable investigation, another scholar has con-
vincingly demonstrated that Rimbaud's itinerary included
no more of Northern Europe than a few hours in England.[2] Such are the dangers of biographical interpretation when applied to so elusive a life and so ambiguous
an *œuvre* as Rimbaud's. One risks revolving in the closed
circle of deriving his life from his works and then interpreting the latter in terms of the former.

Ultimately, however, the objections to biographical
readings of Rimbaud's poetry go beyond specific problems
created by our ignorance of his life. Autobiography is
merely one dimension of a poem's meaning and frequently
a more intermittent and less important one than any
other. For example, that Rimbaud was an obedient child
gives him something in common with the boy in "Les
Poètes de sept ans" but does not account for the persistent
imagery of dampness in the poem. Furthermore, most
commentators on Rimbaud do not make the distinction,
common in present-day American criticism, between the
"I" of the author and the "I" of the speaker of a poem.
Failure to understand this difference leads one into intri-
cate bogs of literalism and effectively precludes any analysis of irony. Only by rejecting the confusion between

2. See A. Adam, "L'Enigme des *Illuminations*," *Revue des Sciences
Humaines*, 60 (1950), 221–45, and V. P. Underwood, "Rimbald le
marin," *Mercure de France*, 340 (1961), 635–48.

autobiography and poetry can we arrive at a coherent reading of *Une Saison en enfer* or most other parts of Rimbaud's work. Verlaine once said, in his customary strange prose, that in the case of Rimbaud "vie et oeuvre sont superbes telles quelles dans leur indiciblement fier *pendent interrupta*,"[3] and if we compare Rimbaud's poetry to Verlaine's own relentlessly autobiographical verse, we realize how right he was.

A certain confusion in critical theory reigns also among those who would read Rimbaud's poems as allegories. A common instance of this is to take the boat in "Le Bateau ivre" as the symbol of a child who is unhappy at home. So simple and univocal an interpretation hardly does justice to the complexity of the poem, and remains so abstracted from the text that it seldom intrudes as we read "Le Bateau ivre." The theoretical objection to allegorical readings of Rimbaud is that, properly speaking, allegory is a historical concept without universal application: allegory is largely a product of Classical, Medieval, and Renaissance culture and depends on a specific worldview, a particular kind of education, and a typological theory of literature. Indeed the usual allegorical interpretations are not even adequate to account for the richness of such works conceived in that tradition as the *Commedia* or the *Faerie Queene*.

There remain the doctrinal readings of Rimbaud's poetry. By this term I mean any criticism that presupposes a system by which Rimbaud produced poetry. The most frequently encountered form of doctrinal interpretation is that derived from the "Lettre du voyant," which explains away difficulties in Rimbaud's work as the results of his "deranging his senses." The noun "voyance" has even been invented to categorize further the demented state in which Rimbaud poured forth his glorious nonsense. To

3. P. Verlaine, *Rimbaud raconté par Paul Verlaine,* ed. J. Mouquet (Paris, 1934), p. 105.

speculate on obscure physiological states and to offer this
as explication for poems provokes the suspicion that the
problems of criticism are merely being eluded. It is too
easy to invoke Rimbaud's *voyance* in the presence of a
difficult poem. Other doctrinal interpretations of Rimbaud's poetry have been made, but most are variants of
biographical criticism, seizing on some trait such as "revolt" or homosexuality to "explain" poems on that basis.
There have also been occasional attempts to codify a
philosophy from which all Rimbaud's work might be
revealed to derive: treatises on alchemy and magic in particular have been examined in such pursuits. One cannot
object to this kind of study except insofar as it tries to be
systematic and abstract, and to regularize Rimbaud's
imagination. Certainly he underwent to some extent the
influence of occultist and hermetic thought, but after the
fashion of poets he used ideas and concepts toward poetic
rather than expository ends.

   In what direction, then, is a more satisfactory analysis
of Rimbaud's poems apt to be found? First of all, literary
history—in the sense of the technical history of poetic
practice—is useful not only in placing Rimbaud's early
work in relation to his contemporaries and defining his
originality, but also in elucidating the themes of his later
poems. We shall have frequent occasion to measure Rimbaud's poetry against that of Victor Hugo, the most influential poet of the nineteenth century; that of Baudelaire, the most original new talent of the mid-century;
and that of the Parnassians, who provide a general standard of poetic taste for the 1860s. Next come questions of
structure, prosody, vocabulary, imagery, symbolism, and
mode of imagination. Here, by freeing ourselves from any
concern other than for the literary practice of Rimbaud
and his use of the poetic heritage, we may profitably approach the problem of shape and meaning in his work.
The question of his poetic development, of the several

changes which his work underwent, will then arise, and
we shall be able to distinguish in it several periods and
kinds of inspiration, without, for that, losing sight of
certain elements of continuity.

In defining the mode of imagination characteristic of
Rimbaud's mature poetry, I shall often have recourse,
with some regret, to the terms myth and mythopoeia. I
am not concerned here with psychological or cultural
theories of myth but with myth as a purely literary phenomenon. For the purposes of this study we may distinguish two relevant aspects of myth, the structural and the
archetypal. In terms of structure, myth is characterized by
an organic, pre-logical vision of the world in which the
lack of distinction between the animate and the inanimate, sentience and lifelessness, is particularly noticeable
and which does not know rational categories of causality.
Such a definition is doubtless inadequate from an anthro-
pological point of view, but it will serve in analyzing a
certain kind of poetry.[4] A complex poem like "Mémoire,"
in which actor and setting are not discrete, partakes of
myth in this sense. As regards mythic archetypes, we are
again concerned with literature and not with extraneous
matters like Jungian psychology; the most obvious example of Rimbaud's use of such material is the journey
through hell which forms the narrative basis of *Une Saison
en enfer,* but we shall find numerous fragments of religious myth and symbol in the last verse poems. Finally,
certain *Illuminations* contain variations on an apocalyptic
myth which is Rimbaud's contribution to romantic visions
of history. Mythopoeia would seem to be the only adequate word to describe the imaginative process at work
in Rimbaud's later poetry, and despite the multiple connotations of the term I shall use it.

In the following chapters only brief and occasional

4. For more discussion of this question see H. Bloom, *Shelley's
Mythmaking* (New Haven, 1959), pp. 1–10.

biographical summaries are given; they are designed to orient the reader in time rather than to present new facts or unusual interpretations. I have felt it unnecessary to discuss Rimbaud's life at greater length because the fullest and most scholarly biography of him is written in English and has been revised to cover discoveries of recent years.[5]

Translations are included for long passages quoted from Rimbaud's poems. Since difficulties of vocabulary and syntax are to be met with even in his early work, I have thought it a useful part of the critical process to make prose renderings into English. These should not, however, be taken as having any esthetic value: they function merely as glosses to clarify problems in semantics and ambiguities of grammar.

Of the numerous commentaries of Rimbaud's poems accumulated over the years I have referred only to those which are pertinent to my discussion; in the case of oft repeated interpretations I have not alluded in footnotes to all the studies in which they may be found. One may legitimately feel dispensed from this task because of the extensive notes in the Pléiade edition of the *Oeuvres complètes* and the Garnier *Oeuvres.*[6] Indeed, the latter contains so abundant a commentary—with appropriate indication of sources—as almost to constitute a variorum edition. For the text of Rimbaud's poems I have followed the Garnier edition except when otherwise noted; for that of his letters, the Pléiade. In matters of punctuation, I have observed the French conventions and Rimbaud's idiosyncrasies, as his editors have recorded them. A line of spaced periods indicates my ellipsis.

5. Enid Starkie, *Arthur Rimbaud* (New York, 1961).
6. *Oeuvres complètes,* ed. Rolland de Renéville and Jules Mouquet (Paris, 1951); *Oeuvres,* ed. Suzanne Bernard (Paris, 1960).

2. Poems of 1870–71: The Emergence of Rimbaud's Voice

Brûlez, *je le veux*, et je crois que vous respecterez ma volonté comme celle d'un mort, brûlez *tous les vers que je fus assez sot pour* vous donner lors de mon séjour à Douai." Thus Rimbaud wrote on June 10, 1871, to Paul Demeny, the repository of a manuscript of his poems of 1870. This impatience with his past poetic inadequacies was to recur later on; it is a leitmotif of Rimbaud's career and one of the reasons why it is often difficult to trace his poetic development. He systematically lost, forgot, or repudiated previous achievements in the enthusiasm of new undertakings. There is every evidence that when he wrote the poems in question, he had already tired of an even earlier style, for he seems never to have mentioned to Izambard and Demeny, his mentors in poetry during 1870, that he had published a piece of verse in January before he knew them.

The origins of Rimbaud's vocation are lost in obscurity. The education he received was firmly oriented toward letters in the usual nineteenth-century fashion; difficult translation and composition exercises in both verse and prose and in French, Latin, and Greek were a staple of it. Thus a command of ancient and modern versification would have been a normal acquisition, but it does not account for his absorption of contemporary poetic idiom. Although we have some of the Latin verse he wrote at school in 1869–70, it does not illuminate this problem, being merely a pastiche, if a remarkable one, of Virgil and other standard authors and quite remote from his French style. All we can postulate is that much experimentation with the alexandrine and poetic diction must have preceded the writing of the first French poem of his we know, "Les Etrennes des orphelins," for the latter shows considerable familiarity with mid-nineteenth-century conventions of phrasing:

— Le rêve maternel, c'est le tiède tapis,
C'est le nid cotonneux où les enfants tapis,
Comme de beaux oiseaux que balancent les branches,
Dorment leur doux sommeil plein de visions blanches!...

> [The maternal dream is the tepid carpet, the cottony nest where curled-up children, like beautiful birds perched on branches, sleep their sweet sleep full of white visions.]

These lines are of course an imitation—at first or second hand—of Victor Hugo, who in his more sentimental moments liked to write about orphans and to compare children with birds. The repetition of *c'est* after a noun is in particular a favorite syntactic device of Hugo's. Nevertheless details like the "tiède tapis" and "nid cotonneux" (a most unusual and apt adjective) bear witness to a genuine and fresh gift for language.[1]

It is difficult to imagine why Rimbaud would have disavowed "Les Etrennes des orphelins" unless, perhaps, a

1. The source seems to be Hugo's "Les Pauvres Gens" (*La Légende des siècles*), which was published in September 1869 by the same *Revue pour tous* that printed "Les Etrennes des orphelins" on January 2, 1870. Coppée has also been suggested as a source; see the Garnier edition, p. 359.

sudden contact with the new Parnassian school of verse
made him impatient with the sentimental poems which
middle-brow provincial newspapers printed. In all likeli-
hood the latter provided his only knowledge of contemporary poetry until the arrival of Georges Izambard at the
Collège de Charleville in January 1870. Izambard, Rimbaud's teacher in *rhétorique,* the penultimate class, was
both quite young and an aspiring poet himself. He had
lived in the capital and was acquainted with the new
French poetry exemplified by Leconte de Lisle and the
contributors to the *Parnasse contemporain* of 1866. The
friendship that developed between him and his brilliant
pupil resulted in a considerable broadening of Rimbaud's
acquaintance with literature and a whole collection of
poems which reflect, with certain distortions, the literary
currents of the day.

This first traceable stage in Rimbaud's poetic development—for we may as well discount "Les Etrennes des
orphelins" and its unknown antecedents—can fortunately
be dated with some precision; a number of his poems
were read or given to Izambard during the spring semes-
ter, and on a visit to the latter at Douai in October Rimbaud copied out, evidently for publication, his works to
date, which he confided to Paul Demeny, a friend of
Izambard's and the author of a volume of verse.[2] It is
this group of poems which eight months later Rimbaud
asked to have destroyed. Fortunately Demeny did not
comply, since otherwise our picture of Rimbaud's poetic
production would be even more eccentric than it is.

The Demeny Manuscript, as this collection is called,
contains twenty-two poems. Some of these are exemplary
imitations of mid-nineteenth-century poets who, under

2. A few problems in dating Rimbaud's early poems still remain.
For a speculative attempt to date them by vocabulary see F. J. Car-
mody, "A Correlation of the Chronology and the Lexicon of Rimbaud's Verse," *French Review, 33* (1960), 247–56.

the spell of Hugo's *Légende des siècles* and Leconte de
Lisle's various volumes, had come to accept the evocation
of legendary, historical, and exotic scenes as a major function of serious poetry. Among other things Rimbaud
wrote a description of the dead Ophelia, which is suitably
colorful, and a "Bal des pendus," where he expresses the
late medieval obsession with death. These poems seem a
bit quaint and Victorian at present, but if we look through
the *Parnasse contemporain* of 1866, the most distinguished
anthology of Second Empire poetry, Rimbaud's efforts
hardly seem inferior to what older and supposedly more
mature poets were writing. In fact these early poems are
so adeptly put together that they seem almost to be
parodies. A particularly pertinent example of Rimbaud's
assimilation of Parnassian ideals is "Soleil et chair" or
"Credo in unam," as he more blasphemously entitled it
in another manuscript:

> Je crois en toi! je crois en toi! Divine mère,
> Aphrodité marine! — Oh! la route est amère
> Depuis que l'autre Dieu nous attelle à sa croix . . .

> [I believe in thee! I believe in thee! Divine mother,
> Aphrodite of the sea! Oh, the road has been bitter
> since the other god hitched us to his cross . . .]

Nothing could have been more normal in 1870 than a
profession of faith in Aphrodite (and not Venus, for
Leconte de Lisle had launched the fashion of transcribing
the Greek names of deities rather than using the traditionally Roman form). As early as 1852 Baudelaire had
protested against the absurdity of the Pagan School and
its polemics against the Vile Galilean, but this kind of
"Hellenism" raged on unabated. The *Parnasse contemporain* is by no means lacking in testimonials to the longev-
ity of the old gods. The Greek pantheon, interpreted as
a symbol of vitality and hedonism, still provided a battle

cry for any poet irritated by the trammels of nineteenth-century life; modern anthropology did not yet exist, and classical religion was romantically conceived of as the apotheosis of Wisdom, Harmony, Nature, and Love. Rimbaud faithfully and eloquently repeats his elders—a proof of how readily Paganism was professed even by those who had not much practical experience of it.

If Paganism was exalted by the poets, one could hardly expect them to sympathize with Louis-Napoléon's cautious *entente* with the Church and the bourgeoisie. Some spared no contempt for his regime and expressed ferociously republican sentiments. The closing years of the Empire were especially marked by a recrudescence of political fervor, and with the outbreak of the Franco-Prussian War and the subsequent fall of Louis-Napoléon, few people refrained from proposing some scheme of national salvation. Victor Hugo was the great prototype of the opposition poet, and Rimbaud, when it came his turn to vilify the Empire, understandably adopted as his model the *Châtiments,* the great nineteenth-century monument of verse satire in which the exiled poet scourged Louis-Napoléon. Rimbaud's republicanism resembles Hugo's in its emotional ardor and doctrinal imprecision; it is therefore not surprising that their satirical techniques are similar. In the following lines Rimbaud is scathing a pair of Bonapartists who dared to call on all Frenchmen, of whatever political color, to rally in defense of the Empire:

Morts de Quatre-vingt-douze et de Quatre-vingt-treize,
Qui, pâles du baiser fort de la liberté,
Calmes, sous vos sabots, brisiez le joug qui pèse
Sur l'âme et sur le front de toute humanité;

. . . .

Vous dont le sang lavait toute grandeur salie,
Morts de Valmy, Morts de Fleurus, Morts d'Italie,
O millions de Christs aux yeux sombres et doux;

Nous vous laissions dormir avec la République,
Nous, courbés sous les rois comme sous une trique.
— Messieurs de Cassagnac nous reparlent de vous!

> [Dead of '92 and '93, who, pale with the strong kiss of
> liberty, calm, broke under your clogs the yoke weigh-
> ing on the soul and brow of all humanity . . . You
> whose blood washed clean all sullied greatness, dead
> of Valmy, of Fleurus, of the Italian campaigns, O
> millions of dark and gentle-eyed Christs; we, bowed
> beneath kings as if under a cudgel, we let you sleep
> with the Republic—Messieurs de Cassagnac recall
> you to us!]

Following a favorite Hugolian pattern, Rimbaud first
evokes a hazy, almost mythical vision of the Revolution
in which proper historical distinctions are somewhat effaced: '92 and '93 are usually considered very different
moments of the Revolution; the battles of Valmy (1792)
and Fleurus (1794) do not have the ominous Napoleonic
associations of the Italian campaigns, and finally the use
of Christ as a kind of common noun casts a rich emotive
glow without much semantic precision. The orotund flow
of apostrophes and appositions succeeds, however, in
welding together these slightly disparate elements into a
sonorous whole, a whole which is shattered by the introduction of the minor provincial journalists Cassagnac into
this recital of glorious proper names. As elsewhere in his
political satires, Rimbaud exploits Hugo's device of
bathos; the satire lacks intellectual force or coherence and
depends solely on verbal incongruity. Naturally such
verse is now as limited in interest as neo-Pagan dithy-
rambs, but in 1870 it was living and relevant; Rimbaud
significantly did not confine himself to Parnassian estheticism but seized on timely themes as well.

In addition to the more ambitious Parnassian and in-
vective styles Rimbaud also tried his hand at lighter verse,

conversational in tone, and in this respect he showed himself to be very much abreast of the poetic problems of the day. The major French romantic poets had gorgeously enriched the vocabulary of the language, but with their preference for elevated subjects and magnificent periods they had rarely—with the exception of Musset—concerned themselves with colloquial verse. All their effort had been spent in liberating poetry from the accretion of decades of hackneyed neo-classical diction. Slowly, however, there grew an interest in more intimate, less lofty poetry; the eloquence of Hugo's later works was such as to discourage any further exploration into verbal grandeur. Banville had begun to experiment with buffoonish styles rather than risk the curse of rewriting Hugo *en pire*, and Baudelaire frequently exploited a quiet, ironic vein. Even Hugo himself sensed the need for a lighter manner; he published *Les Chansons des rues et des bois* (1865) just at a time when younger poets, among whom Verlaine and Coppée are best known, had found that the immediate future of French poetry lay in low-keyed, conversational verse. Rimbaud somehow perceived these only half-discovered resources very early and wrote a number of charming if slight poems in a naïve, engaging style. With both lyricism and humor they treat of adolescent love and its ceremonial. "Roman" is particularly skillful:

I

On n'est pas sérieux, quand on a dix-sept ans.
— Un beau soir, foin des bocks et de la limonade,
Des cafés tapageurs aux lustres éclatants!
— On va sous les tilleuls verts de la promenade.

Les tilleuls sentent bon dans les bons soirs de juin!
L'air est parfois si doux, qu'on ferme la paupière;
Le vent chargé de bruits, — la ville n'est pas loin, —
A des parfums de vigne et des parfums de bière...

II

— Voilà qu'on aperçoit un tout petit chiffon
D'azur sombre, encadré d'une petite branche,
Piqué d'une mauvaise étoile, qui se fond
Avec de doux frissons, petite et toute blanche...

Nuit de juin! Dix-sept ans! — On se laisse griser.
La sève est du champagne et vous monte à la tête...
On divague; on se sent aux lèvres un baiser
Qui palpite là, comme une petite bête...

[You're not serious when you're seventeen. Some nice evening, to hell with beer and lemonade, noisy cafés and their shining lamps. You go out under the green linden trees in the park. The lindens smell good in the good June evenings! The air is sometimes so balmy that you close your eyes. The wind filled with sounds—the town isn't far—brings the scent of grape-vines and beer.

Up there you can see a little scrap of dark blue, framed by a little branch and pinned up with a wretched star, which is melting away in gentle quivers, little and quite white. June night! Age seventeen! You let yourself be overcome. Your sap is champagne and goes to your head. You talk on; you feel a kiss on your lips, palpitating there like a little bug.]

The colloquial tone is perfectly created by the humble, provincial scene evoked, the simple prose-movement of the syntax, and the fancifulness of the star and kiss images. The careful divisions of the material into stanzas and parts also strikes the attention: Rimbaud's earlier verse tends to be meticulously planned in accordance with the principles of order and clarity favored by the Parnassians. The setting is built up in well thought-out steps (the promenade, the evening air, the sky, and the narrator's emotions) so as to prepare the inevitable appearance of a young lady:

III

Le coeur fou Robinsonne à travers les romans,
— Lorsque, dans la clarté d'un pâle réverbère,
Passe une demoiselle aux petits airs charmants,
Sous l'ombre du faux-col effrayant de son père...

Et, comme elle vous trouve immensément naïf,
Tout en faisant trotter ses petites bottines,
Elle se tourne, alerte et d'un mouvement vif...
— Sur vos lèvres alors meurent les cavatines...

> [Your wild heart wanders like Crusoe through ro-
> mances—when, in the pale light of a streetlamp, a
> young lady goes by under the terrible shadow of her
> father's detachable collar. And since she finds you
> incredibly silly, while clicking along in her little high-
> shoes, she turns her head in a quick, lively way—then
> the cavatinas die on your lips.]

The use of the second person and the indefinite *on* provides a delicate ironic balance between participation and
objectivity; Rimbaud avoids at once the dangers of a coy
je or of a remote, impersonal speaker. Much of the charm
of the poem lies, furthermore, in its use of ellipsis: only
acts and gestures are described, and no attempt is made
to elucidate the essentially uninteresting adolescent psychology involved:

IV

Vous êtes amoureux. Loué jusqu'au mois d'août.
Vous êtes amoureux. — Vos sonnets La font rire.
Tous vos amis s'en vont, vous êtes mauvais goût.
— Puis l'adorée, un soir, a daigné vous écrire!...

— Ce soir-là,... — vous rentrez aux cafés éclatants,
Vous demandez des bocks ou de la limonade...
— On n'est pas sérieux, quand on a dix-sept ans
Et qu'on a des tilleuls verts sur la promenade.

> [You are in love. Occupied till August. You are in
> love. Your sonnets make Her laugh. All your friends
> go away, you're ridiculous. Then the adored one, one
> evening, has deigned to write you. That evening you
> go back to the shining cafés, you ask for beer or
> lemonade. You're not serious when you're seventeen
> and you have the green lindens in the park.]

The last stanza with its return to the words and phrases
of the opening one follows a pattern very characteristic of
nineteenth-century French verse: framing lines and refrains were widely used as structuring devices, and Rimbaud's variation on the basic pattern (the words slightly
shift position) demonstrates his precocious skill.

As easy as it is, however, to find models for these poems
of 1870, it would be misleading to imply that they are
completely subservient to the work of other poets. Some
of them contain a distinct element of originality, of which
Rimbaud was probably unaware and which is related to
the particular circumstances of his life. Rimbaud was a
young provincial with no experience of the Paris literary
world and the precise limits of its taste in poetry. He
imitated and was influenced, but perhaps never realized
that certain details of his poems were profoundly contra-
dictory to the esthetic standards of the capital. He learned
positive qualities from Hugo and the Parnassians, but
was doubtless ignorant of various constraints and negative strictures which they automatically observed. It is
known that Izambard, permeated with the taste of the
day, persuaded Rimbaud to modify the last line of a poem
called "A la musique" from the vivid "Et mes désirs bru-
taux s'accrochent à leurs lèvres" to the edulcorated form

"Et je sens des baisers qui me viennent aux lèvres."[3] At times Rimbaud departed even further from accepted canons of decorum; in "Le Forgeron," a patriotic humanitarian poem in the style of Hugo, the rebellious smith cries to Louis XVI, in reference to the latter's ancestors, "Merde à ces chiens-là!" We must remember that the printable vocabulary was still very circumscribed and that to write the *mot de Cambronne* in *Les Misérables* Hugo had felt obliged to follow it with a chapter of apologies and metaphysical justifications. Again, despite all Hugo's hatred for Louis-Napoléon, it is unlikely he would have considered writing anything like the conclusion of "L'Eclatante Victoire de Sarrebruck," where, in response to the cry "Vive l'Empereur": "Boquillon rouge et bleu, très naïf, sur son ventre / Se dresse, et, — présentant ses derrières — : 'De quoi?...' "[4]

It is not merely decency that Rimbaud blithely offends; he also violates the Parnassian cult of linguistic purity with his provincialisms (of which he was perhaps unaware): *maline* for *maligne, aiser* for *accommoder* (cf. "La Maline"), *claire* for *éclaire* (cf. "Les Reparties de Nina"), etc. His later penchant for neologism is already evident in the verb "Robinsonner," the hapax legomenon of "Roman." Nor does he hesitate to repeat words or roots in a way that was considered inartistic and cacophonous: "Les tilleuls sentent bon dans les bons soirs de juin" ("Roman"), "conter tes contes," "Vieilles vieilleries" ("Le Buffet"). Finally, Rimbaud treated in cavalier fashion the sonnet, a form which the Parnassians, with their fondness for arbitrary difficulties, considered particularly beautiful because of its strict rime scheme. In 1870 Rimbaud wrote a number of poems which have the typographical disposi-

3. G. Izambard, *Rimbaud tel que je l'ai connu* (Paris, 1946), p. 41.
4. Boquillon was a comic character created by a contemporary cartoonist. See the Garnier edition, p. 382. The "De quoi" may depend on either "vive" ("on what?") or "empereur" ("of what?").

tion of the sonnet but which on examination prove to be
false sonnets, for the quatrains have different rimes. It is
doubtful if many poets of the day would have considered
these sham forms as anything but wrongheaded and
slovenly.

These little oddities of Rimbaud's early verse do not, I
think, add up to any genuine attempt at innovation; given
the admiration for the Parnassians which he showed in
his letters at that time, it is unlikely that he had as yet
envisaged any break with prevailing modes of verse. What
shortcomings these poems contain, by the criteria of
Parisian poets, must rather be ascribed to Rimbaud's
peculiarly isolated position in the world of letters. He
had become a poet by dint of solitary study in what was
almost a cultural vacuum according to sophisticated
standards, and it is not surprising that he was unaware of
all the Alexandrian refinements of taste which adolescent
prodigies in the capital so easily absorbed. (One thinks
of the considerable reputations as poets which Banville
and Catulle Mendès enjoyed at the age of nineteen.)

Isolation from the Paris literary world had perhaps an
even more significant effect on Rimbaud's work than mere
linguistic provincialism, for the latter, if interesting to
note, hardly creates a real style. The important thing that
Charleville, his age, and his half-peasant, half-bourgeois
background provided Rimbaud with was an astigmatic
view of the world, in which certain areas of experience
are magnified while other commonplace ones vanish. Here
and there in the poems of 1870 we can catch glimpses of a
strangely fresh and vital talent to whom the esthetic, social, and pastoral ideals of Paris are only vaguely known.
An occasional sequence of stanzas bears witness that Rimbaud, for all his brilliant pastiche of his contemporaries,
had an idiosyncratic sensibility which was totally remote
from that of fashionable salon poets.

"Sensationnisme" is a word that has often been used in

defining the original element in Rimbaud's early verse; it was perhaps first suggested by the title of the poem "Sensation," which dates from March 1870:

> Par les soirs bleus d'été, j'irai dans les sentiers,
> Picoté par les blés, fouler l'herbe menue:
> Rêveur, j'en sentirai la fraîcheur à mes pieds.
> Je laisserai le vent baigner ma tête nue.

> [On blue summer evenings I'll go along paths, pricked by wheat-tassels, crushing the tiny grass. Dreamily I'll feel its coolness on my feet. I'll let the wind bathe my bare head.]

Anyone would surely grant that these lines show a remarkable "immediacy of sensation," yet what exactly does such a phrase mean, and how useful is it in describing this poem? If by it we are attempting to state something about the capacity or quality of the poet's sensory apparatus, we are speculating on an unknowable and perhaps irrelevant factor—for after all, poems are made of words, as Mallarmé said, and not experience or good intentions. If, on the other hand, "sensationnisme" designates the abundance of Rimbaud's descriptions of sensuous perceptions, we are on safer ground but we still must qualify the word further. For in "Sensation" as elsewhere in his early work, Rimbaud does not speak of unusual or exotic sensations, but on the contrary of very commonplace ones. Their vividness derives from his way of isolating them, of heightening them by the bareness of his style. Anecdotal material is banished, as are the "themes" or philosophical assertions so dear to most previous French poets. The simplicity and parallelism of the sentence structure give each clause independence and full value; likewise the versification, with its artless, unconcealed caesuras at the sixth syllable, its lack of enjambment, and dense interior rimes in é, has a plain, naïve

movement in which separate phrases are neither under-
stressed nor accentuated at the expense of others. What is
remarkable here is not the sensations described but the
verbal art which makes them so salient.

Yet still more must be said about the question of sensations in Rimbaud's early verse. The fact that certain ones
are commonplace in life does not necessarily mean that
they are commonplace in nineteenth-century French poetry. Rimbaud's rural (rather than pastoral) experience
acquainted him in the most everyday fashion with a
world of sights, smells, and activities that are remote from
the urban streets and bourgeois drawing rooms in which
his fellow poets tended to pass their days. Sometimes in
the midst of a piece of the most banal conception Rimbaud bursts forth with sequences of sensuous impressions
which are quite strange to contemporary taste. Such is the
case with "Les Reparties de Nina." The framework of the
poem is negligible: a young man invites a girl to a seductive excursion into the countryside which she abruptly
declines: "Et mon bureau?" (She evidently has a *bureau
de tabac*, that most dreary of enterprises.) But within this
none too interesting scenario Rimbaud places marvelous
descriptions, such as the proposed walk home past a farm-
house:

> Les bons vergers à l'herbe bleue,
>   Aux pommiers tors!
> Comme on les sent toute une lieue
>   Leurs parfums forts!
>
> Nous regagnerons le village
>   Au ciel mi-noir;
> Et ça sentira le laitage
>   Dans l'air du soir;
>
> Ça sentira l'étable, pleine
>   De fumiers chauds,

> Pleine d'un lent rhythme d'haleine,
>   Et de grands dos
>
> Blanchissant sous quelque lumière;
>   Et, tout là-bas,
> Une vache fientera, fière,
>   A chaque pas...

[Good orchards with blue grass and gnarled apple-trees! You can smell their strong odor a mile around! We'll get back to the village under a half-dark sky. It'll smell of dairy in the evening air; it'll smell of barns full of warm manure-heaps, full of a slow breathing rhythm and big backs shining white under a lamp. And, way over there, a cow will proudly drop dung at every step.]

The three odors, apple-trees, milk, and cow-dung, are presented as normal accompaniments of an evening walk which incite the pleasure of familiarity with no trace of pastoral exaltation or urban disgust. It is difficult to imagine one of the poets whom Rimbaud at the age of sixteen admired speaking of the odor of an apple orchard as being merely "strong"; the poetic tradition would have obliged him to some effusion. The milking of cows, on the other hand, would probably not have inspired him to any comment on odors, for the pastoral tradition had become singularly less concrete since Virgil's time; instead, the cow would have most conveniently served as an example of nature's fecundity or impassive unity. (Hugo and Leconte de Lisle had thus envisaged the cow.) But however a good Parnassian might have coped with apple-trees and the dairy industry, one may legitimately doubt if he could ever have faced the fact, poetically at least, that cows both give milk and defecate—and possibly at the same time. (It is true that the word *fumier* was already used in literature, but its meaning was ordinarily meta-

phoric and pejorative.) Rimbaud's lines are utterly ingenuous in their ignorance of all the complex hierarchy
of poetic subjects which neo-classicism and polite society
had combined to erect. He does not attempt to shock by
jumbling together evocation of apples, dairy foods, and
dung; in this case they simply formed a natural whole in
his mind, and the polite conventions which dissociate the
alimentary and excretory systems were as unfamiliar to
him as the diction of the Comédie Française.[5]

These unwitting innovations of Rimbaud's are particularly interesting if we contrast them with preceding
attempts to enrich the vocabulary of sensation in French
poetry. The first generation of romantic poets broke up
the abstractness and banality of neo-classical verse under
the inspiration of the Bible and translations from foreign
literatures as well as native sources. A modest degree of
descriptiveness re-entered French verse. The taste for
colorful imagery did not cease growing, however, and
toward the mid-century poets began to reach quite far
afield in their search for curious and unusual things to
describe. The neo-Pagan mode which we have mentioned
came into being, along with the most desperate forms of
exoticism; Leconte de Lisle, the most representative of
Second Empire poets, seldom wrote a poem in which he
failed to evoke his native southern hemisphere, the ancient
world, the barbaric days of Scandinavia, or some equally
picturesque environment. But since geography is limited,
the ideal of local color was also supplemented by another
dimension of experience: poets discovered that instead of
reiterating the terror of the polar night, the fascination of
the Indian jungle, or the desecration of modern Greece,

5. This is as good a place as any to note that Rimbaud apparently
had a pronounced provincial accent, a fact which is perhaps not
without importance in view of his oddities of vocabulary, syntax,
and, eventually, of prosody. See the evidence collected by H. de
Bouillane de Lacoste in his edition of the *Poésies* (Paris, 1939), p. 36.

one might elaborate poems on strange and highly culti-
vated sensations. Baudelaire pushed this tendency far—
especially in his lesser poems, for his greatness is independent of the hazards of fashion—and there developed with
him, Gautier, and minor figures a kind of dictionary of
strange sensations, which obviously was no sooner created
than it solidified into cliché. Narcotic dreams, fabrics of
rare texture, exotic decoctions threatened to become as
familiar as descriptions of the Ile-de-France in spring.
Hatred of "nature," love of some obscure ancient age,
scorn of "practical" activities, all these mannerisms were
to be the least valuable but most widely enjoyed of
Baudelaire's legacies, and it is significant to see how Rimbaud reacted to them.

"Encore a-t-il vécu dans un milieu trop artiste," was
Rimbaud's stricture on Baudelaire, whom at the same
time he called "le premier voyant, roi des poètes, *un vrai
Dieu.*" [6] Rimbaud's perception is astonishing; he seizes
immediately on the principal weakness in a writer who
in other respects is both masterly and original. The very
inartisticness of his own environment and the independence of viewpoint which isolation afforded him helped
Rimbaud to see through the sham of Parisian estheticism,
with its insistence on rarefied sensations and exotic climates. Poetry, as he realized, need not go to the Andes or
the *parfumerie* for its subject; by reaching after strange-
ness poets paradoxically risked impoverishing their verse
while attempting to enrich it. Rimbaud, on the other
hand, created a fresh voice in literature by exploiting the
imagery of the commonplace.

There are a number of little poems which, though of no
great weight or moment, demonstrate the curiously bright
effects that Rimbaud obtained from odds and ends of
ordinary existence. Of these poems I find "Au Cabaret-

6. Letter to Demeny, May 15, 1871 (the famous "Lettre du
voyant").

Vert" particularly amusing because it is about satisfying hunger, an experience which perhaps only an adolescent would find poignant enough to write verse about. This is not an evocation of the starved castaway's first meal nor of an *amateur's* feast but an anticipation of the banal satisfaction of banal hunger:

Depuis huit jours, j'avais déchiré mes bottines
Aux cailloux des chemins. J'entrais à Charleroi.
— *Au Cabaret-Vert :* je demandai des tartines
De beurre et du jambon qui fût à moitié froid.

Bienheureux, j'allongeai les jambes sous la table
Verte : je contemplai les sujets très naïfs
De la tapisserie. — Et ce fut adorable,
Quand la fille aux tétons énormes, aux yeux vifs,

— Celle-là, ce n'est pas un baiser qui l'épeure! —
Rieuse, m'apporta des tartines de beurre,
Du jambon tiède, dans un plat colorié,

Du jambon rose et blanc parfumé d'une gousse
D'ail, — et m'emplit la chope immense, avec sa mousse
Que dorait un rayon de soleil arriéré.

[For a week my shoes had been torn on pebbly roads. I was getting to Charleroi. *At the Sign of the Cabaret-Vert:* I asked for bread, butter, and some chilled ham. Happily I stretched my legs under the green table; I looked at the funny pictures in the tapestry. And it was adorable when the girl with huge tits and lively eyes—that one's not afraid of a kiss—laughingly brought me bread, butter, and some warmish ham in a plate with designs on it—white and rosy ham flavored with a garlic clove—and filled up my mug—enormous, with its foam gilded by a belated sunbeam.]

Detail after detail is unsatisfactory by the esthetic of Rimbaud's contemporaries, being neither elegant nor low enough. The word *cabaret* has a neutral sense: it means merely a place to drink and eat, with none of the sordid connotations the word so commonly carries. Ham, bread, butter, and beer (not wine with its long literary background) are treated amply and seriously, whereas the verse of most nineteenth-century poets hardly knows any edibles between ambrosia and humble soup. In their poetry, kings banquet sumptuously and the poor starve on crusts of bread; in other words, food has a moral-political significance rather than being evoked for its own sake. The simple satisfaction of hunger is not an unfamiliar experience, yet Rimbaud's little poem strikes one as far more novel than much of his contemporaries' exotic bric-a-brac. But the finest touch of Rimbaud's originality and audacity is the mention of garlic. Contrary to what many English-speaking people imagine, the French often consider garlic rather vulgar, and in the mid-nineteenth century I dare say mention could be made of it in literature only if the connotations were properly low. Verlaine, in his otherwise quite original "Art poétique," uses the word with opprobrium: "Tout cet ail de basse cuisine." Whether one ate it or not, it had pejorative values for poetry.

"Au Cabaret-Vert," for all its slightness, provides an index of what Rimbaud was doing with the imagery of sensations and with poetic language in general in 1870. He hit upon a middle style in which colloquial words like *tétons* could mingle with more lyrical passages, such as the final line with its elegant inversion. The result is both insouciant and precise, a style suited to cope with the worlds of both imagination and experience. It cannot be too highly prized or wondered at; no nineteenth-century French poet before Rimbaud had achieved such a free, unself-conscious mingling of styles. Hugo had boasted of abolishing the distinction between noble and plebeian

words, but his conception of the latter remained somewhat bookish: essentially he did no more than use the
precise vocabulary of things which neo-classicism had
banished and the "low" words which already enjoyed
some currency in comic literature. Baudelaire likewise
avoided anything smacking of incorrect language, and,
although he created an exceptionally intimate and conversational style, his vocabulary never passes the limits of
the literary tongue. One feels that, like the extraordinary
pornographers of the eighteenth century, Hugo and
Baudelaire could have described almost anything without
breaking linguistic decorum or resorting to the colloquial.
They had an automatic inner check which guided their
pens and which imposed on them a convention of vocabulary which is less narrow but equally as rigid as
Racine's.

Despite his highly literary education, Rimbaud did not
completely absorb the lexical strictures of French letters
and, along with them, a certain elevated point of view
which is inseparable from a distinctly literary vocabulary
and syntax. A style is to some extent the embodiment of
an attitude towards society; schooling and social conventions determine our language as much as the desire for
clarity and expressiveness. We may therefore ask ourselves if Rimbaud's divergences from prevailing literary
language do not also carry with them a new outlook on
his subject matter. It is instructive in this connection to
examine what is perhaps Rimbaud's finest poem of 1870,
and the only one which he evidently did not mean to be
included in the intended holocaust of the Demeny Manuscript.[7] Like a thousand contemporary poems, "Les Effarés" is a description of the poor. Yet it is entirely different from the humanitarian poems of the period: there is

7. There is a copy of "Les Effarés" in Verlaine's handwriting,
which could not have been made before the late summer of 1871.

no exhortation, no sentimentality; in short, there is no
bourgeois *mauvaise conscience* about the existence of the
oppressed. Perhaps no poem in French since Villon conveys so simply and immediately the abjection of the poor.
The title word *effaré* has, as it does elsewhere in Rimbaud's work, a somewhat special sense, unknown to
Littré's dictionary and perhaps dialectal in origin; it suggests more "intimidated" or "dazed" than the usual meaning "frightened." It is Rimbaud's private term for designating the outlook on life proper to the irremediably
downtrodden:

> Noirs dans la neige et dans la brume,
> Au grand soupirail qui s'allume,
> > Leurs culs en rond,
>
> A genoux, cinq petits, — misère! —
> Regardent le Boulanger faire
> > Le lourd pain blond.
>
> Ils voient le fort bras blanc qui tourne
> La pâte grise et qui l'enfourne
> > Dans un trou clair.
>
> Ils écoutent le bon pain cuire.
> Le Boulanger au gras sourire
> > Grogne un vieil air.
>
> Ils sont blottis, pas un ne bouge,
> Au souffle du soupirail rouge
> > Chaud comme un sein.
>
> Quand, pour quelque médianoche,
> Façonné comme une brioche
> > On sort le pain,
>
> Quand, sous les poutres enfumées,
> Chantent les croûtes parfumées
> > Et les grillons,

Que ce trou chaud souffle la vie,
Ils ont leur âme si ravie
   Sous leurs haillons,

Ils se ressentent si bien vivre,
Les pauvres Jésus pleins de givre,
   Qu'ils sont là tous,

Collant leurs petits museaux roses
Au treillage, grognant des choses
   Entre les trous,

Tout bêtes, faisant leurs prières
Et repliés vers ces lumières
   Du ciel rouvert,

Si fort, qu'ils crèvent leur culotte
Et que leur chemise tremblote
   Au vent d'hiver.

[Black in the snow and in the mist, by the large, bright vent-grating, crouched in a half-circle, five children kneeling—poverty!—watch the Baker making heavy golden bread. They see the strong white arm kneading the pale dough and sticking it into a glowing hole. They listen to the good bread cook. The Baker with his fat smile drones an old tune. They nestle together, not one moves, at the red vent's vapor, warm like a breast. When, cake-like as if for some Christmas Eve feast, the bread is brought out, when, under the beams black with smoke, the good-smelling crust sings with the crickets, when this warm hole exudes life, their souls are so thrilled under their rags, they feel so revived, the poor Jesuses covered with frost, that they all crouch there sticking their little pink snouts against the grating murmuring things into the holes, stupefied, saying their prayers and pressing toward this light from heaven opened

up so hard that they burst their pants and their
shirts quiver in the winter wind.]

The opening lines are visually clearer if we recall that
French bakeries have their ovens in the basement with a
vent at sidewalk level through which one can peek at
night and watch the baker going about his tasks. Here the
vent with its iron grating represents a kind of ironic reversal of imprisonment, a sequestration by shutting out,
and the image appropriately evolves from vent to heaven
through a delicately gradated chain of associations: vent
—light—heat—odor—bread—breast—life—heaven. The
absence of anecdote focusses attention on the richness of
the fire and bread symbolism, as does the very formal
sentence structure with its evenly balanced periods. The
association between the bakery and the gift of life is so
marked that one critic has even described the baking as
a symbol of birth, the hieratic *Boulanger* (note the capital)
serving as Creator.[8] I think, however, the symbolism is
less specific and that bread represents a whole complex of
needs, from assurance of shelter and sustenance to the
promise of redemption, for, as in Villon's poetry, the material deprivation from which the outcast suffers threatens
him as a sign of God's indifference. Other poets might
have declaimed against the price of *brioches* or affirmed
society's responsibility toward orphans, but the naïve association Rimbaud makes between food and acceptance
by God is far more immediate and telling; he recreates
the actual conditions and psychology of the *effarés'* life,
rather than presenting it in an objective, sociological fashion which implies contrast with the speaker's privileged
position.

Rimbaud's vision of the poor is quite unique in nineteenth-century French poetry. He was not the first to break

8. C. A. Hackett, *Rimbaud l'enfant* (Paris, 1948), pp. 73–86.

with the eloquent, hortatory, humanitarian manner associated with such subjects, for Baudelaire had certainly
done so before him. Yet in those poems of Baudelaire's
which deal with the dregs of the populace there remains
an ineradicable form of bourgeois mentality; when he
identifies himself with blind beggars (cf. "Les Aveugles")
or ancient crones (cf. "Les Petites Vieilles"), it is because
their physical ugliness justifies his own morbid sense of
guilt. The miserable exist for Baudelaire merely as a mirror, an aid towards further self-wretchedness; they tend
to fall into the category of objects or symbols and lose
their humanness. For Rimbaud, on the other hand, the
outcast is not foreign and exterior, and he could therefore
write about him without Hugo's social indignation or
Baudelaire's morbidity. Rimbaud is free from the guilty
obligation to reprove society and to moralize. It is perhaps
impossible to find a major French poet between Villon
and Rimbaud whose sensibility is so little tempered by at-
titudes associated with the privileged classes. Peculiar social circumstances, adolescent alienation, and his precocious talent provided Rimbaud with a vision of society
unmediated by concern for his own place in the hierarchy;
his perception is true. In a poem like "Les Effarés" one
senses that Rimbaud has reached a point of sensibility
where much of the weight of literary tradition, of current
definitions of poetry, has been unconsciously cast off; he
is free now to create in his own image and to command
literature rather than serve it.

The Franco-Prussian War of 1870-71 had special reper-
cussions on Rimbaud's life and the amount of time he
could devote to his poetic vocation. Like the hero of
Le Diable au corps in 1914, Rimbaud found the German
invasion a schoolboy's dream: *les grandes vacances* had
arrived forever. In the chaos provoked by the fall of the
Empire, the disruption of communications in northeast-

ern France, and the presence of the enemy, boys like Rimbaud were simply left to their own devices, for school buildings and teachers were impressed into the military effort. He now discovered the delights of running away from home and of belying in general his reputation as a model child. Even when the Collège de Charleville lamely reopened in February 1871, Rimbaud did not fall back into the old routine: the taste of freedom had been too strong for him to consent to return to his studies, and the next months were spent in cultivating eccentricities of speech, appearance, and manner in order to establish his otherness in the eyes of Madame Rimbaud and the good people of Charleville.

This period of leisure, though we know little about it, doubtless contributed to the rapidity of Rimbaud's artistic evolution. There is a break in his correspondence between November 2, 1870 and April 17, 1871 and, since none of his poems are dated in manuscript from the winter of 1870–71, we are at a loss to determine what his poetic activities may have been at that time. He was perhaps hard at work, for friends could later remember lines from lost poems.[9] On the other hand, winter may have habitually been a period of lethargy for him, since we have no poems dated from the winters of 1871–72 or 1872–73. (This fact is curious in view of the great fecundity he showed in spring and summer of the same years.) Be that as it may, Rimbaud's style had undergone a considerable change by the spring of 1871, and little in his previous work really prepares us for it. The obscurely vituperative "Vénus anadyomène" and "Le Châtiment de Tartufe," which date from the preceding summer and which dwell on ugly nakedness, vaguely anticipate this new verse, but they are sufficiently awkward in conception and confused in detail

9. These are collected in the Pléiade edition under the title "Bribes."

as to be no more than abortive satires of an essentially simple character. In spite of there being obvious links between the periods of Rimbaud's poetic production, I think it important to insist on the vast changes that occurred whenever he apparently ceased writing for a time and reconsidered the whole enterprise.

Indications of his change in style and poetic orientation are to be found not only in the poems themselves but also in the so-called "Lettre du voyant," of which he wrote two versions in May, one for Izambard, the other for Demeny. Most of this obscure document is not so much an *ars poetica,* however, as a kind of myth of the poet's career, and it can be more fruitfully discussed, I think, in connection with later works. The famous phrases like "JE est un autre" or "dérèglement de tous les sens" are not concrete enough to throw any light on Rimbaud's actual poetic practice: as is often the case in literary history, there is a considerable disparity between the poet's declarations about his art and the exact character of his achievement. Much speculation has been stirred up by Rimbaud's proposal to arrive at the "unknown" through "all the forms of love, suffering, madness," and many biographical conjectures have been made about his use of drugs and magic rites as aids to poetic composition. I think we may easily dismiss these questions as not only unsolvable but as smacking all too suspiciously of nineteenth-century literary gossip with its penchant for demonism. We have heard all too often of Coleridge's opium pipe and Poe's bottle; they are the properties of an age which chose to discuss poetry primarily in terms of inspiration and biographical origins.

But if the bulk of the "Lettre du voyant" does not tell us much about Rimbaud's poems of 1871, part of it definitely indicates that he had been thinking about the dominant forces in nineteenth-century poetry and the directions that it might take. After indignantly passing over all verse between the Greeks and his own century ("rimed prose, a game"), he proceeds to rank his predecessors according to how "voyant" they are. Lamartine, the later Hugo, Gautier, Banville, and Leconte de Lisle are all judiciously evaluated: Lamartine, despite his gift, is "strangled" by his outmoded form; Hugo suffers from an excess of "Jehovahs and pillars"; the "second romantics" (Gautier, Banville, and Leconte de Lisle) are *voyants,* but in comparison with Baudelaire they merely deal in "dead things." Baudelaire, though "his highly touted form is poverty-stricken," remains the chief *voyant.* Of younger poets Verlaine and Mérat (!) are singled out, from a lengthy and disparaging catalogue of forgotten names, as the two *voyants* of the Parnassian school. All these remarks are extremely perspicacious (except for the honor bestowed on the insignificant Mérat) and, despite some obscurity, show a coherent conception of nineteenth-century French poetry. Even though one cannot easily define what Rimbaud means by *voyant,* one senses that there do exist certain bonds, certain common aspirations among the poets whom he singles out. With the exception of Lamartine, perhaps, they worked steadily towards enriching the color of poetic language. Hugo's flamboyant imagery, Gautier's precious, *artiste* manner, Banville's complicated and allusive *Odes funambulesques* ("tight-rope odes"), and Leconte de Lisle's relentlessly exotic landscapes are all distinctive extensions of poetic language in the direction of sensuousness or density of meaning. We should perhaps not insist too much on the etymology of *voyant* in interpreting Rimbaud's use of the word; like "imagination" in English it retains some reference to sight but cannot be exclusively defined in terms of that sense. In fact, one might not exaggerate in suggesting that the *voyant's* gift is what we call imagination; the latter word would not necessarily have occurred to Rimbaud, for it was not widely used in French in its modern sense until

well into the nineteenth century.[10] No French Coleridge
had ever dissected that faculty, and even Hugo, who was
one of its adepts, commonly used terms like "vision" and
"dream" to describe it.

Whatever nuances Rimbaud assigned to his critical vocabulary, it is clear that by April 1871 he had thoroughly
defined his place in the movement of nineteenth-century
poetry: he was exploiting a certain vein of expression
which had been practiced by only a handful of poets—
and imperfectly at that. For in the "Lettre du voyant"
Rimbaud has occasion to speak of "new forms," which
must now be invented to contain the new vision. Again
a semantic problem arises: "form" in nineteenth-century
usage customarily refers to versification, and does not at all
have the breadth of meaning it has acquired in the modern vocabulary of esthetics. On the other hand, Rimbaud's
poems of 1871 are original in virtually every respect *except*
prosody. Perhaps he was using the word in some groping
fashion to imply a complex of innovations in image, vocabulary, and subject. Perhaps, as some think, he actually
foretold his later break with traditional versification. In
any case, his remarks indicate a remarkable grasp of the
history of poetic innovation, a careful analysis of what
had already been accomplished, and a realization of what
remained to be explored.

In sending the two versions of the "Lettre du voyant"
Rimbaud enclosed poems, which he accompanied with
ironic remarks—as if hesitant to declare openly that
they contained in germ the salvation of French poetry.
And just as well, for if they are undoubtedly original, it
would have been difficult for Rimbaud's correspondents
to see just where they were leading. Izambard received
the most horrendous one of the lot. It is variously called

10. See M. Gilman, *The Idea of Poetry in France from Houdar de
la Motte to Baudelaire* (Cambridge, Mass., 1958), especially pp. 237–
69.

"Le Coeur supplicié," "Le Coeur volé," or "Le Coeur du pitre" (Rimbaud sometimes altered his titles in successive copies):

> Mon triste coeur bave à la poupe,
> Mon coeur couvert de caporal :
> Ils y lancent des jets de soupe,
> Mon triste coeur bave à la poupe :
> Sous les quolibets de la troupe
> Qui pousse un rire général,
> Mon triste coeur bave à la poupe,
> Mon coeur couvert de caporal!
>
> Ithyphalliques et pioupiesques
> Leurs quolibets l'ont dépravé!
> Au gouvernail on voit des fresques
> Ithyphalliques et pioupiesques.
> O flots abracadabrantesques,
> Prenez mon coeur, qu'il soit lavé!
> Ithyphalliques et pioupiesques
> Leurs quolibets l'ont dépravé!
>
> Quand ils auront tari leurs chiques,
> Comment agir, ô coeur volé?
> Ce seront des hoquets bachiques
> Quand ils auront tari leurs chiques :
> J'aurai des sursauts stomachiques,
> Moi, si mon coeur est ravalé :
> Quand ils auront tari leurs chiques
> Comment agir, ô coeur volé?

[My sad heart slobbers at the poop, my heart covered with tobacco-spit; they spew mouthfuls of soup at it, my sad heart slobbers at the poop; under the jeers of the soldiery, who all break out laughing, my sad heart slobbers at the poop, my heart covered with tobacco-spit. Ithyphallic and soldierish, their jeers have depraved it! On the rudder there are ithyphallic

and soldierish frescoes. O abracadabratic waves, take
my heart, may it be washed! Ithyphallic and soldierish, their jeers have depraved it. When they've chewed
up their quid, how to act, O robbed heart? There will
be Bacchic hiccups, when they've chewed up their
quid: I'll have stomach retchings, I will, if my heart
is defiled; when they've chewed up their quid, how
to act, O robbed heart?]

The most astonishing things have been written about this
poem, based, as might be expected, on unsubstantiated
anecdotes. Tougher critics consider it a description of
homosexual rape (which Rimbaud putatively underwent
on a putative trip to Paris during the Commune), whereas
others prefer to imagine less ugly accounts of its genesis.
I should prefer to neglect this question entirely and examine the poem's curious imagery.

The setting is hazy with its references to poop and rudder on the one hand, and to soldiers on the other, but
this obscurity is more apparent than real, since, for the
purposes of the poem, barracks and ship can be considered
as interchangeable agents of hostility and oppression. The
nature of the torment which the heart undergoes is likewise more symbolic than anecdotal; all the words pertain-
ing to it concern oral activities of a somewhat disgusting
nature: slobbering, spitting soup, chewing tobacco,
coughing, and vomiting. The torture is less painful than
repulsive: the underlying common image is that of a
sticky fluid of which the heart longs to be washed free,
a sticky fluid which symbolizes the relation between the
heart and its tormentors. The laughter and depraved
jokes are merely another form of dirtying by mouth but
serve to heighten the vaguely erotic content of the whole
action (scabrous jokes, it will be remembered, were considered a kind of sexual aggression by Freud). We cannot
equate this complex of images of defilement at the hands

of an organized force with any specific act; it is all the more gruesome for being completely symbolic and subsumed by the rather Sartrian vocabulary of viscosity. The latter suggests a bond between tormentor and victim which is further emphasized by a degree of complicity on the part of the speaker. His penchant for odd neologisms, his silly use of the triolet form with its reminiscences of courtly medieval verse, and his self-deprecatory, unprotesting submission are as disquieting as his tormentor's brutality. To their cruelty a certain masochism responds.

"Le Coeur volé" stands out from the poems Rimbaud was writing at the same time by its peculiar use of the first person and its lack of circumstantial detail. However, the speaker's ambivalent attitude towards his persecutors as well as the corporeal nature of his sufferings are characteristic: the poems of 1871 are filled with body imagery and the ambivalent emotions which it generates. Time and again we find Rimbaud centering his poems on a tactile sensation, a description of parts of the body, or a physiological function. This corporeal imagery is combined with such varied subject matter that it seems all the more obsessive. Political satires, anti-clerical diatribes, vignettes of life in Charleville—all are informed by a preoccupation with anatomical detail and vital processes. For example, "Les Pauvres à l'église," which sets out to depict the stupid devoutness of the lower classes, turns into a catalogue of physical deformities; typical expressions are "seins crasseux," "vieilles à fanons," "épileptiques," and "qu'attiédit puamment leur souffle." We are at some remove from the discreet and sympathetic description of poverty in "Les Effarés." Few things perhaps inspire such ambivalent feelings as corporeality; the body is a most potent source of symbols, evoking at once thoughts of beauty, erotic pleasure, sexual revulsion, ugliness, and excrement. Fascination and distaste can fuse in the contemplation of nakedness, and this unresolved conflict underlies much of Rimbaud's poetry of this period. "Accroupissements," which Demeny received in the "Lettre du voyant" along with "Le Coeur volé," illustrates rather well the charm of the repulsive which haunted Rimbaud in the spring of 1871. The title itself is exemplary: images of squatting and defecation were among Rimbaud's favorites, and "Accroupissements" describes with some detail a lay brother sitting on his chamber pot in the morning, squatting before the hearth at noon, and crouching in the moonlight:

> Et le soir, aux rayons de lune, qui lui font
> Aux contours du cul des bavures de lumière,
> Une ombre avec détails s'accroupit, sur un fond
> De neige rose ainsi qu'une rose trémière...
> Fantasque, un nez poursuit Vénus au ciel profond.

> [And in the evening, under the moonbeams which outline its ass in light, a shadow with details squats, against a background of rose snow, like a hollyhock— Fancifully a nose follows Venus in the deep heavens.]

The amorous thoughts of the lay brother and the comparison of him with a flower betray the erotic content which the whole action has for the poet. With the greatest gusto he uses a delicate, tender image to describe frère Milotus' gastrointestinal functions: "Quelque chose comme un oiseau remue un peu / A son ventre serein comme un monceau de tripe!" The bird and heap of tripe are played off against one another to obtain a complicated attitude in which digestion is at once a sensual pleasure and a dirty process. This subtle combination of relish and revulsion creates an oddly vivid kind of verse; its authenticity lies in the inherent polyvalence of bodily imagery. Essentially, however, a poem like "Accroupissements" is fragmentary; the curious juxtapositions of buttocks and flowers, birds and tripe are striking details but lack dramatic progression or real import. The concentration on

backsides seems more like a loose scatophilic evocation
than an organized piece of writing; one is uncertain
whether this is some sort of satire (but of what?) or a
rather special erotic fantasy. There is something troubled
and confused about the whole piece, as there is about a
number of other poems of the same period like "Mes
Petites Amoureuses" or "Oraison du soir." Ultimately it
is difficult to say what such poems are about; they exude
a vague, general hostility with erotic undertones, but
which eludes purely literary description. They seem rather
to demand psychological analysis, for the simultaneous
feelings of attraction and disgust generated by the body
are not worked into a coherent pattern. This verse has the
irresolution of fantasy or dream and remains an abortive
exercise in Rimbaud's new imagery.

Although by and large Rimbaud's explorations into
body imagery are crabbed and obscure, he occasionally
succeeded in subordinating it to a genuine design; notably
in "Les Assis," "Les Premières Communions," and "Les
Poètes de sept ans" the obsession with anatomy and physi-
ology serves to elaborate and underscore the subject of
the poems rather than obfuscating it. "Les Assis" exploits
the satiric possibilities of bodily description; the ancient
librarians and habitués of the reading-room are nicely
characterized as engaged in perpetual sexual union with
their chairs:

> Noirs de loupes, grêlés, les yeux cerclés de bagues
> Vertes, leurs doigts boulus crispés à leurs fémurs,
> Le sinciput plaqué de hargnosités vagues
> Comme les floraisons lépreuses des vieux murs;
>
> Ils ont greffé dans des amours épileptiques
> Leur fantasque ossature aux grands squelettes noirs
> De leurs chaises; leurs pieds aux barreaux rachitiques
> S'entrelacent pour les matins et pour les soirs!...
>
> .   .   .   .

Et les Sièges leur ont des bontés : culottée
De brun, la paille cède aux angles de leurs reins;
L'âme des vieux soleils s'allume, emmaillotée
Dans ces tresses d'épis où fermentent les grains.

> [Black with wens, pock-marked, their eyes circled
> with green rings, their knotty fingers clutching their
> thigh-bones, their sinciputs scaly with vague asperities
> like the leprous efflorescence on old walls, they have
> grafted in epileptic loves their fantastic bones onto
> the great black skeletons of their chairs; their feet
> are entwined with the ricketic rungs for the morning
> and for the evening. . . . And the Chairs do not with-
> hold their favors: covered in brown the straw yields
> to the angles of their backsides; the souls of old suns
> rekindle, swathed in these plaited wheat-ears where
> the grains ferment.]

The distinction between animate and inorganic matter
becomes hazy in these lines, where the sitters' bodies resemble some curiously textured wreck and the ricketic
skeletons of the chairs amorously open their arms to their
masters. This world of substance is wonderfully repulsive
and ambiguous with its miasmic half-life; flesh takes on
scaly, fungus-like attributes, while straw and wood exude
warmth and tenderness. Nor is the concentration on bodily detail in the least tangential to the subject of the poem:
the sitters are visibly peculiar physical specimens by their
very definition, in a way that the lay brother of "Accroupissements" is not. At the same time, the grotesque
note never degenerates into obsessive scatology; Rimbaud
has a poetic conception firmly in grasp and develops it
with complete mastery.

Satire like "Les Assis" is a fairly obvious domain for
corporeal imagery, but Rimbaud also employs it in far
more imaginative ways. One of the longest and most curious poems he wrote in 1871 deals with religious fervor as

a kind of physical defilement; this is "Les Premières Communions," the most eloquent of Rimbaud's several anti-Christian pieces of the period. It opens with a familiar, casual evocation of a typical scene of provincial life:

> Vraiment, c'est bête, ces églises des villages
> Où quinze laids marmots encrassant les piliers
> Ecoutent, grasseyant les divins babillages,
> Un noir grotesque dont fermentent les souliers :
> Mais le soleil éveille, à travers les feuillages,
> Les vieilles couleurs des vitraux irréguliers.

> > [Really it's stupid, these village churches, where fifteen ugly brats making dirty marks on the pillars listen to a grotesque ape with stinking shoes rasp out the divine babble. But shining through the trees, the sun awakens the old colors of irregular stained-glass.]

After the catechism class the poet focusses on one of its members, whom the priest has singled out for the quality of her faith. On the eve of her first communion she has a strange experience:

> La veille du grand Jour, l'enfant se fait malade.
> Mieux qu'à l'Eglise haute aux funèbres rumeurs,
> D'abord le frisson vient, — le lit n'étant pas fade, —
> Un frisson surhumain qui retourne : "Je meurs..."

> Et, comme un vol d'amour fait à ses soeurs stupides,
> Elle compte, abattue et les mains sur son coeur,
> Les Anges, les Jésus et ses Vierges nitides
> Et, calmement, son âme a bu tout son vainqueur.

> Adonaï... — Dans les terminaisons latines,
> Des cieux moirés de vert baignent les Fronts vermeils,
> Et tachés du sang pur des célestes poitrines,
> De grands linges neigeux tombent sur les soleils!

[The eve of the great day, the child grows sick. At first, stronger than in the high church with its funereal echoes, the shudder comes—the bed being fresh—a superhuman shudder that rolls her over: "I'm dying . . ." And like a theft of love from her stupid sisters she counts, exhausted and with her hands over her heart, the Angels, the Jesuses, and her resplendent Virgins, and calmly her soul has drunk in her victor. Adonai!—In the Latin endings green-shimmering heavens bathe the golden brows, and spotted with pure blood from celestial breasts great snowy sheets fall onto the sun!]

The experience remains ambiguous: illness, pain, beatitude, and sexual excitement merge in such a way that they seem necessary concomitants. The image of the blood-stained sheets is particularly apt with its multiple associations: being bedridden, the martyr's glory, loss of virginity, and, finally, menstruation, for while the latter is never explicitly mentioned in the poem, it is implied by the theme of sexual initiation, which balances that of spiritual discovery. The precise nature of her suffering and ecstasy is still unknown to the communicant; she is a victim of the mysterious interchangeabilities and secret bonds of body and spirit, pain and pleasure, lust and chastity. Her dreams of divine love metamorphose into frankly erotic ones:

> Des curiosités vaguement impudiques
> Epouvantent le rêve aux chastes bleuités
> Qui s'est surpris autour des célestes tuniques,
> Du linge dont Jésus voile ses nudités.

> [Vaguely immodest curiosities terrify her dream in its chaste blue realms: it has caught itself focussing on the celestial tunics, on the linen in which Jesus veils his naked parts.]

The union of physical illness and religious aspirations persists throughout the poem; they form a complex which defies analysis. Is one merely a function of the other, are they coincidental, or is one a commentary on the other? The pathos of the verse lies in such ambiguities. Finally the torment is so great that the girl awakens:

A son réveil, — minuit, la fenêtre était blanche.
Devant le sommeil bleu des rideaux illunés,
La vision la prit des candeurs du dimanche;
Elle avait rêvé rouge. Elle saigna du nez,

Et se sentant bien chaste et pleine de faiblesse
Pour savourer en Dieu son amour revenant,
Elle eut soif de la nuit où s'exalte et s'abaisse
Le coeur, sous l'oeil des cieux doux, en les devinant :

.   .   .   .

Et faisant la Victime et la petite épouse,
Son étoile la vit, une chandelle aux doigts,
Descendre dans la cour où séchait une blouse,
Spectre blanc, et lever les spectres noirs des toits.

Elle passa sa nuit sainte dans des latrines. . . .

[When she awoke—midnight—the window was white. In front of the blue sleep of the moonlit curtains a vision came over her of Sunday's purity. She had dreamed red. Her nose bled, and feeling very chaste and full of weakness, to enjoy her reviving love amidst God, she thirsted for the night, in which the heart rises and falls under the eye of the soft heavens, whose presence it divines . . . And imitating the Victim and the little bride, her star saw her go down with a candle in her hand to the courtyard, where a shirt was drying—like a white specter, and put to flight the black shadows of the buildings. She spent her holy night in the latrine. . . .]

The bloody nose (ironically recalling the martyr's wounds) and the choice of the outhouse for the holy vigil are the kind of precise, trivial details which make Rimbaud's handling of the theme of divine and profane love both unusual and immediate. The disparity between the Church's language of holiness, purity, and redemption and real life with its dingy courtyards and primitive sanitary conditions becomes monstrously acute. Finally the imagery of bodily discomfort adds a dimension of humble sorrow and anguish to the grandiose, almost baroque theme of the eroticism of Christianity, which otherwise might have seemed remote and Bernini-like. Rimbaud is presenting Christianity as a debilitating force, reprehensive not merely for its perversion of sexual instincts but also because of its secret affinity with weakness. This conception that Christ is not so much an incubus as a disease carrier informs the climax of the poem, in which the communicant, now older and just married, declares that she is frigid, that "Christ has befouled my breath," and that her body "reeks with Jesus' putrid kiss." The poet concludes:

> Christ! ô Christ, éternel voleur des énergies,
> Dieu qui pour deux mille ans vouas à ta pâleur,
> Cloués au sol, de honte et de céphalalgies,
> Ou renversés, les fronts des femmes de douleur.

> [Christ, O Christ, eternal thief of energy, God who for two thousand years vowed to your pallor the brows of women of sorrow, pressed against the ground or thrown back, with shame and head pains.]

All this body imagery, which gives the poem its peculiar color, is curious in its continual shifting between literal and metaphoric meanings: religion is a figurative disease, but it is also related to genuine physical symptoms. The "céphalalgies" are real headaches as well as mental aberrations, just as the communicant's fever cannot be separated from her mystic aspirations.

The mysteriousness of the body with its cryptic reactions and pleasures forms the underlying motif in most of Rimbaud's poems of 1871. In one of them he even succeeds in presenting almost the totality of life as grounded in physical experience. The haunting "Poètes de sept ans" is an evocation of the secret and fascinating sensations which beset an immature creature whose sensual capacities are not yet channeled and directed but attach themselves to a wide variety of things. The poem is divided (like no other one of 1871) into broad, irregular verse-paragraphs rather than by stanzas—which is always a challenge to the poet's inmost sense of form.

> Et la Mère, fermant le livre du devoir,
> S'en allait satisfaite et très fière, sans voir,
> Dans les yeux bleus et sous le front plein d'éminences,
> L'âme de son enfant livrée aux répugnances.

> [And the Mother, closing the Book of Duty, went off satisfied and quite proud, without seeing in his blue eyes and beneath his brow filled with great thoughts her child's soul full of repugnance.]

The first paragraph serves to shut out, to isolate the child's world from authority and prying eyes. The mother goes off, deceived by the symbolic opacity and inexpressiveness of her son's blue eyes, and he is left alone with his most private and immediate preoccupations. The phrase "livrée aux répugnances" is especially well chosen as the conclusion of this passage, for it at once expresses the child's feelings about his mother's world of duties and the distaste which she might feel if she knew the sensations which obsessed him. Now we have the revelation of the child's intimate life:

Tout le jour il suait d'obéissance; très
Intelligent; pourtant des tics noirs, quelques traits,
Semblaient prouver en lui d'âcres hypocrisies.
Dans l'ombre des couloirs aux tentures moisies,
En passant il tirait la langue, les deux poings
A l'aine, et dans ses yeux fermés voyait des points.
Une porte s'ouvrait sur le soir : à la lampe
On le voyait là-haut, qui râlait sur la rampe,
Sous un golfe de jour pendant du toit. L'été
Surtout, vaincu, stupide, il était entêté
A se renfermer dans la fraîcheur des latrines :
Il pensait là, tranquille et livrant ses narines.
Quand, lavé des odeurs du jour, le jardinet
Derrière la maison, en hiver, s'illunait
Gisant au pied d'un mur, enterré dans la marne
Et pour des visions écrasant son oeil darne,
Il écoutait grouiller les galeux espaliers.

[All day long he sweated obedience; very intelligent,
yet dark quirks, certain traits seemed to be proof in
him of acid hypocrisy. In the shadow of the corridors
with their mildewed hangings he passed through
sticking out his tongue, his hands in his groin, and,
in his closed eyes, seeing bright points. A door opened
onto evening: by the lamp you could see him up there
brawling on the staircase under a flood of light falling
from the eaves. In summer, overcome, stupefied, he
especially insisted on shutting himself up in the coolness of the outhouse: he meditated there, at peace
and pricking up his nostrils. When, laved of the day's
odors, the little garden behind the house lit up with
moonlight in winter, lying at the foot of a wall,
covered with clay, and rubbing his dizzy eyes to create
visions, he listened to the swarming sound of the
mangy espaliers.]

The setting for each scene is carefully sketched so that

the child's actions and feelings are geared to particular conditions of air and light, which furthermore are arranged in contrasting sequences: day (the dark corridor), evening (the lantern over the steps), summer (the outhouse —again a closed-in, cool place, dark during the day and comparable to the corridor), and winter (the garden—once again an illuminated night setting). These complex parallelisms and antitheses provide a résumé of the child's life in the changing cycle of the year. The "tics noirs" which characterize him are all the apparently meaningless actions which children relish and which annoy adults: sticking out the tongue, touching the genitals, closing one's eyes and shaking one's head to see "stars," uttering loud, foolish sounds (evidently the sense of *râler* here), and sniffing after disgusting odors. These actions are of course all the more important in that they are not practical but ritual and symbolic: the body's freedom from the constraints of imposed behavior represents the independence of the spirit.

The images of moisture and damp matter which permeate these lines are also worthy of attention: "sweating obedience," "mildewed hangings," "the cool of the outhouse," "laved of the day's odors," "marne" (a clay used to enrich other soil)—constantly the poet evokes humidity, that most obtrusive of atmospheric conditions since it strongly affects the senses both of smell and of touch. Moisture is a particularly apt accompaniment for the child's secret rebelliousness, for, whether betokening germination or decay, it symbolizes the organic processes of life and change. Dampness is fraught with potentiality; it promises new growth and the dissolution of the old. The child is thus attracted to the element representative of his own increasing powers, and the development of the passage concludes appropriately with his sitting half-sunk in the fertile *marne* listening to the teeming future life of the winter-bound espaliers.

The imagery of moisture and liquidness continues curiously through the final lines of the second verse-paragraph, where the child's chosen companions are described:

Pitié! Ces enfants seuls étaient ses familiers
Qui, chétifs, fronts nus, oeil déteignant sur la joue,
Cachant de maigres doigts jaunes et noirs de boue
Sous des habits puant la foire et tout vieillots,
Conversaient avec la douceur des idiots!
Et si, l'ayant surpris à des pitiés immondes,
Sa mère s'effrayait; les tendresses, profondes,
De l'enfant se jetaient sur cet étonnement.
C'était bon. Elle avait le bleu regard, — qui ment!

[Pity! The only children who were his friends were those who, sickly, bare-headed, with eyes watering onto their cheeks, hiding thin fingers yellow and black with mud under old clothes stinking of diarrhea, talked with the gentleness of idiots! And if, having caught him at filthy acts of pity, his mother was horrified, his deep tenderness forced back her shock. That was all right. She had that blue glance—which lies!]

The very filthiness of the poor children constitutes their appeal, for it awakens a pity for living things, a desire to mingle with the dampness of flesh. The ragamuffins have no existence or meaning as personalities but simply as fellow animals. The mother, on the other hand, lives in an abstract world of duties and taboos rather than in one of matter and consequently is separated from her child by the opaque curtain of lying blue eyes which each opposes to the other.

The three concluding verse-paragraphs are constructed in parallel fashion: various facets of the child's imaginary world are related to their points of departure in the real one. First come sexual fantasies:

A sept ans, il faisait des romans, sur la vie
Du grand désert, où luit la Liberté ravie,
Forêts, soleils, rives, savanes! — Il s'aidait
De journaux illustrés où, rouge, il regardait
Des Espagnoles rire et des Italiennes.
Quand venait, l'oeil brun, folle, en robes d'indiennes,
— Huit ans, — la fille des ouvriers d'à côté,
La petite brutale, et qu'elle avait sauté,
Dans un coin, sur son dos, en secouant ses tresses,
Et qu'il était sous elle, il lui mordait les fesses,
Car elle ne portait jamais de pantalons;
— Et, par elle meurtri des poings et des talons,
Remportait les saveurs de sa peau dans sa chambre.

[At the age of seven he composed novels about life in
the great wilderness where banished liberty shines,
woods, suns, riverbanks, plains! He helped himself
with illustrated papers in which, blushing, he saw
Spanish and Italian women laugh. When the daugh-
ter of the workers next door came, wild and eight
years old, with her dark eyes and a calico dress, the
little brute, and when she had jumped on his back
in a corner, shaking her long hair, and he was under
her, he bit her buttocks, for she never wore panta-
loons, and, battered by her fists and heels, took back
with him to his room the taste of her skin.]

The passage at first seems disconnected, but its subjects
actually succeed one another through careful associations. Nature and liberty are joined, as previously, by the
notion of growth and change; the Spanish and Italian
women suggest distant climates, while introducing at the
same time the idea of sexual activity, which is an indispensable aspect of freedom. (The *où*-clause is one of those
hinge-phrases which end by unexpectedly moving quite
far from the initial topic.) The erotic material is now
transposed into real life: the little girl is dark-eyed like

the Mediterranean women (and unlike the blue-eyed mother), while her manners and her calico dress (*indienne*) suggest exotic origins and a strange way of life. The world of adult sexuality in the illustrated papers is now replaced by the confused, indirect eroticism of children with its anal element and hostility. Finally the child retreats to his room where the real experience can be transformed into an imaginative one. The image of the child alone in his room is an important one and recurs, for the room seems to be a projection of himself and to symbolize the mind's space, where scenes of fantasy take place.

The second part of the concluding trio of verse-paragraphs deals with God's authority and the regeneration of mankind which will replace the old Biblical religion:

Il craignait les blafards dimanches de décembre,
Où, pommadé, sur un guéridon d'acajou,
Il lisait une Bible à la tranche vert-chou;
Des rêves l'oppressaient chaque nuit dans l'alcôve.
Il n'aimait pas Dieu; mais les hommes, qu'au soir fauve,
Noirs, en blouse, il voyait rentrer dans le faubourg
Où les crieurs, en trois roulements de tambour,
Font autour des édits rire et gronder les foules.
— Il rêvait la prairie amoureuse, où des houles
Lumineuses, parfums sains, pubescences d'or,
Font leur remuement calme et prennent leur essor!

[He feared the wan December Sundays when, pomaded, on a mahogany stand he read a Bible with cabbage-green edges. Dreams oppressed him every night in his bedroom. He didn't like God but the swarthy men whom, in the tawny evening, wearing overalls, he saw going home to the workers' quarter, where the town-criers with three drumrolls make the crowds laugh and roar over edicts. He dreamed of a love-bound pasture, where gleaming swells of beings,

wholesome scents, golden puberties calmly move and
soar off.]

The passage is constructed as a crescendo of contrasts: the
image of Sunday solitude yields to that of crowds of men
on a working day, and the development concludes with
the vision of beatific throngs—mankind redeemed—on
the luminous plain. The latter is, of course, verdant, unlike the dreary December in which the child must execute
his dull pious duties. We have here the three stages of
humanity's progress: subjugation to an authoritarian god,
consciousness of its own value, and the attainment of the
old god's high state of freedom.[11]

Finally the poem ends with a third picture of the child
alone in his room and contemplating the advent of liberty,
but this last fantasy does not have a specific reference as
do the preceding two, which deal with sex and religion; it
is purely symbolic:

Et comme il savourait surtout les sombres choses,
Quand, dans la chambre nue aux persiennes closes,
Haute et bleue, âcrement prise d'humidité,
Il lisait son roman sans cesse médité,
Plein de lourds ciels ocreux et de forêts noyées,
De fleurs de chair aux bois sidérals déployées,
Vertige, écroulements, déroutes et pitié!
— Tandis que se faisait la rumeur du quartier,
En bas, — seul, et couché sur des pièces de toile
Ecrue, et pressentant violemment la voile!

[And as he especially enjoyed dark things, when, in
the bare room with closed shutters, high and blue,
sourly humid, he read his endlessly meditated novel
full of heavy ochreous skies and drenched forests, of

11. We shall reserve for our discussion of *Une Saison en enfer* a
fuller consideration of nineteenth-century theories of history and
their influence on Rimbaud.

flesh-flowers opened wide in the sidereal woods—
dizziness, crumblings, flights, and pity!—while the
noise of the town went on beneath—alone and lying
on pieces of unbleached cloth and violently antici-
pating a sail!]

Visions of the sky, moist landscapes, boats, and movement
subsume the child's aspirations. The dominant images of
wetness and growth return triumphantly and join with a
new one: that of elevation. The room, high and blue like
the sky, metamorphoses into a ship with its tall sail
piercing the atmosphere, while real life fades away beneath. Grammatically the concluding period is daring and
quite unlike Rimbaud's usual practice: in the abundance
of tightly knit subordinate elements one does not notice
immediately that there is no main verb. This ellipsis
(evidently of *il était* before "seul" or of some verb before
"vertige") is perhaps not of the greatest importance, but
it would seem to contribute to the amazing density of impressions conveyed by these concluding lines.

With "Les Assis," "Les Premières Communions," and
"Les Poètes de sept ans" we reach the highpoint of Rimbaud's poems about Charleville, which are so memorable
in their rich provincial color and ingeniously detailed
imagery. After the summer of 1871 the local and anecdotal side of Rimbaud's inspiration was to vanish, but not
before he had brought it to a high degree of perfection.
Rimbaud succeeded in transforming his native village into
one of those strange places in literary geography which
have their own unmistakable physical and moral atmosphere. Baudelaire's Paris is such a region and so is La-
forgue's. However, few French poets have had Rimbaud's
sense of landscape and none has created out of a non-
descript town and its surroundings so persistent a world
as that of his early poems. The Charleville cycle does not,
of course, account for all of Rimbaud's work in 1870–71;

indeed there are certain poems such as "Le Coeur volé" which in their symbolic mode of expression anticipate his later achievement more clearly than do the local ones. Rimbaud was working in more than one style in 1871, and in the concluding section of this chapter we shall analyze his increasing sense of the value of mythic conceptions. Yet the scenes of life in the Ardennes, though they were to lead to no further exploration of that vein, remain precious—and that precisely because of their uniqueness; Rimbaud's capacities for elaborating a particular style to a high degree of finish only to abandon it constitute perhaps the most rare and fascinating aspect of his poetic gift.

If the "Lettre du voyant" does not furnish any information on Rimbaud's theories of poetic diction, there is one text which does, "Ce qu'on dit au poète à propos de fleurs," a poem which he sent off to Banville in July 1871 and which is an *ars poetica* in the manner of Gautier's "L'Art" or Verlaine's later "Art poétique." In what mood Rimbaud decided to offer Banville this work is not very clear; it might be interpreted either as an attack on the poetry of Banville and his friends or perhaps merely as a clever manifesto. In any case, "Ce qu'on dit au poète à propos de fleurs" is a brilliant defense of many of Rimbaud's characteristic and original stylistic discoveries.

The poem deals with the problem of vegetation and especially of flowers in modern poetry. Since nineteenth-century verse is filled with flowers, they serve as a kind of touchstone for the analysis of style. By singling out this particular point in imagery Rimbaud manages to convey with concision a wealth of ideas on poetic practice. He begins by examining the relation between contemporary poetry, as exemplified by the lily, and present-day life:

> Ainsi, toujours, vers l'azur noir
> Où tremble la mer des topazes,

Fonctionneront dans ton soir
Les Lys, ces clystères d'extases!

A notre époque de sagous,
Quand les Plantes sont travailleuses,
Le Lys boira les bleus dégoûts
Dans tes Proses religieuses!

— Le Lys de monsieur de Kerdrel,
Le Sonnet de mil huit cent trente,
Le Lys qu'on donne au Ménestrel
Avec l'oeillet et l'amarante!

Des lys! Des lys! On n'en voit pas!
Et dans ton Vers, tel que les manches
Des Pécheresses aux doux pas,
Toujours frissonnent ces fleurs blanches!

[Thus ever, toward the black azure, where the sea of
topazes quivers, lilies, these enema-syringes of ecstasy,
will operate in your evening. In our day of breadfruit-
trees, when plants work hard, the lily will drink up
blue stenches in your liturgical proses. The lily of
Monsieur de Kerdrel, the sonnet of 1830, the lily they
give to the minstrel with the carnation and amaranth!
Lilies! Lilies! One never sees any! And in your Poesy,
like the sleeves of soft-footed Magdalenes, there always tremble these white flowers!]

The first stanza plunges us with admirable abruptness into
a quite un-Parnassian style. The opening words echo a
famous and very old-fashioned elegiac line of Lamartine's
("Ainsi toujours poussés vers de nouveaux rivages . . ."),
while "azur noir" (evening) and "la mer des topazes"
(stars) are images of the most novel sort. These elegant
circumlocutions are nicely balanced by the rather mecha-
nistic terms "fonctionneront" and "clystères," which
would not normally find themselves in the company of

such precious expressions. The first stanza serves to establish a certain distance in taste between the speaker and the poetry he is discussing; the effect is electric. The speaker's irreverent language with its mingling of various kinds of words is by implication what diction should be. Next Rimbaud emphasizes the disparity between the plants of today—plants which "function"—and those whose only use is to decorate altars at Eastertime. ("Les bleus dégoûts" suggests incense.) Lilies, furthermore, have historical connotations: they adorned the Bourbon flag (Monsieur de Kerdrel was a royalist); they appealed to the romantics of 1830 for their deathly pallor, and they even figure among the prizes given to poets at the Jeux floraux de Toulouse, a medieval poetic contest which anachronistically survived until Rimbaud's time. In short, lilies are the flowers of obsolete politics and literature. Rimbaud concludes that lilies no longer even *exist* except in verse; like some primitive form of the locomotive or cotton-gin they have been replaced by more efficient flora better adapted to the needs of modern life. Finally he returns to the association between lilies and Christianity—the outmoded religion—and paints a little picture in baroque style which recalls old-fashioned romantic poetry. The speaker's language in these opening stanzas is a dazzling mixture of pastiche, parody, innovation, and serious levity; it is designed to jolt one into a realization of how many linguistic effects French poetry had been overlooking.

The second of the four parts of "Ce qu'on dit au poète à propos de fleurs" is a critique of the French pastoral tradition with its tranquil and familiar botany of the Ile-de-France, which is exemplified by the rose:

> O Poètes, quand vous auriez
> Les Roses, les Roses soufflées,
> Rouges sur tiges de lauriers,
> Et de mille octaves enflées!

Quand BANVILLE en ferait neiger,
Sanguinolentes, tournoyantes,
Pochant l'oeil fou de l'étranger
Aux lectures mal bienveillantes!

De vos forêts et de vos prés,
O très paisibles photographes!
La Flore est diverse à peu près
Comme des bouchons de carafes!

[O Poets, even if you had roses, soufflé-roses, red on
oleander stems, and swollen with a thousand sonnet
octaves! Even if BANVILLE would make them snow
down, blood-red and whirling, blackening the for-
eigner's wild eye in his difficultly sympathetic reading!
The flora of your forests and meadows, O peaceable
photographers, is about as individualized as bottle-
corks.]

The first two stanzas are a parody of the Parnassians'
descriptive technique: the rich adjectival elements they
admired are represented by the expressive if slightly odd
"soufflées" and "enflées d'octaves," while the more orthodox "sanguinolentes" and "tournoyantes" are juxtaposed
for malicious cacophony. The absurd "rouges sur tiges de
lauriers" is a play on words suggested by the name of the
oleander (*laurier–rose*). Finally Rimbaud reaches the crux
of the problem: the Parnassians are photographers; they
are hopelessly committed to descriptions of what can be
seen. Yet no number of lush adjectives will ever make
roses anything but roses: pictorial poetry quickly exhausts
itself, for it is founded on the mistaken notion that the
eye should guide the poet in his choice of subjects. The
eye tends to present one endlessly with the same familiar
sights and therefore offers no scope for the poet's inven-
tiveness:

> Toujours les végétaux Français,
> Hargneux, phtisiques, ridicules,
> Où le ventre des chiens bassets
> Navigue en paix, aux crépuscules;

[Always French vegetation, ill-tempered, tubercular, ridiculous, where basset hounds' bellies navigate peacefully in the twilight.]

Rimbaud's brief against pictorial poetry is not yet finished, however. There remain poets like Leconte de Lisle who have abandoned French vegetation for exotic ones, and it is to them that Rimbaud now addresses himself:

> O blanc Chasseur, qui cours sans bas
> A travers le Pâtis panique,
> Ne peux-tu pas, ne dois-tu pas
> Connaître un peu ta botanique?

[O white Huntsman running bare-legged through the panic pasture, can't you, shouldn't you know a bit of botany?]

The white huntsman recalls the enchanted hunter of romantic legend who was condemned to an eternal flight; like him Leconte de Lisle is metaphorically obliged to roam from country to country in his endless search for landscapes to describe.[12] Yet however far he travels, his descriptions are sadly alike:

> Tu ferais succéder, je crains,
> Aux Grillons roux les Cantharides,
> L'or des Rios au bleu des Rhins, —
> Bref, aux Norwèges les Florides :

[You would follow up, I fear, red crickets with Spanish-fly, Rhine-blue with Rio gold; in short, Norway with Florida.]

12. The image seems to have a parodic reference to Hugo's "Chasseur noir" (*Châtiments*).

Rimbaud satirizes Leconte de Lisle's poetry as a collection
of formulas: his landscapes are differentiated only by
changes of color adjectives and insects. Norway and
Florida are essentially handled in the same way: a few
nouns of local reference and some allusions to climate
constitute all the Parnassian bag of tricks. Yet even if
these poems were less mechanical, the objection remains
that idle descriptions can no longer be considered worthwhile:

> Mais, Cher, l'Art n'est plus, maintenant,
> — C'est la vérité, — de permettre
> A l'Eucalyptus étonnant
> Des constrictors d'un hexamètre;

> [But, dear heart, Art no longer consists—it's the
> truth—in allowing the amazing Eucalyptus its hex-
> ameter-long constrictors.]

The "astonishing" eucalyptus is precisely the kind of obvious local color which Leconte de Lisle strove after, and
his sinuous lines are constrictors because of their stran-
gling effect on poetry. The real objection to Parnassian
exoticism is that, like the roses of the Ile-de-France, its
flora is academic and remote from life:

> Là! ... Comme si les Acajous
> Ne servaient, même en nos Guyanes,
> Qu'aux cascades des sapajous,
> Au lourd délire des lianes!

> [Come now! As if the mahogany trees were only good,
> even in our Guianas, for sapajou monkeys to swing
> on, for lianas to hang on deliriously.]

Even tropical forests are good for something beside pro-
viding picturesque props.

Rimbaud's complaints against contemporary poetry are
twofold: its vision of the world is at once overly selective

and irrelevant. Estheticism lies, of course, at the origin of both faults: the superstition that certain subjects are *a priori* poetical leads to utter monotony and ignores all connection between art and the full range of feeling. Poems about lilies are as hackneyed as they are dry. In addition, this estheticism, which pretends to further poetry by prizing it alone, actually kills literature through the limits it imposes on the imagination. By narrowly defining what is artistic one merely destroys originality and the continuity of art.

Rimbaud's solution to this dilemma is, as one might expect, paradoxical. He urges at once a return to the full range of ordinary experience and a breakthrough into the world of untrammeled imagination. This advice is brilliantly expressed in the concluding parts of "Ce qu'on dit au poète à propos de fleurs":

> Trouve, ô Chasseur, nous le voulons,
> Quelques garances parfumées
> Que la Nature en pantalons
> Fasse éclore! — pour nos Armées!

[Find, O Huntsman, we insist, some odiferous madder-flowers which Nature will make blossom into trousers for our Armies!]

This world of disparate commonplace objects like madder-flowers and the red trousers of the nineteenth-century French army is also one where the least expected transformations take place and metaphor becomes reality. Rimbaud's solution for poetry is an extremist one: the poet must shun all decorums and conventions of language and embrace both the trivial, practical world and the super-reality of imagination. He rejects noble, poetic diction, for it fails by aiming both too high and too low: it is enslaved to reality while being snobbish about it. In a wonderful farrago of images Rimbaud demands new inventions, where all distinctions between the concerns of everyday life and the most extravagant fantasies are abolished:

> Trouve des Chardons cotonneux
> Dont dix ânes aux yeux de braises
> Travaillent à filer les noeuds!
> Trouve des Fleurs qui soient des chaises!
>
> Oui, trouve au coeur des noirs filons
> Des fleurs presque pierres, — fameuses! —
> Qui vers leurs durs ovaires blonds
> Aient des amygdales gemmeuses!

[Find cottony thistles whose knots ten asses with fiery eyes will work to spin! Find flowers which are chairs! Yes, find in the heart of black lodes flowers which are almost stones—wonderful!—which toward their hard blond ovaries have gem-like tonsils!]

The vocabulary of industry and commerce (milling, mining) is the point of departure for these splendid visions with their vivid juxtapositions of colors and textures. These cloth-yielding thistles, flower-chairs, and flower-stones are at once the height of commercial practicality and the utmost in imaginative elegance.

The esthetic expressed in "Ce qu'on dit au poète à propos de fleurs" clarifies in retrospect what Rimbaud was attempting in the poems of the preceding months. We have already seen how in regard to levels of usage and separation of styles Rimbaud had departed from his models. Equally important is his search for subject matter which would be novel but not self-consciously remote. At the same time, however, "Ce qu'on dit au poète" pushes, both by counsel and deed, further into the domain of poetic invention than Rimbaud's preceding poems. The stanzas on fantastic flowers quoted above betray a new breadth of imagination which we may seek in vain elsewhere: the contours of experience vanish, and the poet's creation is absolute and discrete.

Much the same independence from reality can be seen in the famous sonnet on the vowels, which appears to have been written shortly afterwards:[13]

A noir, E blanc, I rouge, U vert, O bleu : voyelles,
Je dirai quelque jour vos naissances latentes :
A, noir corset velu des mouches éclatantes
Qui bombinent autour des puanteurs cruelles,

Golfes d'ombre; E, candeurs des vapeurs et des tentes,
Lances des glaciers fiers, rois blancs, frissons d'ombelles;
I, pourpres, sang craché, rire des lèvres belles
Dans la colère ou les ivresses pénitentes;

U, cycles, vibrements divins des mers virides,
Paix des pâtis semés d'animaux, paix des rides
Que l'alchimie imprime aux grands fronts studieux;

O, suprême Clairon plein des strideurs étranges,
Silences traversés des Mondes et des Anges :
— O l'Oméga, rayon violet de Ses Yeux!

[A black, E white, I red, U green, O blue, vowels: I will tell some day your hidden birth. A, black hairy corset of the bursting flies which buzz around the cruel stench, gulfs of shadow; E, brilliance of vapors and tents, lances of proud glaciers, white kings, quivering flowers; I, purples, spit blood, laughter of beautiful lips in anger or drunk with penance; U, cycles, divine vibrations of the viridian seas, peace of pastures scattered with animals, peace of the wrinkles which alchemy prints on great studious brows; O, supreme Clarion full of a strange stridor, silence traversed by worlds and Angels: O, the Omega, the violet beam of His Eyes.]

13. Biographers date "Voyelles" variously but usually agree in placing it during the summer or early autumn of 1871.

Vast amounts have been written about Rimbaud's choice
of colors: children's alphabet books have been examined,
alchemical solutions proposed, and there is even an abundant literature on the arcane subject of "colored hearing."[14] One scholar has demonstrated, however, that there
are excellent verbal reasons for the assignment of each
vowel's color and order in sequence and that there is no
need to seek for explanations outside the text.[15] Indeed,
Rimbaud's invention of the vowels' colors is quite in keeping with the precepts set forth in the conclusion of "Ce
qu'on dit au poète à propos de fleurs." This world of evil
A's and epiphanic O's is a purely poetic, and, let us finally
say it, mythic creation. For this tendency to invent the
non-existent and to invest the ordinary with strange attributes leads toward myth. "Voyelles" is arranged as a
kind of apocalyptic crescendo in which evil yields to
good. It has the pattern of a Great Chain of Being, a conception frequent in Hugo's poetry. The lower life of the
flies gives place to that of men, who are first described in
their primitive simplicity with their tents and kings and
then presented as the violently emotional beings into
which civilization has perverted them. Nature (including
peaceful animals) is next evoked, for, according to romantic pantheism, plants and dumb creatures still possess the
innocence which man has lost. Finally knowledge, con-

14. An exhaustive account of proposed sources for "Voyelles" is
given in E. Noulet, *Le Premier Visage de Rimbaud* (Brussels, 1953),
pp. 111-87.

15. See C. Chadwick, *Etudes sur Rimbaud* (Paris, 1960), pp. 27-40.
The essential argument of this ingenious explication is as follows:
A is *noir* because the adjective contains that vowel sound; E is *blanc*
as a contrast to *noir*. I is *rouge* because *bleu* or *vert* would make
either a disagreeable alliteration or a pun (*hiver*). O is *bleu* to avoid
the pun *ovaire* and thus *vert* is left for U. The last two vowels are
inverted to avoid a hiatus (*bleu-U*). The author notes that *jaune* and
brun are much rarer in Rimbaud's poetry than the colors used in
"Voyelles."

ceived of as an ennobling force, ushers in a vision of divinity, which is at the top of the hierarchy of creation. This scheme corresponds furthermore to widespread nineteenth-century notions of historical progress and the evolution of humanity.[16] Certain details of the poem remain somewhat arbitrary—I think that on artistic grounds it hardly deserves its great fame—but the general design is clear. It is important in regard to "Voyelles," which has been so extravagantly interpreted, to make the observation that Rimbaud's difficult poems are better clarified by examining them in the light of the nineteenth-century literary traditions in which he was steeped than by searching the poems for anagrams or other devices which he is never known to have used.

Having seen in "Voyelles" the adumbration of a more symbolic and purely imaginative kind of poetry, we are now prepared to embark on an analysis of "Le Bateau ivre," Rimbaud's first long mythopoeic poem, and the masterpiece of that summer of 1871 when he was preparing to remove to Paris and the literary milieu into which Verlaine promised to introduce him. In "Le Bateau ivre" we find a fulfillment of Rimbaud's exhortations to *find* or *invent*. This great work is not at all the concluding piece of the Charleville cycle, as some have seen it; that Rimbaud had played in a boat on the Meuse, or read boys' adventure stories about the sea, is irrelevant. "Le Bateau ivre" introduces a totally new phase in the poet's progressive mastery of his art.

16. Again we must postpone fuller discussion of this question to the chapter on *Une Saison en enfer*.

3. "Le Bateau ivre," "Mémoire," and the Mythic Imagination

MYTH, whether made out of whole cloth or pieced together from classical and other sources, dominates much of romantic and modern poetry. In France the tendency toward myth is quite pronounced in various minor romantic writers, but many of them worked chiefly in prose, and often their achievements cannot be judged on any grounds other than good intentions.[1] It was not until the mid-nineteenth century, with the later work of Hugo, Gérard de Nerval, and Lamartine, that a corpus of important myth-centered poetry accumulated. Rimbaud's evolution toward this mode of imagination is therefore part of a larger movement in French literature which, though obscure at the time—Nerval was little known and Hugo's most audacious poems, *Dieu* and *La Fin de Satan,* remained unpublished until after his death—seems, from our vantage point, of considerable scope.

The characteristics of mythopoeic poetry will emerge more clearly as we examine "Le Bateau ivre," but we might make the distinction—which is especially pertinent in this case—that a myth is not an allegory, it is not a

1. For a detailed account of the turning to myth in nineteenth-century French poetry see H. J. Hunt, *The Epic in Nineteenth-Century France* (Oxford, 1941).

structure of simple, univalent symbols which can be translated into concepts. The integrity of myth refuses to be violated by reduction into abstract terms: its symbols are too rich in suggestiveness and interrelations for us to say that Rimbaud's boat represents something else. Nor is the life of a boat meaningless because boats are inanimate: we cannot press a rational order on this poem and insist that it conform. The world of myth must be understood on its own terms, and careful examination of the poem is indispensable.

Comme je descendais des Fleuves impassibles,
Je ne me sentis plus guidé par les haleurs :
Des Peaux-Rouges criards les avaient pris pour cibles,
Les ayant cloués nus aux poteaux de couleurs.

J'étais insoucieux de tous les équipages,
Porteur de blés flamands ou de cotons anglais.
Quand avec mes haleurs ont fini ces tapages,
Les Fleuves m'ont laissé descendre où je voulais.

[As I was going down impassive Rivers, I no longer felt myself guided by the haulers: screeching redskins had taken them as targets, nailing them naked to colored stakes. I was indifferent to any crew, bearing Flemish wheat or English cottons. When along with my haulers this uproar was over, the Rivers let me go on where I wanted.]

"Le Bateau ivre" is divided into a number of parts, whose discreteness and unity are assured by rhetorical devices. Several parallelisms relate the first two stanzas: the use of "Fleuves" and a form of *descendre* in lines one and eight, the mention of the haulers' massacre in the third line of each stanza, the imperfect tenses in lines one and five as contrasted with the compound tenses which follow them, and so forth. It is important to note the tenses here as elsewhere in the poem: the juxtaposition of *passé simple* and *passé composé* (lines two, seven, and eight) serves a particular function. The *passé composé*, the punctual past tense of ordinary speech, is used as a neutral, unemphatic tense, whereas the *passé simple*, with its more limited and literary usage, is reserved for dramatic effect. It is the *passé simple* which marks the sudden, magical liberation of the boat—a liberation all the more startling in that at first it is only felt and not seen (for, like a beast of burden, the boat cannot see its back). The sharply punctual, almost historical "je ne me sentis plus" cutting across the flowing durative imperfect "descendais" vividly isolates this moment of transformation when the boat gratuitously ceases to resemble other boats. Its surprise is contrasted with the rivers' attitude, since, though animate like everything else in the poem, they seem not to notice this metamorphosis. The boat's reaction to the massacre of the haulers anticipates its later adventures, where there is emphasis on colorful visual detail and indifference to suffering; thus the description of the massacre serves to set a prevailing mood. In this case, however, the boat's insouciance is quite explicable: its will is finally being asserted over the orderliness of the world represented by images of commerce. The boat and the Indians have triumphed over the shipping industry and European trade, and the fact is underscored by the emphatic position of "voulais" at the end of the second stanza.[2]

The next three stanzas describe the boat's *physical* initiation into the sea world (as distinguished from the spiritual one, which comes later):

Dans les clapotements furieux des marées,
Moi, l'autre hiver, plus sourd que les cerveaux d'enfants,

2. I am indebted for certain details of this analysis to B. Weinberg, "'Le Bateau ivre' or the Limits of Symbolism," *PMLA,* 72 (1959), 165–93.

Je courus! Et les Péninsules démarrées
N'ont pas subi tohu-bohus plus triomphants.

La tempête a béni mes éveils maritimes.
Plus léger qu'un bouchon j'ai dansé sur les flots
Qu'on appelle rouleurs éternels de victimes,
Dix nuits, sans regretter l'oeil niais des falots!

Plus douce qu'aux enfants la chair des pommes sures,
L'eau verte pénétra ma coque de sapin
Et des taches de vins bleus et des vomissures
Me lava, dispersant gouvernail et grappin.

> [Into the furious clash of the tides I, the other winter,
> more heedless than children's brains, I ran! And the
> uprooted Peninsulas have not undergone a more tri-
> umphant hubbub. The storms blessed my maritime
> vigils. Lighter than a cork I danced on the waves,
> which they call eternal rollers of victims, ten nights,
> without regretting the silly eye of the lighthouses.
> Sweeter than the flesh of unripe apples is to children,
> the green water penetrated my hull of fir and washed
> me of spots of blue wines and vomit, dispersing rud-
> der and grappling-hook.]

The comparison of the boat with an obstinate child
brings out an important association in the poem. Earlier
the Indians had evoked the world of children's books, and
the word "tapage," used of the massacre, commonly designates children's uproar. The opposition between the boat
and children, on the one hand, and men, on the other, is
constant: eating green apples is an unwise childish penchant, and later the boat speaks of wishing to show exotic
fishes to children (stanza fifteen). The boat and children
are related through their common love of impetuosity and
disorder: the third stanza describes the boat's entry into
the sea with violent expressions. "Je courus" is opposed
both by tense and energy of meaning to the peaceful

"descendais" of an earlier stanza, and its rhythmically isolated place in the line heightens it. "Les Péninsules démarrées" suggests great masses in movement (the optical illusion by which, from a boat, the land seems to be moving), and the verb *subir* accentuates the triumph with which the boat imposes its will for the first time.

Stanza four, in language suddenly become gentle, confirms the benevolence of the ocean, which is hostile only to men. Their lighthouses are contemptuously called not *phares* but "falots," which means "foolish" as well as "lanterns," and their absurd fear of the sea is mocked by quoting one of their phrases: "rouleurs éternels de victimes," a parody of *le père* Hugo's sonorous verses on the perils of the deep (cf. "Oceano nox"). The grandiose Hugolian expression contrasts sharply with the simplicity of the boat's language and its homey similes. Finally the recurring *passé simple* of the fifth stanza marks the end of the boat's physical initiation into sea life: it has now become one with its element, and the last traces of the world of men are effaced. With the rudder and hook vanishes the world of orderly movement.

The long middle section of "Le Bateau ivre" (stanzas six to fourteen) opens with the boat's spiritual entrance into the ocean world, which a sudden shift of style sets into great relief:

> Et dès lors, je me suis baigné dans le Poème
> De la Mer, infusé d'astres, et lactescent,
> Dévorant les azurs verts; où, flottaison blême
> Et ravie, un noyé pensif parfois descend;
>
> Où, teignant tout à coup les bleuités, délires
> Et rhythmes lents sous les rutilements du jour,
> Plus fortes que l'alcool, plus vastes que vos lyres,[3]
> Fermentent les rousseurs amères de l'amour!

3. There is some question whether one should read "*nos* lyres" or "*vos* lyres." Verlaine's copy (the only source for the text) seems

[And from then on I bathed in the Poem of the Sea
infused with stars and lactescent, devouring the
green azure, where, like a pallid, ecstatic bit of flot-
sam, a pensive drowned man sometimes sinks down—
where, dyeing suddenly the blueness, with delirium
and slow rhythms under the glimmers of day, there
ferments the bitter reddening of love, stronger than
alcohol and vaster than your lyres!]

Vast images of space, light, and color suddenly invade the
poem. These stanzas seem to describe first the night sea,
milky with phosphorus, dotted with reflected stars, hori-
zonless, and indistinguishable from the sky.[4] Then dawn
comes: "rutilements" suggests breaking day and "rous-
seurs" the color which "dyes" the blue sea, while the
rhythms of the waves are accentuated by the long, low
fingers of light. Dawn is an appropriate symbol of a new
spiritual experience, and into the light imagery are woven
highly emotive words which convey the boat's ecstasy. The
experience is esthetic ("Poème," "lyres"), physical ("dévo-
rant," "alcool") and so overwhelming as to be compared
with death; the *noyé ravi* recalls Leopardi's famous line "E
il naufragar m'è dolce in questo mar." The adjective
"amères" should not surprise us: pleasure and pain are
closely related and readily turn into one another. This is

---

to have "nos," but *n* and *v* are easily confused, and he might have
made a mistake. I prefer the reading "vos" because it emphasizes the
boat's differentness from mankind and because there is no *nous*
implied anywhere in the poem.

4. The expression "azurs verts," like the "nuit verte" of stanza
ten, the "mers virides" of "Voyelles," the "herbe bleue" of "Les
Reparties de Nina," and the "cresson bleu" of "Le Dormeur du val,"
has been attributed to Rimbaud's taste for Latinisms. The adjective
caeruleus applies both to green and blue things, and this usage may
have inspired the poet's fond confusion of the two colors. See
R. Faurisson, "A-t-on lu Rimbaud?" *Bizarre*, nos. 21–22 (1961),
pp. 14–15.

not an edulcorated joy but the most voluptuous self-im-
molation. Finally the word "amour" occurs at the climax
of the passage. This term must be understood in the
special sense it acquired in nineteenth-century poetic
usage; the romantic pantheists employed it to describe
total communion and harmony with the universe. Its
connotations are at once metaphysical and sensuous. The
boat's immersion in the sea perfectly exemplifies the romantics' desire to abolish the barriers between subject and
object, to achieve a unity of spirit.

The stanzas we have just considered are the emotive
peaks of the poem; yet many more stanzas remain, and we
must now pay particular attention to Rimbaud's subtle
ways of sustaining his tone and varying his images. The
central part of "Le Bateau ivre" consists of six stanzas
beginning with *je* or *j'ai* and also showing certain other
parallelisms of sentence structure. The first three continue
to elaborate light and weather imagery:

Je sais les cieux crevant en éclairs, et les trombes
Et les ressacs et les courants : je sais le soir,
L'Aube exaltée ainsi qu'un peuple de colombes,
Et j'ai vu quelquefois ce que l'homme a cru voir!

J'ai vu le soleil bas, taché d'horreurs mystiques,
Illuminant de longs figements violets,
Pareils à des acteurs de drames très antiques
Les flots roulant au loin leurs frissons de volets!

J'ai rêvé la nuit verte aux neiges éblouies,
Baiser montant aux yeux des mers avec lenteurs,
La circulation des sèves inouïes,
Et l'éveil jaune et bleu des phosphores chanteurs!

[I know the skies bursting with lightning, and the
waterspouts and the surf and the currents: I know
evening, dawn reaching high like a people of doves,
and I have sometimes seen what man has thought to

see! I have seen the low sun, spotted with mystic horrors and lighting, with long violet clots which resemble the actors of ancient dramas, the waves rolling at a distance in shutter-like quivers. I have dreamed the green night with dazzled snows, a kiss rising slowly to the sea's eyes; the circulation of unknown saps and the yellow and blue awakening of singing phosphorus.]

Only two difficulties of meaning present themselves here: the simile of the second stanza seems to mean that the long beams of light glancing on the waves move back and forth like actors in a shadow play or some other simple form of theater. The kiss and eye metaphor of the third stanza is more ambiguous; the eyes of the sea would seem to be its surface (eyes have been called "pools" after all), while the kiss, which could be in apposition to "nuit" or "neiges," might describe the approach of night from the horizon or the rising of bubbly foam to the water's surface. In any case these three stanzas deal with knowledge of the universe as symbolized by evening, dawn, sunset, and night; it is as if the boat saw the archetype of each hour. "Je *sais* le soir," says the boat with an emphatic, unusual use of *savoir*. This definitive vision is what man can only think to see (and again the boat emphasizes its difference from mankind).

Each of the preceding three stanzas contains, in simile or metaphor, a hint of living creatures: doves, actors, singing phosphorescences. Yet essentially the boat is alone in a seascape. Now lands, plants, and animals come into view:

J'ai suivi, des mois pleins, pareille aux vacheries
Hystériques, la houle à l'assaut des récifs,
Sans songer que les pieds lumineux des Maries
Pussent forcer le mufle aux Océans poussifs!

J'ai heurté, savez-vous, d'incroyables Florides
Mêlant aux fleurs des yeux de panthères à peaux
D'hommes! Des arcs-en-ciel tendus comme des brides
Sous l'horizon des mers, à de glauques troupeaux!

J'ai vu fermenter les marais énormes, nasses
Où pourrit dans les joncs tout un Léviathan!
Des écroulements d'eaux au milieu des bonaces,
Et les lointains vers les gouffres cataractant!

[I followed for whole months the swell, like a hysterical dairy-stable, in its assault on the reefs, without
imagining that the Maries' luminous feet could force
the snout of the wheezing Oceans! I have run into,
you know, unbelievable Floridas, where among the
flowers are mingled the eyes of panthers with human
skin! Rainbows stretched out like reins under the
horizon of the seas to greenish herds! I have seen the
enormous swamps fermenting, fish-traps where a
whole Leviathan rots in the rushes! Avalanches of
water in the middle of calms and the far distances
cataracting toward the abyss!]

The cows of the sea seem at first to be merely a metaphor
for the waves forced back into the sea by the headland of
the Camargue (where the village of the Saintes-Maries is
situated). But the green herds of the next stanza are more
concrete, and the panther-men melting into the flowers
are definitely more than just a figure of speech. Mythic
poetry is animistic and does not know rational distinctions
between animals, plants, and inert matter; it has the archaic, pre-logical vision of the world as instinct with mysterious life. In the third stanza, Leviathan is put on the
same plane with gigantic whirlpools, as if they were comparable entities. In connection with animism we should
also note a peculiar stylistic device which supports it: the
nouns of "Le Bateau ivre" are largely in the plural, cre-

ating a blurred effect of multiplicity, pullulation, and plenitude. The so-called poetic plural is, of course, common in French, but it is seldom carried to such lengths and with so specific an effect.

In addition to the abundant plurals another distinctive stylistic trait lends a feeling of portentous life to this passage as well as to many others in the poem. The definite article is constantly used before nouns, even when, as in "pareille aux vacheries hystériques," a partitive article or other construction would be demanded by normal usage. This insistent use of the definite article ends by creating a strange class of beings, by investing almost any noun with a demonstrative particularity, as if the thing it designated were too individual to be confused with others of its kind. This curious grammar is not exclusive, furthermore, to "Le Bateau ivre" and is present in many of Rimbaud's poems.[5]

To conclude the central part of "Le Bateau ivre" Rimbaud uses a very formal rhetorical device: an enumeration of nouns summarizing the preceding stanzas—weather and animals—and devoid of a main verb.

Glaciers, soleils d'argent, flots nacreux, cieux de braises!
Echouages hideux au fond des golfes bruns
Où les serpents géants dévorés des punaises
Choient, des arbres tordus, avec de noirs parfums!

> [Glaciers, silver suns, nacreous waves, ember skies! Hideous strandings in brown gulfs where the giant serpents, devoured by bedbugs, tumble down from gnarled trees with black scents!]

We have now reached a turning point in the poem where we must once again consider the question of tenses. The central section is written in the present (for statal

---

5. "Voyelles" is a relevant example and the *Illuminations* exploit this device quite thoroughly.

matters) and the *passé composé,* but the latter is ambiguous and requires some analysis. Since it may serve either as a present perfect or as a preterite, it does not clearly define the relation of past to present; it does not indicate whether the boat is still continuing its wanderings or whether they belong to an irrevocable, historical past. One's first impression is that, in contrast to the *passés simples* of the introductory stanzas, the *passés composés* indicate that the adventure is not over, that the past events are part of one continuing experience. Finally, however, by a very subtle transition Rimbaud corrects in retrospect the meaning of this tense, but not without our first having received from it a false feeling of immediacy. He slips in a conditional perfect, which implies remoteness and irremediability, and then passes into the iterative imperfect with its sense of "used to":

J'aurais voulu montrer aux enfants ces dorades
Du flot bleu, ces poissons d'or, ces poissons chantants.
— Des écumes de fleurs ont bercé mes dérades
Et d'ineffables vents m'ont ailé par instants.

Parfois, martyr lassé des pôles et des zones,
La mer dont le sanglot faisait mon roulis doux
Montait vers moi ses fleurs d'ombre aux ventouses jaunes
Et je restais, ainsi qu'une femme à genoux...

Presque île, ballottant sur mes bords les querelles
Et les fientes d'oiseaux clabaudeurs aux yeux blonds.
Et je voguais, lorsqu'à travers mes liens frêles
Des noyés descendaient dormir, à reculons!

> [I should have liked to show children those sunfishes of the blue wave, those golden fishes, those singing fishes. Foams of flowers rocked my driftings and ineffable winds occasionally winged me. Sometimes when I was martyred, weary of poles and zones, the sea, whose sob made my gentle roll, brought up to

me her shadow-flowers with yellow suckers. And I
remained like a kneeling woman . . . Like a kind of
island tossing on my sides the quarrels and droppings
of blond-eyed noisy birds. And I sailed on, when
through my fragile ties drowned men sunk backwards
to sleep.]

As the tenses shift, the character of the boat's experiences
also changes; the energetic quest for the ocean's mysteries
yields to languor. The boat thinks, for the first time and
as if regretfully, of the existence of sympathetic creatures,
children, and is attracted more by flowers than by the
rigors of strange climates (vaguely categorized as the "poles
and zones"). A series of words suggests failing strength and
feeble movement: "bercer," "dérade" (a neologism from
dérader: "to be dragged out of harbor by winds"), "lassé,"
"roulis doux," "une femme à genoux" (implying that the
boat is leaning forward to look at the flowers). The boat
has again become conscious of its physical self: the third
stanza even seems to indicate that it is topheavy with the
weight of the birds, while its hull ("frêles liens") has become so disintegrated that drowned men may pass through
the chinks. This passage balances stanzas three to five,
which described the boat's physical sensations on entering
the sea, for the form of "Le Bateau ivre" is cyclical, and
we are now returning to the original point of departure.

Another elaborate rhetorical pattern (still in the imperfect tense) leads us further back toward the civilized
world:

Or moi, bateau perdu sous les cheveux des anses,[6]
Jeté par l'ouragan dans l'éther sans oiseau,

6. The odd expression "les cheveux des anses" can best be ex-
plained, I think, by reference to Latin: *cheveux* renders *comae,*
which means both hair and foliage. *Anse (de panier)* is an architectural and geometrical term for a kind of curve; like *sinus* it is here
applied to a bay because it describes the shape of the shoreline.

Moi dont les Monitors et les voiliers des Hanses
N'auraient pas repêché la carcasse ivre d'eau;

Libre, fumant, monté de brumes violettes,
Moi qui trouais le ciel rougeoyant comme un mur
Qui porte, confiture exquise aux bons poètes,
Des lichens de soleil et des morves d'azur;

Qui courais, taché de lunules électriques,
Planche folle, escorté des hippocampes noirs,
Quand les juillets faisaient crouler à coups de triques
Les cieux ultramarins aux ardents entonnoirs;

Moi qui tremblais, sentant geindre à cinquante lieues
Le rut des Béhémots et les Maelstroms épais,
Fileur éternel des immobilités bleues,
Je regrette l'Europe aux anciens parapets!

[Now I, a boat lost in the foliage of coves, thrown by
the storm into the birdless ether, I, whose water-
drunken carcass would not have been salvaged by the
Monitors and the Hanseatic sailing ships; free, smok-
ing, covered with violet mists, I, who pierced the
reddening sky that looks like a wall covered with—
a delicious jam for good poets—lichens of sunlight
and mucus of blue sky; who ran, speckled with electric satellites, a wild plank, escorted by black sea-
horses, when the Julys beat down with cudgels the
burning funnels of the ultramarine skies; I, who
trembled, hearing a hundred leagues around the
moaning of the Behemoths in heat and the dense
Maelstroms, I, eternal drifter of the motionless blue,
I miss Europe and its ancient cliffs.]

The first and last stanzas of this lengthy period are related
by proper names ("Monitors," "Hanses," "Europe"), so
that it forms an elegant circle. All the stanzas are, furthermore, connected by parallel images: the boat is being

tossed into the air, pierces the sky, is thrown about by summer storms which merge sea and sky, and runs endlessly through the "immobilités bleues," an expression which suggests the unity of ocean and atmosphere. What these images convey is the boat's fragile lightness and passivity, which have already been hinted at in the preceding stanzas. However, should the boat's drunken subjugation to the sea be interpreted as the reason for its missing Europe? That is to say, are the clauses dependent on "moi" causal or adversative in meaning? I think the adversative sense is a better reading, partly because it gives "Je regrette l'Europe . . ." greater dramatic relief and partly because the experiences described in the clauses dependent on "moi" summarize the boat's original desires: to be drunken with water, to be free, to enjoy a kind of esthetic pleasure ("confiture exquise aux bons poètes"), to move recklessly and irregularly, and to see the animals and phenomena of the deep. Thus, *although* the boat has done these things, its mind returns to home. These four stanzas are almost a résumé of the central section of the poem (stanzas six to fourteen), and the boat expresses its surprise that, having utterly achieved its yearnings, it should then long for Europe.

The next stanza introduces a curious new element:

J'ai vu des archipels sidéraux! et des îles
Dont les cieux délirants sont ouverts au vogueur :
— Est-ce en ces nuits sans fonds que tu dors et t'exiles,
Million d'oiseaux d'or, ô future Vigueur?

> [I have seen sidereal archipelagos! and islands whose ecstatic skies are open to the sea-wanderer: is it in these limitless nights that you sleep and retire, million golden birds, O future Vigor?]

The ecstatic sky imagery recurs but with a new nuance: the heavens are now the symbol of conceivable but unattainable aspirations. "Vigor" is exactly what the boat has lost—if it ever had it, for the adjective "future" has interesting implications. Has the boat's journey taken place in real time and space, or was it merely a now fading dream, symbolic of what is to take place in the future? We must postpone considering this problem, for the last stanzas of the poem are related alternatively rather than sequentially.

Mais, vrai, j'ai trop pleuré! Les Aubes sont navrantes.
Toute lune est atroce et tout soleil amer :
L'âcre amour m'a gonflé de torpeurs enivrantes.
O que ma quille éclate! O que j'aille à la mer!

> [But, truly, I have wept too much. The dawns are heartbreaking. Any moon is horrible and any sun bitter. Acrid love has filled me with intoxicating torpor. O let my keel burst! Let me dissolve into the sea!]

"J'ai trop pleuré!" abruptly places us in a new phase of the journey, for there has been no question of weeping previously. The boat suddenly realizes what has been apparent from the imagery of the preceding eight stanzas: that its sea-change leads ultimately to dissolution, that its weakness is a prelude to disgust and the desire for death. "L'âcre amour" (the noun significantly recurs just this one time to designate again the boat's total sea experience) leads to a kind of love-death.

Suddenly in a brilliant metamorphosis the boat is placed in a new perspective:

Si je désire une eau d'Europe, c'est la flache
Noire et froide où vers le crépuscule embaumé
Un enfant accroupi plein de tristesses, lâche
Un bateau frêle comme un papillon de mai.

> [If I want European water, it is the cold, black puddle where, in the sweet-scented twilight, a squat-

ting child full of melancholy sets off a boat fragile as
a May butterfly.]

The sea has dwindled to a landlocked puddle, and the
boat's fragility is now understandable, since it is only a
toy. The boat's bond with children is also clearer: they
are its only companions, and the sea adventure was their
communal dream. However, there are implications for
the future in the description of the landscape with its
delicate alternation of connotations (A. "noire," B. "embaumé," A. "tristesse," B. "mai"). The ground on which
the child squats is cold and dark, but the evening air is
fragrant with approaching spring, and the boat brings
to mind a butterfly. As in the stanza on "future Vigor,"
height symbolizes the promise of the future, and the turn
of the season reinforces the sense of expectation. The child
will grow and free himself from the tyranny of the adult
world.

But we must not conclude that the boat is merely a
symbol of the child and his dreams, for the cycle of growing power and dissolution through which the boat passes
is not identical with a child's aspirations. We must beware of the urge to make a facile epitome of the poem.
The boat is to some extent equated with the child, but
it is also a more general symbol and ultimately irreducible.
To make clear that the poem is about a boat and not an
allegory about a child, Rimbaud concludes it with a final
picture of the boat's abjection:

Je ne puis plus, baigné de vos langueurs, ô lames,
Enlever leur sillage aux porteurs de cotons,
Ni traverser l'orgueil des drapeaux et des flammes,
Ni nager sous les yeux horribles des pontons.

[I can no longer, bathed in your languor, O waves,
follow close on the cotton boats, or pass haughty
flags and shell-fire, or swim under the terrible eyes
of the prison-ships.]

The cycle has come full swing; the boat is suddenly back in the world of organized shipping, where it had been before its magical liberation. But now the other ships are menacing and more powerful than the enervated "carcasse ivre d'eau." (There is also a symbolic correspondence here with the child's inferior position in the world of men: the stanzas interreact.)

We may define the shape and emotive content of a mythopoeic poem like "Le Bateau ivre," but it is impossible to translate it into a coherent allegory. The association between boat and child, for example, is intermittent and most pronounced at the beginning and end of the work. The boat's voyage corresponds somewhat with the cycle of life—or love, or even artistic inspiration, if one likes—but the details of imagery (for example, that of commerce in the first and last stanzas) do not easily lend themselves to such readings. Finally, the sea is so polyvalent a symbol in literature as to defy any neat categorizing of it. Numerous allegorical interpretations are generated by the poem, but none is so definitive as to exclude the others. Such is the nature of myth: it may be used but never exhausted by ratiocination.

Rimbaud is said to have composed "Le Bateau ivre" as a kind of showpiece to take with him to Paris in September 1871; it was to demonstrate the scope of his talent to the circle of Parisian poets to whom Verlaine had announced the arrival of a provincial genius.[7] Certainly the poem was infinitely beyond the powers of any of the little literary figures who saw it, but greatness can be a liability, and coupled with Rimbaud's surliness it could not fail to incite enmity. Furthermore the originality of "Le Bateau ivre" undoubtedly disconcerted Verlaine's friends as much as its beauty struck them. As yet there were few published

7. E. Delahaye, *Rimbaud, l'artiste et l'être moral* (Paris, 1923), p. 41.

and widely known poems in French which departed so radically from the traditional forms of narration. Even Banville, who was an intelligent if minor poet, could not quite understand the beginning of "Le Bateau ivre," if we are to believe Verlaine. "Verlaine used to tell me," wrote one contemporary, "that when Rimbaud read his poem ["Le Bateau ivre"] to Banville, the latter objected that it would have been a good idea to say at the beginning, 'I AM a boat who . . .' The young savage didn't make any reply, but on the way out he shrugged his shoulders and muttered, 'Vieux c...' "[8] Banville and his Parnassian friends felt they held the key to perdurable beauty, and this rather neo-classical outlook shut them off from innovations like Rimbaud's mythopoeia. They believed in clear-cut metaphors and similes and were understandably thrown off by anything so elusive as "Le Bateau ivre."

Rimbaud was fortunately not destined to become a man of letters in the ordinary sense of the word. A month or two of contact with Parisian literary circles sufficed to alienate him from all but the most bohemian souls. His atrocious manners became famous, but perhaps his social reputation was also due to his own boasts about his way of life and to the malevolence of Verlaine's friends. Many anecdotes about Rimbaud's behavior in Paris have come down to us, but biographers differ on their interpretation, and in any case the accuracy of such stories is frustratingly suspect. It is difficult to say at this remove exactly how Rimbaud and the *littérateurs* parted company, but one may legitimately suppose it had something to do with the mediocrity and pretentiousness of the latter. The literary world which from the provinces had seemed so brilliant proved on closer examination to consist largely of dabblers. Verlaine remained an exception, however; his ad-

8. Quoted in Colonel Godchot, *Arthur Rimbaud "ne varietur,"* 2 (Nice, 1938), 141. The source of this anecdote is a letter from Delahaye to Godchot.

miration for Rimbaud (which led shortly to a more intimate relationship) was so immense that he allowed it to
estrange him from his family and fellow-poets.

The autumn and winter of 1871 form an obscure period
in the history of Rimbaud's poetic career. Just as in 1870
and 1872, we cannot positively date any poems from the
cold months, while the change of style apparent in the
springtime poems indicates that some profound transformation had occurred in his esthetic.[9] The stages and
causes of this change cannot however be traced. Debauchery with Verlaine does not seem to me to offer an
adequate reason for poetic innovation, though some
critics associate the two with alarming ease. Nor does the
influence of Verlaine's work, reinforced by his presence,
seem very decisive. Verlaine was in a fallow period and
had written very little since 1869; indeed, his encounter
with Rimbaud may have saved his talent from extinction.[10] However, the stimulus of discussions with the
older poet is a factor not to be discounted in plotting
Rimbaud's poetic development. Whatever the case may
have been, the poems dated from 1872 are cast in a totally
new mold: they resemble their predecessors neither in
prosody, sentence structure, nor imagery.

The manuscript of "Mémoire" bears no date, but editors group it with the poems of 1872 for fairly obvious
reasons of style. It is worthwhile considering this poem in
connection with "Le Bateau ivre," for it has the same
meter and mythic character while showing the increasing
ellipsis of Rimbaud's last verse. "Mémoire" is a difficult

9. The satiric and buffoonish verse of the *Album zutique* dates
from this period, but it is of little importance for Rimbaud's poetic
development.

10. The Pléiade edition (ed. Y.-G. Le Dantec, Paris, 1954) attempts
to date his poetry with whatever means are available. It does not
seem that Verlaine wrote much between *La Bonne Chanson* and his
Wanderjahr with Rimbaud.

poem, but careful reading can discover its general design. The first of its five parts evokes a river under the morning light:

I

L'eau claire; comme le sel des larmes d'enfance,
L'assaut au soleil des blancheurs des corps de femmes;
la soie, en foule et de lys pur, des oriflammes
sous les murs dont quelque pucelle eut la défense;

l'ébat des anges; — Non... le courant d'or en marche,
meut ses bras, noirs, et lourds, et frais surtout,
                              d'herbe. Elle
sombre, ayant le Ciel bleu pour ciel-de-lit, appelle
pour rideaux l'ombre de la colline et de l'arche.

> [Clear water, like the salt of children's tears, the assault on the sun by the whiteness of female bodies; the silk of oriflammes, made of abundant pure lilies, under the walls once defended by some maid; the play of angels—no; the golden flow on its way moves its arms, black and heavy and above all cool with grass. She sinks down, having the blue sky as a canopy, summons to serve as her curtains the shadow of the hill and arching bridge.]

The first stanza is syntactically rather casual. The loose string of appositions is very different from the rigorous and oratorical sentence structure of "Le Bateau ivre"; key words and themes of the poem are emitted as if by chance. Actually they are arranged in a crescendo of hyperbole; "sel des larmes d'enfance" doubly enriches the initial image of clear water: salt reflects light brilliantly while childhood and tears suggest the nostalgia of a time long since gone, for, as the title indicates, "Mémoire" is concerned with the past. The female bodies appropriately represent a sinuous feminine river gleaming under the

sunlight. The masses of lilies bordering the river and
castle shine like silk oriflammes, the medieval flag of the
French kings; lilies are equally associated with the mon-
archy, and the allusion to Joan of Arc further establishes
us in a remote and fabulous world. The play of light is
finally termed an angels' game to emphasize the mythic
atmosphere, but having reached this climax of metaphoric
embellishment the poet disclaims his periphrasis and returns to a more sober description of the river. The arms
of the river are its grassy banks, which it is said to move
in its meanders. The "elle" has no precise reference; as
in other parts of the poem, we must accept this pronoun
without antecedent and attempt to understand its relations with the surrounding imagery. "Elle" here is clearly
the river; the water has already been associated with a
female body, and many rivers are feminine in French, as
well as the word *rivière*. With their two genders, the romance languages offer extraordinary possibilities for animistic expression; here the river is not a woman simply by
metaphor: as the poem unfolds it becomes impossible to
separate them into the classic tenor and vehicle of a figure
of speech. Neither is the concrete term for which the other
is substituted. This ambiguity is pursued in the last lines
quoted above, for both women and rivers have beds
covered by *ciels* ("sky" or "canopy").

II

Eh! l'humide carreau tend ses bouillons limpides!
L'eau meuble d'or pâle et sans fond les couches prêtes.
Les robes vertes et déteintes des fillettes
font les saules, d'où sautent les oiseaux sans brides.

> [Ah! the watery pane spreads out its limpid broth.
> The water fills with pale bottomless gold the awaiting
> beds. The faded green dresses of girls make willows
> from which jump reinless birds.]

"Elle sombre . . ." in the preceding stanza suggests spreading out as well as sinking, which prepares us for the evocation of the pond that the river forms in its course. The interjection "Eh" and the exclamation points underscore the sudden widening of the watercourse as it expands into the waiting ("prêtes") bed. ("Couches" has a rich if vague meaning here, suggesting wrappings, thickness, and warmth.) In a typically animistic reversal (cf. the river's moving the land in stanza two) girls' dresses make willows rather than the other way round. Rimbaud is determined to shake off the classical structure of metaphor and achieve a less logical but more elemental unity.

> Plus pure qu'un louis, jaune et chaude paupière
> le souci d'eau — ta foi conjugale, ô l'Epouse! —
> au midi prompt, de son terne miroir, jalouse
> au ciel gris de chaleur la Sphère rose et chère.

> [Purer than a louis, a warm and yellow eyelid: the marsh-marigold—your conjugal pledge, O Bride—turns toward the south and, dimly reflecting light, vies with the dear, rosy Sphere in the sky pale with heat.]

The imagery of reflection and brightness reaches its climax in this evocation of noon, where the relation between river and sun (already suggested in the second line of the poem) is made more explicit. The capital letters of "Epouse" and "Sphère" help isolate and emphasize the two major poles, the river and the sun, from the welter of life about them. As in old fertility myths the landscape seems dependent on the union of sexual forces. Thus the marsh-marigold symbolizes, through its watery roots and sun-like blossoms, the unity of noon. The image of the flower as eyelid stresses the drowsy heat of the hour, which complements the mention of beds in previous stanzas.

The third and middle part of "Mémoire" is by far the

most difficult both in general sense and in detail. Here the river and sun change in both relationship and modality:

III

Madame se tient trop debout dans la prairie
prochaine où neigent les fils du travail; l'ombrelle
aux doigts; foulant l'ombelle; trop fière pour elle;
des enfants lisant dans la verdure fleurie

leur livre de maroquin rouge! Hélas, Lui, comme
mille anges blancs qui se séparent sur la route,
s'éloigne par delà la montagne! Elle, toute
froide, et noire, court! après le départ de l'homme!

[Madame stands too straight in the nearby meadow,
where the sons of work snow down; a parasol in her
fingers; stepping on the white flower, too proud for
it; children reading in the flowering green their book
bound in red morocco! Alas, He, like a thousand
angels taking leave on the road, goes away over the
mountain! She, quite cold and black, runs! after the
departing male.]

The female element suddenly and sarcastically becomes "Madame," a word redolent of bourgeois life, and her actions (standing too straight, despising the flower) evidently constitute some offense, which is punished, or at least followed, by the man-sun's setting. But of course the sun goes down inevitably, even in a mythic world, so that his departure assumes the character of a natural cataclysm as well as that of a voluntary withdrawal. There is a fine balance of ambiguity in this passage, which prevents one from simply interpreting it as an allegory of nature or of mankind. The two are both present, inseparable, but not quite identical.

With the transformation of the river and sun into more

anthropomorphic terms the landscape also modifies gently, but not beyond recognition. The "ombelle" (a word which Rimbaud uses vaguely to designate a white flower[11]) replaces the "lys" of earlier stanzas, and the hill (upon which the castle apparently stands, in accordance with medieval custom) turns into a mountain. These small changes contribute to the continuous feeling of growth and movement in the poem, as well as to the shimmering evanescence of its visual effects. The children, who have been hinted at in the opening line and also suggested by the "girls' dresses" of the willow trees, seem to be present as necessary witnesses of mythic action; as in "Le Bateau ivre" they participate naturally in the world of suprarational events. Finally the snow of "fils du travail" adds plenitude and movement to the scene, though without one's being able to determine whether Rimbaud wrote the plural of *fil* or *fils*. Because of the descending motion and whiteness suggested by the verb "snow" they seem related to the sun and its beams; it is fitting that Rimbaud intensify the light imagery (the parasol is also part of it) just before the landscape dims into twilight.

The evening which settles over the scene is not only that of day but also the waning of the year; time is telescoped in a curious fashion as the river-woman laments spring, summer, and the grass which once covered her arm-banks:

IV

Regret des bras épais et jeunes d'herbe pure!
Or des lunes d'avril au coeur du saint lit! Joie
des chantiers riverains à l'abandon, en proie
aux soirs d'août qui faisaient germer ces pourritures!

11. For a study of the approximate character of Rimbaud's botanical terms see W. M. Frohock, "Rimbaud amid Flowers," *Modern Language Notes*, 76 (1961), 140–43.

Qu'elle pleure à présent sous les remparts! l'haleine
des peupliers d'en haut est pour la seule brise.
Puis, c'est la nappe, sans reflets, sans source, grise :
Un vieux, dragueur, dans sa barque immobile, peine.

> [Longings after the thick, young arms of pure grass!
> The gold of April moons in the heart of the holy
> bed! The joy of abandoned shipyards overcome by
> August evenings, which made rotting things germi-
> nate! Let her weep at present under the ramparts!
> The breath of the poplars up there is the only breeze.
> After, there's the surface without reflections, spring-
> less, gray: an old dredger struggles in his motionless
> boat.]

The landscape continues its metamorphoses: the willows
yield to the more austere poplars, and the pond is no
longer part of a moving river but "springless." The children have vanished leaving in their place an old man em-
prisoned on the wintry, lifeless water. The relation of the
poem to its title is gradually emerging as the pond comes
to be a link between past and present, which, like memory, can be dredged. *Mémoire,* it should be recalled,
designates the faculty and total content of memory, not
a recollection like *souvenir.*

The old man speaks the final stanzas:

V

Jouet de cet oeil d'eau morne, je n'y puis prendre,
ô canot immobile! oh! bras trop courts! ni l'une
ni l'autre fleur : ni la jaune qui m'importune,
là; ni la bleue, amie à l'eau couleur de cendre.

> [The toy of this dreary eye of water, I cannot pluck,
> O immobile boat! Oh arms too short! either flower:
> neither the yellow one which importunes me there,
> nor the friendly blue one in the ash-colored water.]

The eye image of part II returns in a new form—and not unexpectedly, for the effect of metamorphosis in time is created by just such interrelations in the poem. Flowers also recur, but this time they appear to be waterlilies. It is difficult to assign an exact symbolic value to them, but the yellow one seems associated with past scenes (the marsh-marigold, sunlight) and, like memory, it importunes, whereas the blue flower, related to the water and the present, suggests oblivion. (It is worth recalling that some flowers have a connection with memory in traditional symbolism, e.g. the lotus and forget-me-not.) In any case, the old man's impotent dissatisfaction is further accentuated by the immobility of his boat, his enslavement to the past. The hopelessness of his situation is enlarged on in the last stanza, where, after an evocation of dead banks, the pond expands to the horizon:

> Ah! la poudre des saules qu'une aile secoue!
> Les roses des roseaux dès longtemps dévorés!
> Mon canot, toujours fixe; et sa chaîne tirée
> Au fond de cet oeil d'eau sans bords, — à quelle boue?

> [The dust of the willows shaken by a wing! The roses of the reeds long ago withered! My boat forever stationary, and its chain caught, in the depths of this boundless eye of water, in what mud?]

"Mud"—the accretions of memory inspire disgust, and the poem concludes in a vision of total monotony, curiously reminiscent of some of Baudelaire's verses on the past like "Spleen," where the present is the time of ebbing life and changelessness. Like "Le Bateau ivre" "Mémoire" is suggestive of many things: the cycle of life, the incompatibility of the sexes, and so forth, but these "themes" are merely resonances and cannot, individually or if multiplied many times, account for this strange myth which preserves its inviolable coherence.

"Mémoire" is an extraordinarily supple and delicately woven poem; "Le Bateau ivre" seems almost stiff in comparison with its conventional syntax and the firm contours of its imagery. Even its versification, despite some Verlainean disregard for the caesura after the sixth syllable of the alexandrine, is timid beside that of "Mémoire." Rimbaud had almost abandoned the alexandrine by 1872, and in this, his last poem in the form, he seems determined to destroy its traditional solidity. The rimes, for example, are all feminine, which, while it does not have much significance for the ear, is nevertheless an infraction of consecrated rules. More important is the play of interior rimes, enjambment, sentence fragments, and frequent strong pauses within lines:

Madame se tient trop debout dans la prairie
prochaine où neigent les fils du travail; l'ombrelle
aux doigts; foulant l'ombelle; trop fière pour elle;
des enfants lisant dans la verdure fleurie
leur livre de maroquin rouge! . . .

There is only one classical caesura in these lines (after "ombelle"), and it is assimilated to other strong pauses and obscured by the rime with "elle." In fact, these are alexandrines for the eye alone; their actual form is as shifting and sinuous as the subject of the poem itself.

The distance which separates "Mémoire" from "Le Bateau ivre" is enormous in regard to artistic evolution if not time, but both poems reflect Rimbaud's essential artistic concern from the summer of 1871 on: the creation of allusive, elliptic poems remote from anecdote and specific reference. The meaning of these poems is furthermore inseparable from their structure; the "new forms" which Rimbaud had demanded in the "Lettre du voyant" were finally achieved. From this point on our principal task is to analyze the unity of sense and shape which characterizes Rimbaud's later work, but before approaching *Une Saison en enfer* or the major *Illuminations,* we have first to examine more fully the poetic results of Rimbaud's association with Verlaine: the emergence of a new prosody and the symbols of spiritual life in the last verse poems.

permitted himself at most an occasional odd caesura in the alexandrine. It is sufficient, on the other hand, for us to note that over two-thirds of Rimbaud's 1872 poems are in verse forms new either to him or to the language in order to realize the magnitude of the change which he underwent.

Before examining this change, however, we must also take into account Verlaine's previous work, for prosodic innovation was a communal undertaking with the two poets and Verlaine's verse was also profoundly affected. The latter's *Romances sans paroles* are more or less contemporary with Rimbaud's last verse poems, and it is not surprising that Verlaine originally wished to dedicate the *Romances* to his friend, since Rimbaud's presence can be felt in many stylistic traits. Unlike Rimbaud, Verlaine began his poetic career as a modest innovator in prosody, and his name eventually came to be associated with the expression *vers libérés* (but not *libres*). His early *Poèmes saturniens* do not seem very "liberated" when read today, but the public of 1866 could have seen some daring in the lack of alternance between masculine and feminine rimes in certain poems and in such oddly articulated alexandrines as "L'inflexion des voix chères qui se sont tues," with its 7/5 division. However, Verlaine did not really make a program of poetic license, and it is impossible to detect any further liberation of his prosody in his two subsequent volumes, *Fêtes galantes* and *La Bonne Chanson*. One is inclined to think that Verlaine's early audacities of versification resulted more from indifference to the Parnassian cult of restriction than from any intense desire to renovate.

Unfortunately we have more adequate information about Verlaine and Rimbaud's personal relations in 1872–73 than about their literary theories at that time. Most of their notions about poetry must be deduced from analysis of what they wrote. Even the letters between the two

4. The Last Verse Poems: The Renovation of Prosody and the Symbolism of Spiritual Quest

IN approaching Rimbaud's last verse poems—those of 1872—we must devote some attention to a subject which up to now has concerned us only in passing: versification. Curiously enough, the poet who made genuine innovations in imagery, vocabulary, and myth-making remained rather conventional and even conservative in regard to prosody. He confined himself largely to well-worked forms like alexandrines arranged in regular stanzas or sonnet patterns and *octosyllabes* grouped in quatrains. The few other forms he tried were equally commonplace: the triolet ("Le Coeur volé"), verse-paragraphs of alexandrine couplets ("Les Poètes de sept ans"), and traditional combinations of short and long lines such as 8/4 and 12/6 (e.g., "Les Effarés"). The alexandrine and the *octosyllabe* are the most widely used French verse lengths, yet Rimbaud was surely acquainted with some of the experiments in lines of less than eight syllables or of an uneven number of syllables (*vers impairs*) which poets like Hugo and Verlaine had attempted. Still he showed no inclination in 1871 to abandon the mainstream of French prosody and

which were destroyed by Verlaine's father-in-law might
not have been very illuminating had they survived, since
the few samples of them we have barely touch on literature. However, the name of one little-known writer is
preserved in Verlaine's half of the extant correspondence,
and from it we may infer something about their new interests, for the obscure Favart is by no means the sort of
literary figure one might expect Verlaine or Rimbaud to
know or mention.

For most of us the name Favart, if it means anything
at all, conjures up no more than a little street alongside
the Opéra-Comique. Charles-Simon Favart (1710–92)
earned this commemoration for being one of the best-
loved librettists of the eighteenth century. His works have
long since disappeared from the stage, but the curious
interest in him which Verlaine and Rimbaud showed in
1872 makes some investigation of his libretti pertinent.
The mention of Favart in their correspondence occurs in
April 1872, after Rimbaud had left Paris to allow Verlaine some chance of reconciliation with his wife. Verlaine
wrote in a postscript, "Parle-moi de Favart, en effet."[1]
Although this request implies that Rimbaud had com-
municated his fondness for Favart to Verlaine, we cannot
say with certainty which of the two poets first discovered
the librettist. Verlaine owned a copy of Favart's *Ninette
à la cour* by July of the same year, yet it may have been
acquired at Rimbaud's instigation.[2] Verlaine also claimed
years later that Rimbaud had studied old libretti at the
Charleville library, a statement which seems to establish
Rimbaud's priority.[3] On the other hand, Verlaine once
mentioned having started work on an "opéra-bouffe 18e

1. Letter of April 2. Verlaine's letters to Rimbaud are included
in the Pléiade Rimbaud.
2. See the list of objects Verlaine left in Paris when he set off for
Belgium in Rimbaud's company, *Correspondance, 1* (Paris, 1922), 69.
3. *Les Poètes maudits* (Paris, 1900), p. 17.

siècle" in the days before he met Rimbaud, which certainly suggests that by 1872 he was aware, if not of Favart,
of similar writers, and of course *Fêtes galantes* demonstrate some study of eighteenth-century culture.[4] The
problem is also obscured by another remark in Verlaine's
letter of April 2, 1872: "C'est charmant, *l'Ariette oubliée,*
paroles et musique! Je me la suis fait déchiffrer et chanter!
Merci de ce délicat envoi!" The "ariette oubliée" might
be an eighteenth-century piece, except that the adjective
"oubliée" given as part of the title would then be surprising; it suggests a pseudo-old-fashioned song of Rimbaud's manufacture instead of a genuine old *ariette.* For
an eighteenth-century librettist *ariette* was simply a technical term (like *air,* which replaced it) and would hardly
have been qualified with so romantic a term as "oubliée."
On the other hand—such are the obscurities of this question—Rimbaud did not know music any more than Verlaine did, so he could hardly have been sending along his
own work with accompaniment. Whatever the case may
be, the phrase "ariette oubliée" later returns in the plural
as the title of a section of *Romances sans paroles,* and the
epigraph for these poems is taken from *Ninette à la cour.*

On the surface Verlaine and Rimbaud's preoccupation
with Favart might seem inconsequential, except for the
fact that Favart was a librettist, not a poet, and both Verlaine and Rimbaud were evolving new verse forms.
French verse which is specifically intended for musical
setting is, as a matter of course, freer in prosody than ordinary poetry, for the exigencies of melodic development
and variety do not favor a continuous flow of *octosyllabes*
or alexandrines. Nor is it free verse like La Fontaine's, for
the latter is not especially suited to musical setting. La
Fontaine often likes generous contrasts between line
lengths like the famous "Même il m'est arrivé quelquefois

4. *Correspondance, 1,* 97.

de manger / Le berger" and similar effects which do not lend themselves readily to melody. Librettists, on the other hand, prefer slight changes in line length; an extra syllable or two can easily be absorbed into a melodic line or an insufficient number of them can be prolonged without difficulty. The following sequences are typical of the approximations of song:

> Je vends des bouquets,
> De jolis bouquets,
> Ils sont tous frais (bis)
>
> C'est l'image
> D'un objet charmant
> C'est l'hommage
> D'un tendre amant.[5]

Alternation of such similar lines as those of four and five syllables is not felt to be clearly articulated and elegant in normal French verse, where combinations like 12/8, 8/4, etc. are the rule.

Favart's prosody differs in still another way from that of the poet who does not write with an eye to being set to music: he handles the mute *e* in a special fashion. The last example quoted above is not a combination of three-, four-, and five-syllable lines, as it would be in ordinary verse, but a sequence of lines of four and five syllables, for, in music, the feminine lines may acquire an extra syllable at the end. Songs even admit of such haphazard versification as the following:

> Dans nos prairi–es
> Toujours fleuri–es
> On voit sourir–e
> Un doux zéphire.[6]

5. C. Favart, *La Fée Urgèle* (Paris, 1766), pp. 10–11.
6. *Ninette à la cour* (Paris, 1755), p. 24.

The *-ies* endings have two syllables; the *e* of *sourire* is pronounced despite the hiatus with *un,* but *zéphire* counts only as two syllables. (Obviously one must consult the musical accompaniments to realize all the possible irregularities of such verse.) The mute *e* can be suppressed at will for convenience or for colloquial effect; in *Ninette à la cour* we find "Com' la cloche . . . ," "je suis vot' sarviteur . . . ," and "Demain tu s'ras ma femme . . ."[7]

Considering the evident importance which Verlaine and Rimbaud attached to Favart and probably by way of him to the prosody of song, we are not surprised that both of them devoted themselves in 1872 to the composition of gracile lyrics in unusual verse forms. What is really curious, however, is the different way in which each poet profited from their common endeavors: as we analyze their separate *oeuvres,* it is apparent that the difference lies not simply in the number of prosodic licenses each one accumulated but in their divergent manners of conceiving the possibilities of verse.

Verlaine's volume, *Romances sans paroles,* reflects in many ways the mentality of a known, respected younger poet whose piety towards the traditions of French poetry was genuine. He shifted the balance of his verse lengths toward short or *impair* ones, using for the first time lines of six, nine, and eleven syllables. Yet this does not constitute a revolution in prosody; it is merely the exploration of a tendency already present in his own early work and in certain volumes of Hugo's. About half the *Romances* do not have the traditional alternation of masculine and feminine rimes, but there again Verlaine merely carries to greater lengths a practice with which he was already familiar. In only one poem does he attempt something which might have been denounced as cacophonous; the

7. *Ninette à la cour,* pp. 4, 46, 53.

sixth of the "Ariettes oubliées" rimes masculine and feminine endings together:

> C'est le chien de Jean de Nivelle
> Qui mord sous l'oeil même du guet
> Le chat de la mère Michel;
> François-les-bas-bleus s'en égaie.

There is a rather calculated effect in Verlaine's prosodic
novelties, as if he were attempting to startle but not to
outrage. Furthermore, no poem is unusual in several ways
at once. Each has its one curious trait and resembles an
exercise in a single problem, rather than a general attempt
to explore the possibilities of versification.

At the same time it would be unjust to imply that Verlaine's association with Rimbaud led to no more than a
few warmed-over prosodic audacities on his part. Phrases
in his letters of that period indicate that he was conscious
of attempting something quite new: "ma poétique de plus
en plus *moderniste*" he spoke of in September 1872.[8]
Later: "Je fourmille d'idées, de vues nouvelles, de projets
vraiment beaux." Most interesting of all is his project for
a preface "où je tombe *tous les vers,* y compris les miens,
et où j'explique des idées que je crois bonnes."[9] The
preface never got written, but some of its notions may
have been embodied in the famous "Art poétique," composed in April 1874 but not published until 1882. The
place of this poem in Verlaine's *oeuvre* has sometimes
been mistaken because of its date of publication; to be
exact, "Art poétique" reflects the esthetic concerns of
Verlaine just after his association with Rimbaud and the
composition of *Romances sans paroles:*

> De la musique avant toute chose,
> Et pour cela préfère l'Impair

8. *Correspondance, 1,* 46.
9. *Correspondance, 1,* 97–98.

> Plus vague et plus soluble dans l'air,
> Sans rien en lui qui pèse ou qui pose.

"Music" is the key term to this conception of poetry, and it is a matter of both prosody and sense: the tenuousness of the unusual *vers impair* should be matched by a certain vagueness in diction. The very title *Romances sans paroles,* "songs without words," suggests the ineffable wedding of melody and evocation which Verlaine was striving for. The example which Verlaine gives of "music" in "Art poétique" is furthermore patterned after the first of the "Ariettes oubliées" in his volume:

> C'est des beaux yeux derrière des voiles,
> C'est le grand jour tremblant de midi,
> C'est, par un ciel d'automne attiédi,
> Le bleu fouillis des claires étoiles.
>
> ("Art poétique")

> C'est l'extase langoureuse
> C'est la fatigue amoureuse,
> C'est tous les frissons des bois
> Parmi l'étreinte des brises,
> C'est, vers les ramures grises,
> Le choeur des petites voix.
> (*Romances sans paroles*)

The imprecise pronoun reference of "c'est" and the casual accumulation of images create the suggestive obscurity common in song. Sharp contours and detailed pictorial effects are strictly avoided; instead of an explicit dramatic situation the speaker merely evokes, as it were, fragments of an experience. This is not difficult verse in the sense of containing complicated symbols or recondite allusions; its vagueness is rather an attempt at naïveté, a refusal of rhetorical rules. Verlaine's conception of the music of poetry is narrow but nonetheless legitimate insofar as it appears to be based on the study of song.

Thanks to "Art poétique" we can determine fairly well what Verlaine's poetic preoccupations were in 1872–73. Rimbaud, on the other hand, presents us with a more complex problem in keeping with the greater complexity of his talent. Doubtless Rimbaud shared Verlaine's theories of musicality, for he also searched for images dim in outline and for a certain lyric obscurity, but we are most of all struck by his prosodic innovations. The latter were enormous, since unlike Verlaine he was restrained by little piety toward literary tradition; one may indicate in a simple, schematic fashion all Verlaine's audacities in versification, but a full analysis of new prosodic devices in Rimbaud's later poems would be exceedingly involved. From the conventional patterns of his earlier verse, Rimbaud passed in 1872 to such a multiplicity of new forms that one can merely point out the major aspects of them. It is as if he had suddenly attempted to make up for lost time after his earlier neglect of the possibilities of versification. His least innovation was the use of short and *impair* lines or the suppression of the distinction between masculine and feminine rimes.

First of all, Rimbaud seems to have realized, perhaps under the influence of Favart, that expressive rhythmic effects can be obtained by adding or subtracting a syllable here or there in an otherwise regular poem:

> l'enfant
> Gêneur, la si sotte bête,
> Ne doit cesser un instant
> De ruser et d'être traître,
>
> Comme un chat des Monts-Rocheux,
> D'empuantir toutes sphères!
> Qu'à sa mort pourtant, ô mon Dieu!
> S'élève quelque prière!
>
> ("Honte")

> [The annoying child, the so stupid beast, must never stop a moment from scheming and betraying, from stinking up all spheres, like a Rocky Mountain cat! Yet at his death, O my God, may some prayer be raised!]

The addition of an extra syllable to the penultimate line provides a majestic cadence in keeping with the sudden shift of tone. On the other hand, however, variations of one syllable are not always detectable by the ear: since the rules of French prosody do not take into consideration pause or vowel quantity, verse is often phonetically more irregular than it looks on paper, and Rimbaud's juxtaposition of similar line lengths can be merely a logical representation of the way verse really sounds. Rimbaud evidently made the important discovery that, working primarily by ear, he could create harmonies quite in keeping with the traditional outlines of French verse while not concerning himself overly with syllable counting:

> Néanmoins ils restent,
> — Sicile, Allemagne,
> dans ce brouillard triste
> et blêmi, justement!

> [Nonetheless, they remain, Sicily, Germany, in this sad and wan fog, properly!]

The ear does not feel any shock at the increased length of the last line. Rimbaud came to realize that the number of syllables is merely one factor determining the shape of a line of verse and not always the most important one. Elements of pause and vowel quantity can completely obscure the length of a line, and feminine rimes can alter meters. Furthermore some traditional verse is regular for the eye alone and does not even contain the requisite number of syllables. In a joking vein and against his usual practice, Rimbaud wrote these spurious *décasyllabes:*

> — Calmes maisons, anciennes passions!
> Kiosque de la Folle par affection.
> Après les fesses des rosiers, balcon
> Ombreux et très bas de la Juliette.
>
> ("Bruxelles")

[Calm houses, former passions! Pavilion of the woman mad from affection. After the rosebush branches, the shadowy and very low balcony of Juliet.]

Rimbaud is parodying here the many poets, including Verlaine, who persistently cheated at syllable counting: by stretching a point the *i*'s of "anciennes" (or "passions") and "Juliette" can be counted as full syllables, but as a matter of fact they are pronounced as consonants rather than whole vowels. The arbitrariness of this practice is emphasized by the fact that "kiosque" and "affection" are treated normally and according to speech. "Bruxelles" is a rambling association of exotic images which has no great poetic merit, but it is amusing in its outrageous use of accepted false lines.[10]

The most extraordinary example of Rimbaud's experimentation with line lengths is "Bonne Pensée du matin"; here it is not simply a question of intercalating an occasional extra syllable, as Favart might have done, but an attempt to revise the whole notion of line length in French. The traditional habit of counting all mute *e*'s as real syllables was by Rimbaud's time quite out of line with French phonology, yet, at the same time, certain "mute" *e*'s had and still have an audible and affective value, especially in heightened language. In "Bonne Pensée du matin" Rimbaud steers between the two ex-

---

10. Verlaine was especially shameless in undermining the traditional counting of line lengths while clinging to it; cf. these dubious *octosyllabes* (*La Bonne Chanson XVIII*): "Nous sommes en des temps infâmes / Où le mari-age des âmes / Doit sceller l'uni-on des coeurs."

tremes of ignoring the mute *e*'s and giving them all full syllabic value. It would be possible to analyze the poem into a maze of lines of six, seven, eight, nine, and ten syllables, but I think the first four stanzas are best taken as combinations of three *octosyllabes* followed by a shorter line:

> A quatre heures du matin, l'été,
> Le sommeil d'amour dure encore.
> Sous les bosquets l'aube évapore
>   L'odeur du soir fêté.
>
> Mais là-bas dans l'immense chantier
> Vers le soleil des Hespérides,
> En bras de chemise, les charpentiers
>   Déjà s'agitent.
>
> Dans leur désert de mousse, tranquilles,
> Ils préparent les lambris précieux
> Où la richesse de la ville
>   Rira sous de faux cieux.
>
> Ah! pour ces Ouvriers charmants
> Sujets d'un roi de Babylone,
> Vénus! laisse un peu les Amants,
>   Dont l'âme est en couronne.

[At four o'clock on a summer morning the sleep of love still lasts. Under the thickets dawn evaporates the scent of the festive night. But over there, in the great building-yard, toward the Hesperides' sun, the carpenters are already at work in shirtsleeves. Calm in their wilderness of moss, they prepare the precious panels where the city's wealth will laugh under artificial skies. Oh, for these charming workmen, ruled by a Babylonian king, Venus! leave a bit those lovers whose souls are crowned with satisfaction.]

These are very special *octosyllabes* of course. "Bras de

chemise" receives its normal three-syllable pronunciation, for counting all three *e*'s according to the traditional method would be grotesque to the ear. On the other hand, the *e*'s after certain long syllables may have or even need a certain value: "heures" might be lightly prolonged; "immense" should doubtless have a small final syllable in order to separate the *s* from the following sibilant, and "richesse" by its rhythmic position demands fullness and length. These small variations create an *octosyllabe* which actually corresponds to French phonology. Mechanical syllable-counting, which is no real test of meter, is replaced by the test of the ear with its insistence upon taste and normal usage. Such prosody is infinitely subtle and requires intelligent collaboration on the part of the reader; no mere schoolbook directions for scansion can account for it. The final stanza of "Bonne Pensée du matin" is again best analyzed according to good pronunciation:

> O Reine des Bergers!
> Porte aux travailleurs l'eau-de-vie,
> Pour que leurs forces soient en paix,
> En attendant le bain dans la mer, à midi.

[O Queen of Shepherds! Bear brandy to the workers, so that their strength may be at peace until the bath in the sea at noon.]

"Reine" counts as two syllables because of its accentuated, vocative function, and the *e* of "forces" must be pronounced to avoid assimilation of the *c* to the *s* of "soient." "Eau-de-vie," on the other hand, should not be graced with an extra syllable in the middle. Taking these considerations into account, this stanza assumes a dynamic, crescendo-like pattern: each line grows longer than the preceding one until the final, classically articulated alexandrine provides a point of rest.

To pause parenthetically over a question of content—

for "Bonne Pensée du matin" is too remarkable to use solely as an example of prosody—these lines follow the pastoral convention with its gentle humblefolk, benign landscape, and ethos of love. This mode of literature evidently came to Rimbaud's attention through Favart, whose *opéras-comiques* are often self-consciously naïve trifles about the virtuous rustic life and the urgency of love. Their frank artificiality must have charmed Rimbaud, who in "Bonne Pensée du matin" attempted to wed this note to his own richly colored style. To the imagination for landscape, atmosphere, and epidermic sensation which he possessed and which the neo-classical authors of pastoral rather lacked, he added old-fashioned mythological trappings, like the Hanging Gardens of Babylon and the cult of Cypris, goddess not only of love but of nature. In this respect "Bonne Pensée du matin" stands alone in Rimbaud's poems of 1872; though other poems of the period are song-like in movement, none shows the same delight in the conceits of eighteenth-century libretti. This is Rimbaud's version of the *fête galante* which haunted Verlaine, but, whereas the latter felt only the elegiac, erotic element in neo-classical pastoral, Rimbaud was attracted by its fabulous, fairytale-like atmosphere.

So far we have considered only Rimbaud's innovations in the handling of line length and mute *e*'s and ignored the oddities of rime which occur in our examples. This second aspect of his versification now requires some treatment in itself. Theorists have always claimed that French verse is unique, at least in Western Europe, for its dependence on constant and perfect rime. Even librettists like Favart, who do not fear irregularities of line length, avoid departures from accepted practice in this respect. It is therefore all the more surprising that Rimbaud not only ceased to distinguish between masculine and feminine rimes or to alternate them (as Verlaine had sometimes refused to do) but even abandoned rime altogether at times:

Tel, j'eusse été mauvaise enseigne d'auberge.
Puis, l'orage changea le ciel, jusqu'au soir.
Ce furent des pays noirs, des lacs, des perches,
Des colonnades sous la nuit bleue, des gares.
("Larme")

[Drinking this way I looked like a bad inn sign. Then
the storm changed the sky until evening. There were
black countries, lakes, perches, colonnades under the
blue night, railway stations.]

Zut alors, si le soleil quitte ces bords!
Fuis, clair déluge! Voici l'ombre des routes.
Dans les saules, dans la vieille cour d'honneur,
L'orage d'abord jette ses larges gouttes.
("Michel et Christine")

[What the hell if the sun leaves this place! Flee, bright
flood! Here comes the shadow on the roads. In the
willows, in the old great courtyard the storm at first
flings its heavy drops.]

English has approximate rimes like *auberges/perches* and
bords/honneur, but they are unknown in French poetry
after the Middle Ages. We do not have to look so far,
however, to find the prototype of this versification: the
immemorial tradition of French folk songs, which ignores
and antedates the canons of modern French prosody. Any
collection of them which has not undergone excessive
editing or modernization should contain examples of intermittent or negligent rime. To take a very familiar folk
song, "A la claire fontaine" shows a mixture of rime and
assonance: [11]

A la claire fontaine
M'en allant promener,

11. I use assonance in the normal English sense; in French it
usually means a one-sound rime such as *peu/feu.*

> J'ai trouvé l'eau si belle
> Que je m'y suis baigné.
> L'y a longtemps que je t'aime,
> Jamais je ne t'oublierai.

Thus there are excellent antecedents for Rimbaud's negligence of rime, although they have been largely ignored by students of French prosody.[12] It is difficult to say, of course, to what extent Rimbaud took folk music into account during his period of experimentation with verse forms, but the possibility is not to be excluded: once one begins to study the prosody of sung texts in the work of someone like Favart, one is easily tempted to inquire more broadly into the matter. Rimbaud's handling of rime in 1872 certainly suggests some such inspiration, and Izambard claimed that one of Rimbaud's poems was actually patterned on a folk song which he heard him sing at Douai in 1870: "Avène, avène, / Que le beau temps t'amène. . . ." According to Izambard, this furnished the pattern of the "Chanson de la plus haute tour": "Qu'il vienne, qu'il vienne, / Le temps dont on s'éprenne. . . ."[13] This one example is curious if not conclusive in estimating Rimbaud's interest in folk song.

Wherever Rimbaud's new notions of prosody came from, he did not hesitate to develop them to the utmost

12. Remy de Gourmont wrote an essay on "Le Vers populaire" (in *Esthétique de la langue française*, Paris, 1955, pp. 171–86), but in general this aspect of French prosody has been neglected. Indeed little has been written on the history of post-medieval French versification that goes beyond elementary facts. In particular the nineteenth-century innovations remain unexplored.

13. Izambard, *Rimbaud*, pp. 128–31. Izambard also gives the musical notation and a reference to an anthology of folk songs. Oddly enough, however, the version of the "Chanson de la plus haute tour" which more closely corresponds to the song "Avène, avène . . ." is the one used in *Une Saison en enfer* and which one would assume to be posterior to that of May 1872.

limits. Thus he composed one poem without a single true rime; "Bannières de mai" is perhaps unique in French verse for its subtle harmonies:

> Aux branches claires des tilleuls
> Meurt un maladif hallali.
> Mais des chansons spirituelles
> Voltigent parmi les groseilles.
> Que notre sang rie en nos veines,
> Voici s'enchevêtrer les vignes.
> Le ciel est joli comme un ange.
> L'azur et l'onde communient.

[In the bright linden-branches dies a sickly hunting call. But spiritual songs flutter among the currants. As our blood laughs in our veins, the grape-vines intertwine. The sky is pretty like an angel. The azure and the wave commune.]

An extremely delicate play of echoes ties together the endline words, and the more one studies it, the more complex it appears. Much the same may be said of the interior rimes, assonances, and alliterations. One only regrets the slightly stiff, closed-couplet form of the sentence structure: the constraint and patient invention which his novel replacement for rime imposed on him evidently discouraged Rimbaud from attempting anything more elaborate in the way of syntax or meter (which is merely the common *octosyllabe*). He never again experimented in so thorough-going a fashion with half-rimes, yet this one effort is far from negligible: indeed it is probably the only regular blank verse poem in French which is more than a historical curiosity.

At some time—we do not really know when—Rimbaud pushed his prosodic invention even further and created what was to be known in the 1880s as *le vers libre*. There are four sections in the manuscript of the *Illuminations* which are clearly cast in a form of verse; two of them ("Marine" and "Mouvement") have always been recognized as such because of their typographical arrangement, whereas the other two ("Départ" and "Veillées" 1) are disposed on the page in so prose-like a fashion that most commentators have assimilated them to the prose *Illuminations*. The latter two are nonetheless unrelated to Rimbaud's genuine prose poems; indeed they are closer to verse patterns than "Marine" or "Mouvement," and we shall begin with them. "Veillées" 1 is held together by a complicated echo of rimes (both interior and endline) in *é* and *i:*

> C'est le repos éclairé, ni fièvre, ni langueur, sur le lit
> ou sur le pré.
> C'est l'ami ni ardent ni faible. L'ami.
> C'est l'aimée ni tourmentante ni tourmentée. L'aimée.
> L'air et le monde point cherchés. La vie.
> — Etait-ce donc ceci?
> — Et le rêve fraîchit.

> > [It's clear-minded rest, neither fever nor languor, on the bed or meadow. It's the friend, neither ardent nor weak. The friend. It's the loved one, neither tormenting nor tormented. The loved one. The air and the world unsought for. Life. Was it this? And the dream cools.]

The first sentence consists of three balanced phrases of seven, six, and seven syllables respectively, the first and third also riming. Numerous parallelisms interrelate the following three lines, and the two short final lines constitute a classically divided alexandrine with interior rime. In short, "Veillées" 1 consists of recognizable fragments of traditional verse and rime effects. "Départ" is constructed of similar prosodic elements:

Assez vu. La vision s'est rencontrée à tous les airs.
Assez eu. Rumeurs des villes, le soir, et au soleil, et
   toujours.
Assez connu. Les arrêts de la vie. — O Rumeurs et
   Visions!
Départ dans l'affection et le bruit neufs!

> [Seen enough. Vision was found at every point. Had
> enough. Murmur of cities, in the evening, and in the
> sun, and always. Known enough. The decrees of life.
> O Murmur and Vision! Leaving for new affection
> and noise!]

Each of the first three lines consists of an initial rime
phrase followed by twelve or thirteen syllables divided
like an alexandrine into two or three equal parts—some
allowance being made, of course, for the extra syllable
of the second line. Odd as this pattern may seem, it is
nonetheless a verse form as rightfully as are those curious
Chinese or Hebrew poems whose structure is so remote
from English or French conceptions. In no way should
"Départ" or "Veillées" I be assimilated to prose, which
is organized around sentence structures rather than rime
and verse lengths.

Finally "Marine" and "Mouvement" are the poems
which many critics have claimed as the first examples of
unrimed free verse in French. The former, which is short,
will serve as an illustration:

Les chars d'argent et de cuivre —
Les proues d'acier et d'argent —
Battent l'écume, —
Soulèvent les souches des ronces.
Les courants de la lande,
Et les ornières immenses du reflux,
Filent circulairement vers l'est,
Vers les piliers de la forêt, —

Vers les fûts de la jetée,
Dont l'angle est heurté par des tourbillons de lumière.

> [The chariots of silver and copper—the prows of steel
> and silver—beat the foam—raise the roots of the
> brambles. The currents of the moor and the immense
> ruts of backwash run circularly toward the east,
> toward the pillars of the forest, toward the piles of
> the pier, whose angle is hit by whirls of light.]

"Marine" is a curious study in metaphorical structure—a
careful ambiguity being maintained as to whether the sea
is a metaphor for land or vice versa or whether the two
are being described as analogies of one another—but its
fame is due to its form, which breaks totally with rime
and sharply articulated rhythms. One feels however that
despite the imaginative effort which such a poem must
have demanded, "Marine" is more facile and less well-knit
than "Départ" or the song poems of 1872. Rimbaud was
perhaps of the same opinion, for he did not, so far as we
know, pursue unrimed free verse beyond "Marine" and
its companion piece "Mouvement."

Rimbaud's achievements in prosody before he abandoned verse for prose are unique and impressive. At a moment when French verse was coming to seem uncomfort-
ably archaic and remote from the living language, he
made an attempt to salvage what was still viable in it
while discarding the more minute, old-fashioned rules
governing rime and line length. Rimbaud did not—before
"Marine" and "Mouvement"—break totally with the tradition of French versification but, like the romantics before him, modified its detail. He preserved above all its
essential movement, which, as he understood, is not dependent on mere mechanics. In this respect Rimbaud's
last verse is precious; the next generation of poetic innova-
tors, for whom the *vers libre* was supreme, tended to reject
out of hand the classic forms of French prosody rather

than to redeem and adapt them to contemporary taste. Yet finally there is something even more remarkable about Rimbaud's last verse pieces: they are not merely exercises but ripened poems, and we must now consider them as such.

Like "Mémoire," which we have already examined, Rimbaud's other last verse poems usher in new thematic material as well as prosodic innovations. Critics have never been able to single out as many possible sources for the poems of 1872 as they have for Rimbaud's earlier work, for none of them bears much resemblance to any previous French poetry. Lacking literary sources, however, some have attempted to find autobiographical allusions here and there; perhaps there are references to incidents of Rimbaud's life in these poems, but if so, they are neither sufficiently frequent nor obvious to make such interpretations coherent. Furthermore we cannot even be very certain about Rimbaud's activities and preoccupations in 1872. He returned to Paris in May after spending the early spring in Charleville, left France in Verlaine's company for Belgium and England, and eventually went home to the Ardennes in December, but from this period we have few letters and no satisfactory eyewitness account of his life, Verlaine's correspondence being of little help here. In short, we know nothing—save what the texts themselves tell us—about the inspiration of Rimbaud's last verse.

It is therefore understandable that we demur when assured that a poem entitled "Jeune Ménage" is about Verlaine and Rimbaud's sexual relations or about Verlaine's marriage. (Why not, for that matter, about someone else's?) The poem hardly seems so specific:

La chambre est ouverte au ciel bleu-turquin;
Pas de place : des coffrets et des huches!

Dehors le mur est plein d'aristoloches
Où vibrent les gencives des lutins.

Que ce sont bien intrigues de génies
Cette dépense et ces désordres vains!
C'est la fée africaine qui fournit
La mûre, et les résilles dans les coins.

Plusieurs entrent, marraines mécontentes,
En pans de lumière dans les buffets,
Puis y restent! le ménage s'absente
Peu sérieusement, et rien ne se fait.

[The bedchamber is open to the dark-blue sky. No room: coffers and chests! Outside the wall is full of birthwort where sprites' gums vibrate. This certainly is the work of genies' intrigues, this extravagance and this futile bustling about! It's the African fairy who supplies blackberries and the leaded panes in the corner. Several of these malcontent godmothers enter the sideboards like beams of light, then stay there! The couple has frivolously gone out and nothing gets done.]

Rimbaud is here working with the conventions of romance and fairy tale. The theme of young lovers persecuted by intriguing supernatural powers—evil godmothers and sprites—is a familiar one in legend, and the fabulous character of the situation is emphasized by the bond between the lovers and nature: their bedroom, appropriately furnished in medieval fashion with caskets suggestive of treasure, is open to the sky, and food is automatically furnished by a sympathetic fairy. Nothing here demands an allegorical interpretation: the poem is an exercise in a certain tone and tradition of narrative whose lightness and playful quality had begun to interest Rimbaud. "Mémoire" is not dissimilar in its use of myth-like ma-

terial, even though it is a considerably richer and more
subtle poem.

Another related piece, which seems obscure if we take
no account of the conventions Rimbaud is experimenting
with, is "Michel et Christine." Here the symbolic marriage
in nature is handled not simply with levity but in a
thoroughly parodic fashion. The poet first invokes an
apocalyptic storm in which he alone remains unsheltered:

> Mais moi, Seigneur! voici que mon esprit vole,
> Après les cieux glacés de rouge, sous les
> Nuages célestes qui courent et volent
> Sur cent Solognes longues comme un railway.
>
> Voilà mille loups, mille graines sauvages
> Qu'emporte, non sans aimer les liserons,
> Cette religieuse après-midi d'orage
> Sur l'Europe ancienne où cent hordes iront!
>
> Après, le clair de lune! partout la lande,
> Rougis et leurs fronts aux cieux noirs, les guerriers
> Chevauchent lentement leurs pâles coursiers!
> Les cailloux sonnent sous cette fière bande!

> > [But I, Lord! now my soul is flying, after the skies
> > gleaming red, under the heavenly clouds that run and
> > fly along a hundred marshes long as a railway. Here
> > come a thousand wolves, a thousand wild seeds,
> > borne, not without morning-glory vines as well, by
> > this religious afternoon storm over ancient Europe,
> > where a hundred hordes will rove. Afterwards the
> > moonlight! All over the plain red-faced warriors
> > against the black sky slowly ride their pale steeds!
> > The pebbles resound beneath this proud troop!]

The "religious" storm with its warriors, wolves, and weeds
flying through the air derives from the vision of the
plague-bearing riders in Revelation 6, the colors red,

black, and pale being direct reminiscences of St. John.
Perhaps the repeated use of numbers as well owes something to that part of the Bible. This pseudo-allegorical
cortege is followed by a burlesque vision of beatific union
corresponding to the descent of the New Jerusalem at the
end of the Apocalypse:

> — Et verrai-je le bois jaune et le val clair,
> L'Epouse aux yeux bleus, l'homme au front rouge,
> ô Gaule,
> Et le blanc Agneau Pascal, à leurs pieds chers,
> — Michel et Christine, — et Christ! — fin de l'Idylle.

> [And shall I see the yellow wood and bright valley,
> the blue-eyed Spouse, the red-browed man, O Gaul,
> and the white Paschal Lamb at their dear feet—
> Michel and Christine—and Christ!—end of the Idyll.]

The Lamb of God, the central symbol of Revelation, is
grotesquely joined in a trinity with two lovers from a
popular pastoral and romantic play of the nineteenth
century, and the three of them patriotically bear the colors
of the French Republican flag, to which much sentimental
attachment was proclaimed in Rimbaud's day. The whole
picture is a parody of God smiling on France—"fille aînée
de l'Eglise"—and is broken off by the triumphant cacophony of "Michel et Christine,—et Christ!" Like much comic
writing, "Michel et Christine" has a certain degree of
exuberant incoherence—not to say nonsense—which one
should not be tempted to overinterpret.[14]

"Mémoire," "Bonne Pensée du matin," "Jeune Ménage," "Michel et Christine"—in all of these poems we
have seen Rimbaud resorting to old-fashioned sources for

14. There appear to be other allusions, amusing if haphazard, to
Scribe's *Michel et Christine*, which treats of a soldier returning from
war to find his loved one. See Starkie, *Rimbaud*, pp. 200–01.

themes and images. He blends together material from the
realms of fairy tale, pastoral literature, medieval culture,
pagan mythology, and sacred legend in the syncretic manner of a medieval or Renaissance poet. Though the result-
ing poems differ greatly from one another, they have in
common a certain lightness of tone and fancifulness of
imagery which distinguishes them as a group from Rimbaud's previous work. Although each one is interesting
in some way—for a charming image or a curious prosodic
effect—we shall confine ourselves now to a series written
in the first person singular and related by a common
mood of spiritual quest. After his earlier violent anti-
clericalism, Rimbaud turned in 1872 to a curiously religious, if not very Catholic inspiration. We learn from a
letter of Verlaine's that Rimbaud referred to some of his
poems as "prayers," and that the life the two poets were
to lead together would be a *via crucis*.[15] The famous lost
Chasse spirituelle evidently dated from this period, and
thus it seems likely that the poems of spiritual aspiration
which we shall now examine were only part of a larger
group.[16] However, rather than defining beforehand the
theme of these pieces, we must begin by studying their
evocative powers. "Larme" is an appropriate place to start.

Loin des oiseaux, des troupeaux, des villageoises,
Que buvais-je, à genoux dans cette bruyère
Entourée de tendres bois de noisetiers,
Dans un brouillard d'après-midi tiède et vert?

Que pouvais-je boire dans cette jeune Oise,
— Ormeaux sans voix, gazon sans fleurs, ciel couvert! —

15. Verlaine's aforementioned letter of April 2, 1872 and his un-
dated one which follows in the Pléiade edition.
16. For what little is known about *La Chasse spirituelle* see the
"historique des *Illuminations*" in the notes to the Pléiade edition,
pp. 691–92.

Boire à ces gourdes jaunes, loin de ma case
Chérie? Quelque liqueur d'or qui fait suer.[17]

[Far from the birds, the flocks, the village girls, what
was I drinking, on my knees in this patch of heather
surrounded by new-grown hazel trees, in a warm,
green afternoon fog? What could I have been drinking from this young Oise—voiceless small elms,
flowerless turf, sultry sky!—drinking from these yellow gourds, far from my dear cabin? Some golden
liquor provoking sweat.]

Delicate repetitions of sounds, rhythms (the tripartite pattern of lines one and six), and categories of descriptive
details create an almost ritualistic evocation of isolation
and expectancy. The recurring "loin de," "boire," and
"que —ais–je" emphasize the impression of a strange action in a strange spot. The latter's secrecy is stressed by
the image of the soft, warm, closed-in thicket, while the
repetition of the description of place, "—Ormeaux sans
voix, gazon sans fleurs, ciel couvert!—," conveys the feeling of absent phenomena which may manifest themselves.
The adjectives "tendres" and "jeune," like the diminutive
"ormeaux," further contain a hint of promise and future
transformation. Within the framework of lulling repetition there is also a growing sense of suspense each time a
form of the verb *boire* recurs: the poet is first merely
kneeling before some sort of water, then he is contemplating a source of the Oise (the name of that river being
probably used for its sonority), and finally he becomes
aware of strange yellow gourds, whose unfamiliarity is

17. For "Larme" I have (quite exceptionally in this chapter) given
the version of the poem quoted in *Une Saison en enfer* rather than
that of the May 1872 manuscript. The later version is shorter, denser,
and more dramatic.

underscored by the demonstrative "ces." The action of drinking becomes more and more a portentous and mysterious symbol, just as the wood comes to seem more and more a magical place shut off from the rest of the earth and mankind. Yet at the height of this development the atmosphere of enchantment breaks off with the disappointed words "Quelque liqueur d'or qui fait suer," whose lame rhythm, after the flowing measures which precede, expresses the poet's sorrow.

The poet remains kneeling in vain, like the drinker on a "peculiar inn sign," until the moment of transfiguration occurs:

> Je faisais une louche enseigne d'auberge.
> — Un orage vint chasser le ciel. Au soir
> L'eau des bois se perdait sur les sables vierges,
> Le vent de Dieu jetait des glaçons aux mares;
>
> Pleurant, je voyais de l'or — et ne pus boire. —
>
> [I looked like a suspicious inn sign. A storm came to drive away the sky. In the evening the water from the woods sank into the virgin sand; God's wind flung icicles into the ponds. Weeping, I saw gold—and could not drink.]

The virgin sand and the icicles, which contrast with the impure, soupy atmosphere of the first two stanzas, suggest a new purity which will permit the poet to drink and be refreshed, but he is unfit and unable to do so. The real gold—as opposed to the unquenching yellow liquor—which the poet finally sees is doubtless a reminiscence of the alchemists' search for the true metal, and the change of temperature and clearing of the sky also suggest a chemical experiment, but it would be imprudent to push the analogy too far: the gold is generally symbolic of some attainment—whence the tears of the poet who can only glimpse but not reach it.[18]

The crippled vision of "Larme" is associated at once with godhead ("le vent de Dieu"), nature, and magic, but in so deft and delicate a way that we cannot define this relation in abstract terms. At best we can compare it with other poems of the same period where imagery of dampness and thirst is present, in order to ascertain if the latter has some general symbolic tenor. Fortunately such poems are not lacking; the fascination which Rimbaud early showed for impressions of coolness and moisture (cf. "Les Poètes de sept ans") only increased in 1872.

"Comédie de la soif" is constructed as a kind of dramatic scene, where the poet, despite his thirst, refuses the beverages which are offered to him. First his grandparents speak:

1. Les Parents

> Nous sommes tes Grands-Parents,
> 　Les Grands!
> Couverts des froides sueurs
> De la lune et des verdures.
> Nos vins secs avaient du coeur!
> Au soleil sans imposture
> Que faut-il à l'homme? boire.

MOI. — Mourir aux fleuves barbares.

> Nous sommes tes Grands-Parents
> 　Des champs.
> L'eau est au fond des osiers :
> Vois le courant du fossé

18. For alchemical imagery in Rimbaud see Starkie, pp. 159–70. Many curious *rapprochements* are made here, though one may doubt that alchemical symbols retain much of their original value when transplanted into Rimbaud's poems.

>   Autour du château mouillé.
>   Descendons en nos celliers
>   Après le cidre et le lait.[19]

MOI. — Aller où boivent les vaches.

[We are your Grandparents, the old ones! Covered
with the cold sweat of the moon and greenery. Our
dry wines were cheering! In the frank sunlight what
does man need? drink. I: death in barbaric rivers.
We are your Grandparents from the fields. Water is
at the roots of the willows: see the flow in the moat
around the damp castle. Let's go down to our cellars
for cider and milk. I: let's go drink where the cows
do.]

The spectral voice of his grandparents reaches the poet
from the cemetery, where they lie under the cold light of
the moon. They recall with gusto the condition of the
living—their cheerful wines and "frank" sunlight—and
urge drinking onto the poet as the most pleasant and essential part of life. Indeed, their state in death is no more
than an ultimate absorption into thirst-quenching dampness. The cellar which they maintained so carefully against
the summer heat is comparable to the tomb they now enjoy. When they describe themselves as "from the fields,"
we must understand that the expression designates not
only the land they tilled but that they now lie under. They
conceive of life quite materialistically as a brief space in
the sun, during which man fortifies himself with drink,
until he returns to the primordial wet earth. The poet,
however, abruptly refuses their view of the world—his
second comment being especially curt because of its lack
of rime. He will not make any distinction between the
beverages proper to man and swamp water.

19. I omit the semicolon after "celliers" in accordance with one
manuscript. See the Garnier edition, p. 432.

Nous sommes tes Grands-Parents;
    Tiens, prends
Les liqueurs dans nos armoires;
Le Thé, le Café, si rares,
Frémissent dans les bouilloires.
— Vois les images, les fleurs.
Nous rentrons du cimetière.

MOI. — Ah! tarir toutes les urnes!

[We are your Grandparents. Here, take liqueurs from
our cupboards; tea, coffee, so rare, bubble in the
kettles. "See the pictures, the flowers; we are back
from the cemetery." I: Ah, dry up all urns!]

After the grandparents' description of their hoarded and
prized drinks, the parents evidently return from a visit
to the cemetery, bearing religious pictures (such as are
given to children) and flowers. The poet's only reaction
is to invoke the emptying of all urns, that is, of all material
satisfactions for thirst, for they are meaningless to him.

In answer to his scorn of real liquids, "Spirit" next
comes to offer him the delights of imaginary ones:

2. L'Esprit

Eternelles Ondines
    Divisez l'eau fine.
Vénus, soeur de l'azur,
    Emeus le flot pur.

Juifs errants de Norwège,
    Dites-moi la neige.
Anciens exilés chers,
    Dites-moi la mer.

[Eternal Undines, part the fine water. Venus, sister
of the blue, stir the pure wave. Wandering Jews of

Norway, tell me of the snow; dear former exiles, tell me of the sea.]

"Spirit" is the muse of the imagination and accordingly speaks in a "poetic" pastiche quite unlike the style of the grandparents. The mythological references, the self-conscious apostrophes, and the rather formal "dites-moi . . ." construction are insipid enough to make one anticipate the poet's refusal of "Spirit's" aid:

> MOI. — Non, plus ces boissons pures,
> Ces fleurs d'eau pour verres;
> Légendes ni figures
> Ne me désaltèrent.

[I: No, no more of these pure beverages, these water-flowers for glasses; legends and figures do not slake my thirst.]

The irrelevant preciousness of poetry is stigmatized as trying to drink out of flowers.

The poet's friends next press upon him drinks associated with bars and drunkenness, floods of wine and absinthe, but he replies with indifference:

> J'aime autant, mieux, même,
> Pourrir dans l'étang,
> Sous l'affreuse crème,
> Près des bois flottants.

[I would just as soon—more, even—rot in the pond under the horrid scum by the marshy woods.]

He would just as soon die as live by material liquids. Finally, the poet dreams of wandering off in search of some beverage to quench his thirst:

4. LE PAUVRE SONGE

Peut-être un Soir m'attend
Où je boirai tranquille
En quelque vieille Ville,
Et mourrai plus content :
Puisque je suis patient!

Si mon mal se résigne,
Si j'ai jamais quelque or,
Choisirai-je le Nord
Ou le Pays des Vignes?...
— Ah! songer est indigne

Puisque c'est pure perte!
Et si je redeviens
Le voyageur ancien,
Jamais l'auberge verte
Ne peut bien m'être ouverte.

[Perhaps some evening awaits me when I shall drink
in calm in some old city and die more satisfied—since
I'm patient! If my pain lessens, if I ever have gold, will
I choose the North or the Land of Vines? Ah, it's un-
worthy to dream, because it's sheer loss. And if I become again the traveler I was, the green inn can never
open for me.]

The literal sense of drinking fades gradually away in this
fourth section; the poet realizes that he cannot reach the
"green inn" by wandering, that on the contrary this
spiritual spot will remain closed to him if he attempts to
locate it geographically. The notions of patience and
resignation furthermore suggest a kind of inner discipline
and adaptation to his unquenchable thirst, a new awareness of how vast and hopeless it is. Although the "green
inn" for which he longs is not a physical place any more
than his thirst is literal, the image evokes somewhat the

natural world seen as a totality, and in the conclusion of
the poem the poet associates himself with the life of the
woods:

5. CONCLUSION

Les pigeons qui tremblent dans la prairie,
Le gibier, qui court et qui voit la nuit,
Les bêtes des eaux, la bête asservie,
Les derniers papillons!... ont soif aussi.

[The pigeons that tremble in the field, the hunted
animals that run and see the night, the water creatures, the beast of burden, the last butterflies—are
also thirsty.]

Having cut himself off from mankind the poet experiences
a community with animals, for whom also the condition
of life is an immaterial thirst. This bond of the poet's
with non-human souls is characteristic of French romantic
sensibility, which tended to ascribe to other living creatures than man higher capacities for spiritual attainment.
Here animals share with the poet a yearning which is at
once a desire for dissolution of the self and for absorption
into the organic world of nature:

Mais fondre où fond ce nuage sans guide,
— Oh! favorisé de ce qui est frais!
Expirer en ces violettes humides
Dont les aurores chargent ces forêts?

[But to melt where that unguided cloud melts—Oh!
favored by the cool! To expire in these damp violets
with which dawn lades the wood?]

Thirst turns into something more like a wish to drown in
dampness and penumbra—the "violets" being ambiguously both flowers and the half-light of dawn. The night of
the preceding stanza has yielded to a new day, which the

poet hopes will bring essential satisfaction. His longings are at once ascetic and life-loving, an urge towards both disincarnation and re-embodiment, a pantheistic version of the mystics' experience of losing the self in order to participate in life more fully.

"Comédie de la soif" establishes thirst and dissolution as symbols of immaterial longings of a religious character. This imagery is reworked and further elaborated in "Le loup criait . . .":

> Le loup criait sous les feuilles
> En crachant les belles plumes
> De son repas de volailles :
> Comme lui je me consume.
>
> Les salades, les fruits
> N'attendent que la cueillette;
> Mais l'araignée de la haie
> Ne mange que des violettes.
>
> Que je dorme! que je bouille
> Aux autels de Salomon.
> Le bouillon court sur la rouille,
> Et se mêle au Cédron.

[The wolf howled under the leaves as he spat out the beautiful feathers from his meal of fowl: like him I am being consumed. The lettuces, the fruits wait to be picked; but the spider in the hedge only eats violets. Let me sleep, let me boil on Solomon's altars. The broth runs off the rust and mingles with the Cedron.]

Starvation is a complementary symbol of spiritual yearning, for the body is sloughed off to liberate the soul: the delicate images of the almost immaterial spider and the wolf giving up his meal (as if fowls had no more to them than feathers) illustrate the poet's *ascesis* while further associating him with the natural world. Violets again symbolize pantheistic communion. The final stanza, with its evocation of the Holy Land—the ideal, tranquil spot toward which the spirit turns—passes abruptly from the theme of disincarnation through abstinence to that of resorption into the beauty of the world. "Le loup criait . . ." is thus an elliptic, condensed use of the material of "Comédie de la soif" and is best read in the light of the latter poem.

The destruction of the self of which Rimbaud writes is willful and epitomized in paradoxical titles like "Comédie de la soif" and "Fêtes de la faim." The second is a song of starvation:

> Ma faim, Anne, Anne,
> Fuis sur ton âne.
>
> Si j'ai du *goût,* ce n'est guères
> Que pour la terre et les pierres.
> Dinn! dinn! dinn! dinn! Mangeons l'air,
> Le roc, les charbons, le fer.

[My hunger, Ann, Ann, flee on your ass. If I have any taste, it's only for earth and stones. Ding! ding! ding! ding! Let's eat air, rock, coal, iron.]

Eating what is inedible and lacks nourishment is a rather infantile fantasy, and Rimbaud appropriately casts his poem in the form of a naïve, childish song with an aimless opening phrase, onomatopoetic words, and doggerel-like rime. The note of ingenuous piety which is present in "Le loup criait . . ." takes on a forlorn character here as the Flight into Egypt (in which an ass often figures) seems to be confusedly evoked along with the Virgin's mother. Plaintiveness is an essential element in the tone of these poems, for it conveys the uncertainty and lost feeling of the spirit embarking on the quest for a higher state.

The four climactic poems of this cycle of spiritual aspiration are grouped together under the title "Fêtes de la patience." To the themes of thirst, hunger, and wasting away they add new symbols and something very like an account of mystical illumination. In the first of the series, "Bannières de mai," the poet rejects his patience in misfortune (the word "patience" has something of its etymological sense of "suffering") and calls on summer to take him into her protection, as if he were an insect or animal:

> Qu'on patiente et qu'on s'ennuie
> C'est trop simple. Fi de mes peines.
> Je veux que l'été dramatique
> Me lie à son char de fortune.
> Que par toi beaucoup, ô Nature,
> — Ah moins seul et moins nul! — je meure.
> Au lieu que les Bergers, c'est drôle,
> Meurent à peu près par le monde.

> [That one be patient and a prey to ennui is too simple. Enough of my troubles. I want the dramatic summer to attach me to her chariot of chance. Let me, less alone and less null, enormously die through you, O Nature. Whereas Shepherds, it's funny, die more or less anywhere.]

Men ("les Bergers") die haphazardly, but the poet hopes to live the life of the season and to die with it. He aspires to become a "fils du soleil," as Rimbaud put it elsewhere, one generated of the sun and dependent on it:

> Je veux bien que les saisons m'usent.
> A toi, Nature, je me rends;
> Et ma faim et toute ma soif.
> Et, s'il te plaît, nourris, abreuve.
> Rien de rien ne m'illusionne;
> C'est rire aux parents, qu'au soleil,

Mais moi je ne veux rien à rien;
Et libre soit cette infortune.

[I am willing to be used up by the seasons. To you,
Nature, I yield, along with my hunger and all my
thirst. And please feed, quench. Nothing gives me
illusions about anything. Laughing at the sun is like
laughing at parents. But I don't want anything from
anything. And let this misfortune be free.]

The poet conceives of nature as the only refuge from the
sufferings of the self which has fallen into utter indifference. By a dialectic shift his acedia and discouragement
cease to be a source of individual misfortune and become
the means whereby he loses himself in the life of the
season. His very weariness with himself permits his release. This notion is not unlike the old spiritual paradox
of losing life in order to regain it.

"Bannières de mai" uses traditional pastoral imagery
and does not add any theme to those we have encountered
so far except that of absorption into summer. With the
"Chanson de la plus haute tour," however, the important
symbol of the castle enters "Fêtes de la patience." The
castle is at once suggestive of aspiring spirituality and
isolation; in it the poet hovers between the world of men,
which he has put behind him, and the union of purified
souls which he anxiously awaits:

> Oisive jeunesse
> A tout asservie,
> Par délicatesse
> J'ai perdu ma vie.
> Ah! Que le temps vienne
> Où les coeurs s'éprennent.

[In idle youth, a slave to everything, by thoughtful-
ness I've lost my life. Ah! let the time come when
hearts will love.]

The life which the poet fears having lost through excessive concern with others is the true one, not that of the world. He resolves nevertheless to persist in his retreat:

> Je me suis dit : laisse,
> Et qu'on ne te voie :
> Et sans la promesse
> De plus hautes joies.
> Que rien ne t'arrête,
> Auguste retraite.
>
> J'ai tant fait patience
> Qu'à jamais j'oublie;
> Craintes et souffrances
> Aux cieux sont parties.
> Et la soif malsaine
> Obscurcit mes veines.

[I told myself: desist and don't let yourself be seen, even without the promise of higher joys. Let nothing stop you, august retreat. I have been patient for so long; may I never remember again. Fears and sufferings have vanished into the heavens. And the unhealthy thirst darkens my veins.]

The torment of the soul which Rimbaud calls patience is somewhat like the Dark Night of the mystics, which occurs between the initial steps toward union with God and its ultimate realization. The preliminary fear and suffering have abandoned the poet, who longs for forgetfulness of the past in order to focus himself on his consuming thirst. An extraordinary simile expresses the monstrous intensity of his experience:

> Ainsi la Prairie
> A l'oubli livrée,
> Grandie, et fleurie
> D'encens et d'ivraies

> Au bourdon farouche
> De cent sales mouches.

[Like a meadow abandoned to oblivion, overgrown
and flowering with incense and tares under the fran-
tic hum of a hundred filthy flies.]

The wild meadow with its fantastic and sinister aspect
symbolizes the poet's disquiet at his solitary labors of
spiritual elevation and his fear that they may not be
fruitful. The Biblical and liturgical associations of "en-
cens" and "ivraies" prepare a further use of Catholic
vocabulary:

> Ah! Mille veuvages
> De la si pauvre âme
> Qui n'a que l'image
> De la Notre-Dame!
> Est-ce que l'on prie
> La Vierge Marie?

[Ah! the thousand widowhoods of this poor soul, who
only has the picture of Our Lady. Should one pray
to the Virgin Mary?]

The spirit is widowed while awaiting the moment when
hearts will unite, and it can glimpse beatitude only in a
cheap religious image (the images d'Épinal, with which
French children are familiar). That Christian ways of
thinking have not been specifically alluded to before this
point need not surprise us: these poems are syncretic and
undoctrinal to such a degree that a reference to the Virgin
Mary as intercessor merely expresses the poet's feeling of
abandonment and not any theological conception.

The "Chanson de la plus haute tour" ends with a song-
like repetition of the first stanza and its prayer for the
time to come "où les coeurs s'éprennent." This prayer is
partially answered in "L'Eternité," where the poet passes

beyond the barrier of temporality and the recollection of the world of mankind:

> Elle est retrouvée.
> Quoi? — L'Eternité.
> C'est la mer allée
> Avec le soleil.

[It is found again. What? Eternity. It's the sea gone with the sun.]

Air and sea, eternity and endless space fuse together in this vision of summer light. The curious use of the past participle of *aller* is particularly remarkable in the way it suggests the movement of the seascape out toward infinity. The imagery of light is further developed in subsequent stanzas:

> Ame sentinelle,
> Murmurons l'aveu
> De la nuit si nulle
> Et du jour en feu.

[Vigilant soul, let us murmur the avowal of night's nullity and the flaming day.]

The soul in its tower has come to the end of its lonely vigil: the brief summer night has vanished as well as time, and the poet has realized the one ultimate truth which is the sun. Lightness is associated with sunshine, and in this purification by fire the poet soars over mankind:

> Des humains suffrages,
> Des communs élans
> Là tu te dégages
> Et voles selon.

[From human approval, from communal aspirations you are now free and fly as you wish.]

Fire is also, however, symbolic of rigor, and the poet's experience of illumination is not a banal ecstasy but a timeless, sustained trial—free from hope in the future as from regret for the past:

> Puisque de vous seules,
> Braises de satin,
> Le Devoir s'exhale
> Sans qu'on dise : enfin.
>
> Là pas d'espérance,
> Nul orietur.
> Science avec patience,
> Le supplice est sûr.
>
> Elle est retrouvée. . . .

[Since from you alone, satin embers, Duty breathes forth without one's wishing to say: enough! No hope is there, no beginnings. Knowledge with patience, the torture is certain.]

The poet's conquest of truth can be made only at the price of pain—unless he should be favored in his undertaking by divine intervention. In "Age d'or," where from visions of eternity he passes to an even higher state of illumination, an angel intercedes:

> Quelqu'une des voix
> Toujours angélique
> — Il s'agit de moi, —
> Vertement s'explique :
>
> Ces mille questions
> Qui se ramifient
> N'amènent, au fond,
> Qu'ivresse et folie;

> Reconnais ce tour
> Si gai, si facile :
> Ce n'est qu'onde, flore,
> Et c'est ta famille!

[One of the voices, always angelic, sharply scolds (it is talking of me): these thousand questions with their ramifications only lead in the end to delusion and folly. Learn this notion, so gay and simple: all is only wave and flower, and it's your family.]

Nothing is more simple or lighthearted than true knowledge, which consists in realizing the unity of all creation in the sunlight. The world of men and the soul's former wretchedness are summarily dismissed:

> Le monde est vicieux;
> Si cela t'étonne!
> Vis et laisse au feu
> L'obscure infortune.
>
> O! joli château!
> Que ta vie est claire!
> De quel Age es-tu,
> Nature princière
> De notre grand frère! etc...

[The world is vitiated, as if that surprised you! Live and cast in the fire your obscure misfortune. O pretty castle! How bright your life is! To what age of the world do you belong, princely nature of our big brother?]

The image of the bright castle reaches its plenitude of meaning here: it symbolizes the sumptuous and harmonious architecture of creation in which dwell the community of hearts that the poet has longed for. The eternity of aspiration has turned into a Golden Age of fulfillment, where no feeling of effort subsists from the arduous stages of illumination which preceded. The imagery reverts to a more naïve and child-like plane with its angels, "pretty" castle, and big brother in order to express the naturalness and ease of this final vision.

Mysticism, Christianity, magic, pantheism—all these beliefs have been mentioned in the course of our discussion without any one of them being equated with Rimbaud's thought. Much less can one even suggest all the possible sources there might be for the themes and symbols of this poetry. The essential problem is that Rimbaud's "mystical" poems are syncretic after the manner of much nineteenth-century religious literature. They have an artistic coherence and pattern but no clear theological grounding—unlike, say, St. John of the Cross' verse, which Rimbaud's recalls sometimes in its intensity. Rimbaud's last verse poems draw on heteroclite fragments of religious myth and symbolism rather than on any dogmatic conception of God, creation, and the soul. Thus he makes use at the same time of pagan sun-worship and the Virgin Mary's function as intercessor. Most generally we can describe Rimbaud's myth of spiritual adventure as a process of disincarnation and suffering which leads to a dissolution and renewal of the self in the world of all creation save mankind—light, flowers, water, and angels. Each poem is constructed around one or more of the key themes of the tower or castle, the sun, patience, thirst, hunger, and retreat from the world, and each deals with some point along the journey to eternity. Without much difficulty we could, by using traditional allegorical methods, make these poems conform to various systems of religious thought: for example, the sun can be Christ in liturgical typology, and so one might readily Christianize the whole cycle. Such an interpretation, however, would be as unjustified and vain as it would be ingenious. Discretion must be used in the case of a poet like Rimbaud in order not to simplify or over-categorize his imagination. It is not possible to assert that Rimbaud had any clear conception of spiritual exercise or ever attempted to pursue such practices; on the contrary, his notions of spiritual aspiration were most likely poetic and bookish. Nonetheless he created a cycle of poems comparable in imagination with very remarkable devotional poetry and of unquestionable religious force. It is one of the anomalies of nineteenth-century French literature that writers like Rimbaud, Hugo, and Nerval, who were hostile to churches, produced works of intense spirituality. In the course of examining *Une Saison en enfer,* we shall have occasion to consider at greater length the character of non-orthodox nineteenth-century religious thought and Rimbaud's in particular.

5. *Une Saison en enfer* and the
Dialectics of Damnation

UNE Saison en enfer is dated April–August 1873, and its composition therefore coincided with a rather dramatic sequence of events in Rimbaud's life: the last quarrel-ridden months of his liaison with Verlaine, the latter's attempt to shoot him in Brussels, and the sudden, irremediable experience of solitude forced on him by the elder poet's imprisonment. It hardly seems questionable that the work was inspired to some extent by Rimbaud's torturous relations with Verlaine, who is caricatured in one section of it; yet on the other hand, many themes of *Une Saison en enfer* must derive from preoccupations which remain unknown—for, like the two previous winters, that of 1872–73 is a blank in Rimbaud's career. That he spent part of it in London with Verlaine and part in the Ardennes with his family is virtually all we know. One may conjecture, as many critics do, that some of the last verse poems or some of the *Illuminations* were written at that time, but nothing allows us to affirm this with certainty. Nor do any letters survive which might suggest in what direction Rimbaud's thought and poetics were developing. About all we can be sure of is that *Une Saison en enfer* was not his first attempt at a prose poem.[1]

1. There are prose poems by Rimbaud in the aforementioned list of objects which Verlaine left in Paris in 1872 (see ch. 4, note 2).

Une Saison en enfer is the first of Rimbaud's poems to deal unmistakably with Christianity since his anti-clerical diatribes of 1871. His preoccupation with religious themes—in the most general sense—is evident in the last verse poems, but the latter hardly anticipate the painful attempt to come to grips with Christian doctrine which forms the basis of *Une Saison en enfer*. What precipitated Rimbaud's renewed concern with his childhood faith constitutes one of the most fascinating and mysterious elements in his biography. Curiously enough, Verlaine's conversion occurred not long after Rimbaud confronted the challenge of Catholicism, and one suspects that for both poets their relations assumed some almost metaphysical significance. However, this is sheer speculation.

In any case, it is almost certain that around the time when he was working on *Une Saison en enfer* Rimbaud studied the Gospel of St. John and sketched out his own version of three episodes from sacred history.[2] What he planned to do with these drafts is of course unknown. It is tempting to think that he was planning a really modern gospel—in accordance with his own conception of modernity—in order perhaps to confound Renan's then famous *Vie de Jésus*. Unlike scholars and humanitarians of the period, he would surely not have been put off by any elements of magic or metaphysics, however strange, that are found in Scriptures. It is significant in this respect that he chose as his source St. John, the most theological and cryptic of the evangelists. Unfortunately the three fragments we possess do not inform us clearly about his attitude toward Jesus. They have been called "skeptical and sarcastic," but, given the subtle and paradoxical character of Rimbaud's prose, it is impossible to infer his intentions from disconnected fragments. The following paragraph, dealing with the changing of water into wine at the Wed-

2. The evidence for dating is that they are written on the back of drafts for *Une Saison en enfer*.

ding in Cana and Jesus' arrival in Capernaum (John 2),
may be taken as typical of their ambivalent tone:

> Jésus n'avait point encor fait de miracles. Il avait,
> dans une noce, dans une salle à manger verte et rose,
> parlé un peu hautement à la Sainte Vierge. Et per-
> sonne n'avait parlé du vin de Cana à Capharnaum,
> ni sur le marché, ni sur les quais. Les bourgeois,
> peut-être.[3]

> [Jesus had not yet performed any miracles. He had,
> during a wedding, in a pink and green dining room,
> spoken a bit arrogantly to the Holy Virgin. And no
> one had talked of the wine of Cana in Capernaum,
> either at the market place or on the docks. The
> bourgeoisie, perhaps.]

This use of modern language and conceptions to present
Jesus' life hardly seems to be sarcastic in itself; clergymen
frequently sin far more in this direction. With no real
plan or context into which we might place these lines it
is difficult to say whether they are disparaging or slyly
laudatory. At the same time, and partly perhaps for the
same reason, they are singularly lacking in the density
and evocativeness characteristic of Rimbaud's mature
work. It is always perilous to attempt to rewrite a text of
such authority as the Bible, and Rimbaud fortunately
does not seem to have long pursued this somewhat sterile
enterprise. Instead, he channeled his Biblical preoccupations into *Une Saison en enfer,* which reflects serious examination of the Gospel.

Une Saison en enfer is first of all a myth of fall and
redemption; the plan of the work is, in this respect,
parallel to the Christian notion of the life of the individual and of mankind, without by any means being

3. Jesus' remark to Mary, to which Rimbaud alludes, is "Woman,
what have I to do with thee? mine hour is not yet come" (John 2:4).

identical with it. The brief introductory section is an account of the narrator's fall from his former happy state and permits us to sense the differences which separate Rimbaud's conceptions from those of Christianity:

> Jadis, si je me souviens bien, ma vie était un festin où s'ouvraient tous les coeurs, où tous les vins coulaient.
> Un soir, j'ai assis la Beauté sur mes genoux. — Et je l'ai trouvée amère. — Et je l'ai injuriée.
> Je me suis armé contre la justice.
> Je me suis enfui. O sorcières, ô misère, ô haine, c'est à vous que mon trésor a été confié!

> [Long ago, if I remember well, my life was a feast where all hearts opened, all wines flowed. One evening I seated Beauty on my lap—And I found her bitter—And I reviled her. I armed myself against justice. I fled. O witches, wretchedness, hatred, to you I confided my treasure!]

The poet's former state is expressed in exclusively symbolic rather than theological terms, and we must therefore refrain from defining it beyond observing that the feast implies the communion of souls. Likewise the actual cause of his fall remains unexplained. Rimbaud is not concerned with developing a total philosophy of history and the individual *ab origine;* consequently he indicates the prior, blissful condition of the narrator schematically by blending together unspecific paradisaical images. This prologue is furthermore a summary in which future themes of the poem are suggested: art and beauty, alienation from society, and the temptations of the supernatural. The process of the poet's self-damnation is next described, for the prologue is, in point of time, the speech of one already arrived at the lower depths:

Je parvins à faire s'évanouir dans mon esprit toute l'espérance humaine. Sur toute joie pour l'étrangler j'ai fait le bond sourd de la bête féroce.

J'ai appelé les bourreaux pour, en périssant, mordre la crosse de leurs fusils. J'ai appelé les fléaux, pour m'étouffer avec le sable, le sang. Le malheur a été mon dieu. Je me suis allongé dans la boue. Je me suis séché à l'air du crime. Et j'ai joué de bons tours à la folie.

[I succeeded in banishing all human hope from my heart. On every joy, to strangle it, I pounced stealthily like a ferocious beast. I called the executioners in order, dying, to bite the butts of their guns. I called on disasters to smother me with sand, with blood. Misfortune was my god. I stretched out in the mud. I dried myself in the breath of crime. And I've played good tricks on madness.]

Hell inspires the urge toward self-destruction and physical violence: this theme is to be developed in countless ways in the course of the following chapters, where the state of the body occupies as important a position as does that of the soul in Christian thought.

The possibility of salvation occurs to the narrator as he is menaced with ultimate annihilation—for we must observe that Rimbaud's hell is metaphoric in the sense that its inhabitants are still living:

Or, tout dernièrement, m'étant trouvé sur le point de faire le dernier *couac!* j'ai songé à rechercher la clef du festin ancien, où je reprendrais peut-être appétit.

La charité est cette clef. — Cette inspiration prouve que j'ai rêvé!

[Now just recently, on the point of giving my last croak, I thought of searching out the key of the one-

time feast, for which I might regain appetite. Charity
is the key.—This inspiration proves I was dreaming!]

Charity, which the poet derisively rejects as a possible
path of redemption, is a key concept in *Une Saison en
enfer*. The word recurs continuously with subtle shifts
of meaning, but for the moment we need only recognize
its close associations with the Gospel and with Christianity. As the greatest of the three theological virtues and
the one which bears most on the conduct of life (faith and
hope are less tangible) charity can be almost synonymous
with Christian demeanor. Here the narrator summarizes
the temptation and repudiation of Christian faith which
will form a major theme of subsequent chapters. As elsewhere in this prologue, the briefest of allusions is used
to foreshadow the body of the work.

Finally the poet is reproved by the devil, for, despite
the fact that this hell is an abode for the living, Rimbaud
carefully preserves the medieval imagery of damnation
both for humor and as a structural element in the poem:

> "Tu resteras hyène, etc...," se récrie le démon qui
> me couronna de si aimables pavots. "Gagne la mort
> avec tous tes appétits, et ton égoïsme et tous les
> péchés capitaux."

> ["You will remain a hyena, etc.," protests the demon
> who crowned me with such lovely poppies. "Go to
> death with all your appetites, and your egotism, and
> all the deadly sins."]

Opium poppies bespeak oblivion, and the narrator, mind-
less now of his former state, sets out to describe life in the
hell of the living from the point of view of one who is
irremediably damned and has only a brief space left before his final dissolution:

Ah! J'en ai trop pris : — Mais, cher Satan, je vous en conjure, une prunelle moins irritée! et en attendant les quelques petites lâchetés en retard, vous qui aimez dans l'écrivain l'absence des facultés descriptives ou instructives, je vous détache ces quelques hideux feuillets de mon carnet de damné.

[Ah! I've had enough. But, dear Satan, I beg of you, a less irritable look! and, while waiting for my few last-minute cringings, I will tear out for you, who appreciate in writers the lack of descriptive or instructive powers, these few hideous pages from my recordbook of damnation.]

The chapters of *Une Saison en enfer* are, at least provisionally, the record of a soul lost to good and committed to self-destruction.

The "carnet de damné" consists of several parts arranged in a descending scale of spiritual and physical perdition. The first and longest section, "Mauvais sang," is in some ways the most obscure, which may be ascribed to its origins, for in May 1873 Rimbaud described his work in progress as a "livre nègre" rather than a poem about hell, and it is certainly this chapter to which the epithet is most applicable.[4] Rimbaud's initial conception of his book was apparently modified in form and imagery, if not in subject, after his rupture with Verlaine, and he merely adapted the fragments of his "livre nègre" to fit the pattern of *Une Saison en enfer.*

"Mauvais sang" is an introduction to the dialectics of salvation and damnation which will inform subsequent chapters: it is not yet an account of hell but merely a series of propositions, as it were, about possibilities open to the spirit. Its geographical realm is therefore earth, where dwell those who are still not committed to either

4. See the letter of May 1873 to Delahaye.

heaven or hell. The "I" of "Mauvais sang" is, like that
of the rest of the poem, neither autobiographical nor
allegorical save in a shadowy and intermittent fashion.
The narrator has the peculiarity of constantly shifting
identity to accommodate himself to each new step in his
dialectic. He first appears as a splendid and cynical bar-
barian, hostile to civilization with its industrious ways
and moral constraints:

> J'ai de mes ancêtres gaulois l'oeil bleu blanc, la
> cervelle étroite, et la maladresse dans la lutte. Je
> trouve mon habillement aussi barbare que le leur.
> Mais je ne beurre pas ma chevelure. . . .
>
> D'eux, j'ai : l'idolâtrie et l'amour du sacrilège; —
> oh! tous les vices, colère, luxure, — magnifique, la
> luxure; — surtout mensonge et paresse.
>
> J'ai horreur de tous les métiers. Maîtres ou ouvriers,
> tous paysans, ignobles. La main à plume vaut la main
> à charrue. — Quel siècle à mains! — Je n'aurai
> jamais ma main. Après, la domesticité mène trop
> loin. L'honnêteté de la mendicité me navre. Les
> criminels dégoûtent comme des châtrés : moi, je suis
> intact, et ça m'est égal.

[From my Gallic ancestors I have blue-white eyes, a
narrow brainpan, and clumsiness in a fight. I find my
clothes as barbaric as theirs. Only I don't butter my
hair. . . . From them I have: idolatry and love of
sacrilege—oh, all the vices, anger, lust—magnificent,
lust—above all lying and laziness. I have a horror of
all work. Bosses, workers, all are ignoble peasants.
The hand that guides the pen is as good as the one
that guides the plow—what an age of hands!—I'll
never have my hand. Afterward domesticity leads too
far. The respectability of beggardom appalls me.
Criminals are as disgusting as eunuchs: I'm intact and
that's all right with me.]

The narrator stands totally outside society unlike beggars and common criminals, whom he recognizes as merely being prisoners of the order they seem to reject. There is more than a hint of the supernatural about his freedom; like all mythic heroes he is somehow superior to other men and enjoys special protection of a divine or infernal sort:

> Mais! qui a fait ma langue perfide tellement, qu'elle ait guidé et sauvegardé jusqu'ici ma paresse? Sans me servir pour vivre même de mon corps, et plus oisif que le crapaud, j'ai vécu partout. Pas une famille d'Europe que je ne connaisse. — J'entends des familles comme la mienne, qui tiennent tout de la déclaration des Droits de l'Homme. — J'ai connu chaque fils de famille!

> [But! who has made my tongue so perfidious that it has guided and safeguarded my laziness up to this point? Without even making use of my body to support myself and idler than a toad I've lived everywhere. Not a family in Europe I don't know.—I mean families like mine that owe everything to the declaration of the Rights of Man. I have *known* each family's son!]

The theme of strange powers culminates in the scabrous and boasting final pun. The function of this opening passage is multiple. To begin with, it provides a complete image of Satanic perfection, from the insolent distaste for all things constructive through the fondness for perverting good by idolatry and offending God's scheme of things by unnatural acts. Rimbaud takes care to establish the attributes of God's counterpart in hell, lest we be tempted to think of the devil as a mere subordinate punisher rather than as one of the twin poles of the moral world. We see evil here in its anagogical form: not as specific or contingent but absolute. The ironically colloquial form of the discourse, however, precludes any melodrama; on the contrary, the fundamental paradox of barbaric urbanity operates to persuade a seductive inversion of values. The assumption of the Satanic mask by the narrator stresses the fact that there are two races of men, the children of Abel and those of Cain, and on the basis of this distinction he will now proceed in the body of "Mauvais sang" to postulate a complex series of antitheses on the theme of the two races. As this passage draws to an end, we are situated in present time—the nineteenth century—and the narrator's social origins become clearer: he belongs to the undifferentiated horde of serfs whose individual existence begins only with the French Revolution and their legal recognition.

At this point the narrator suddenly loses his mythic attributes of absoluteness and power; he is placed in a scheme of history and society, where we find him among the subdued:

> Si j'avais des antécédents à un point quelconque de l'histoire de France!
> Mais non, rien.
> Il m'est bien évident que j'ai toujours été race inférieure. Je ne puis comprendre la révolte. Ma race ne se souleva jamais que pour piller : tels les loups à la bête qu'ils n'ont pas tuée.

> [If only I had antecedents at some point in the history of France. But no, nothing. It's quite evident to me that I've always been of an inferior race. I can't understand revolt. My race never rose up except to plunder: like wolves around the animal they haven't killed.]

These nameless masses, too indifferent and too lazy to revolt, nevertheless succeed in perverting the ideals of civili-

zation like the crusaders who sacked Christian Byzantium
and the East while believing in their holy mission:

> Je me rappelle l'histoire de la France fille aînée
> de l'Eglise. J'aurais fait, manant, le voyage de terre
> sainte; j'ai dans la tête des routes dans les plaines
> souabes, des vues de Byzance, des remparts de Solyme;
> le culte de Marie, l'attendrissement sur le crucifié
> s'éveillent en moi parmi mille féeries profanes.

> [I recall the history of France, eldest daughter of the
> Church. As a serf, I would have made the trip to the
> Holy Land; in my mind I have roads through the
> Swabian plains, images of Byzantium, of the ram-
> parts of Jerusalem; the cult of Mary, pity for the
> crucified Jesus well up in me amid a thousand pro-
> fane magic visions.]

He longs for all the extravagance, fanaticism, and superstition of medieval Christianity:

> — Je suis assis, lépreux, sur les pots cassés et les orties,
> au pied d'un mur rongé par le soleil. — Plus tard,
> reître, j'aurais bivaqué sous les nuits d'Allemagne.
> Ah! encore : je danse le sabbat dans une rouge
> clairière, avec des vieilles et des enfants.

> [I, a leper, am seated on shards and nettles, at the
> foot of a wall devoured by the sun.—Later, as a mer-
> cenary, I would have bivouacked under German
> nights. Ah! still again: I dance the witches' sabbath
> in a red clearing with old women and children.]

Leprosy, the feared yet holy disease of Christianity, the
bloody Thirty Years' War, and the round of the Witches'
Sabbath—the peasants' ancient tribute to the powers of
evil—equally enchant him. "Je n'en finirais pas de me
revoir dans ce passé." Yet he never confuses himself with
the leaders of Christendom: "Je ne me vois jamais dans

les conseils du Christ; dans les conseils des Seigneurs, — représentants du Christ." He remains submerged in the masses who contribute in no way to the ordering of society but merely submit to the forces of civilization while seizing every occasion to ignore its interdictions. His attachment to Christianity lies in the latter's by-products of superstition and regard for the devil. But the nineteenth century with its hegemony of the bourgeoisie and its democratic governments changed the traditional nature of European life by forcing identity, responsibility, education, and the vote on the population at large:

> Qu'étais-je au siècle dernier : je ne me retrouve qu'aujourd'hui. Plus de vagabonds, plus de guerres vagues. La race inférieure a tout couvert — le peuple, comme on dit, la raison; la nation et la science.

> [What was I in the last century? I can only recognize myself today. No more vagabonds, no more vague wars. The inferior race has covered everything—the people, as they say, reason, the nation, and science.]

The poet scorns the era when his own inferior race has assumed all power and created its ideals of reason, progress, and science. He mockingly uses the vocabulary of advanced political thinkers who saw in science the liberation of mankind, the replacement for the old hierarchy of birth, and the means towards a perfect world: "La science, la nouvelle noblesse! Le progrès. Le monde marche! Pourquoi ne tournerait-il pas?" "Nous allons à l'*Esprit*," he ironically declares, using a word much beloved of nineteenth-century fabricators of theories of history, who called Spirit or *Geist* the new state toward which the world was moving.[5] His barbaric soul is not satisfied with

5. There are a multitude of French romantic theories of history, of varying tendencies. Rimbaud was actually acquainted with some of the radical thinkers who had taken refuge in London after the Commune.

promises of heaven on earth or technology regnant but
yearns for the old Christian world dominated by the
supernatural, God and Satan, grace and damnation, when
real nobility and freedom were possible. He longs for an
anagogical, non-secular view of the universe. That day is
past, however, and he remains an anachronism with his
thirst for sin and redemption:

> Le sang païen revient! L'Esprit est proche, pour-
> quoi Christ ne m'aide-t-il pas, en donnant à mon
> âme noblesse et liberté. Hélas! l'Evangile a passé!
> l'Evangile! l'Evangile.
>
> J'attends Dieu avec gourmandise. Je suis de race
> inférieure de toute éternité.

> [The pagan blood comes back. The Holy Ghost is
> near, why doesn't Christ help me by giving my soul
> nobility and freedom! Alas! The Gospel has passed!
> The Gospel! The Gospel! I gluttonously await God.
> I am of an inferior race from all eternity.]

His spirit is still that of the old inferior race with its
desire for revelations and the supernatural. As the thought
returns of his native brutishness, the narrator begins
dreaming of the possibilities for barbaric life still left in
the world: if no escape in time is possible, change in place
suffices to recapture his proper moral climate:

> Me voici sur la plage armoricaine. Que les villes
> s'allument dans le soir. Ma journée est faite; je quitte
> l'Europe. L'air marin brûlera mes poumons; les
> climats perdus me tanneront. Nager, broyer l'herbe,
> chasser, fumer surtout; boire des liqueurs fortes
> comme du métal bouillant, — comme faisaient ces
> chers ancêtres autour des feux.
>
> Je reviendrai, avec des membres de fer, la peau
> sombre, l'oeil furieux : sur mon masque, on me jugera
> d'une race forte. J'aurai de l'or : je serai oisif et brutal.

Les femmes soignent ces féroces infirmes retour des pays chauds. Je serai mêlé aux affaires politiques. Sauvé.

[Here I am on the Breton shore. Let the cities light up in the evening. My day is done, I'm leaving Europe. The sea air will burn my lungs; lost climates will tan me. Swim, trample grass, hunt, above all smoke; drink liquors strong as boiling metal—as my dear ancestors did around their fires. I'll come back with limbs of iron, dark skin, a furious look: by my mask they'll think I'm from a strong race. I'll have gold; I'll be lazy and brutal. Women take care of these ferocious invalids back from the hot countries. I'll go into politics. Saved.]

The salvation he conceives of is at once ironic and serious: a triumph of barbarism and violence in the modern world cannot actually replace the vanished redemption of Christianity, but it is preferable to the insipid, morally neutral life of modern civilization. The vision breaks off, however, in a fit of lassitude, which, along with self-irony, always marks a transition in the dialectic of "Mauvais sang" to a new *prise de position:* "Maintenant, je suis maudit, j'ai horreur de la patrie. Le meilleur, c'est un sommeil bien ivre, sur la grève."

The poet now drops the insolent mask he has worn up to this point and proceeds to face his dilemma in a new light:

On ne part pas. — Reprenons les chemins d'ici, chargé de mon vice, le vice qui a poussé ses racines de souffrance à mon côté, dès l'âge de raison — qui monte au ciel, me bat, me renverse, me traîne.

[You can't leave. Let's again follow the roads here, burdened with my flaw, the flaw that sank its roots of suffering by my side from the age of reason on—

that rises into the sky, batters me, throws me down,
drags me.]

The "vice" of which the poet speaks is not one of the
seven deadly sins, for here the word has, as often in
French, its etymological sense of "flaw" or "defect" with
no moral connotations. Quite to the contrary, the poet's
failing might seem to be a virtue: "La dernière innocence
et la dernière timidité. C'est dit. Ne pas porter au monde
mes dégoûts et mes trahisons." Considering anew his position, the narrator suddenly admits that it is not native
sinfulness which informs his character but rather innocence: the dialectic has moved a step further. Yet innocence when coupled with timidity is only a source of
squeamishness ("dégoûts") and a refusal of others ("trahisons"); it ceases to be an operative virtue and cannot lead
to spiritual perfection. In irritation at the uselessness of
his purity the poet invokes bestiality and Satanic perfection as a viable escape from his dilemma; the Gospel has
passed, but hell perhaps remains. A burst of what one
might call mercenary or Foreign Legion imagery takes up
the previous theme of quitting Europe for savage lands:

> A qui me louer? Quelle bête faut-il adorer? Quelle
> sainte image attaque-t-on? Quels coeurs briserai-je?
> Quel mensonge dois-je tenir? — Dans quel sang
> marcher? . . .
> — Ah! je suis tellement délaissé que j'offre à
> n'importe quelle divine image des élans vers la per-
> fection.
> O mon abnégation, ô ma charité merveilleuse! ici-
> bas, pourtant!

[Whom to sell myself to? What beast must I worship?
What sacred image are we attacking? Whose heart
shall I break? What lie must I tell?—Whose blood
shall I walk in? . . . Ah! I am so alone that I offer

to any divine image my yearnings for perfection. Oh
my abnegation, Oh my marvelous charity! Here on
earth, though!]

In the state of solitude to which his timid innocence con-
demns him the poet turns indifferently toward visions of
grace or intimations of evil. Savagery is a replica of sanctity, hell's state of grace. There are two divine images,
heavenly and infernal, and the poet's longings after perfection may fix themselves on the absolutes of either God
or Satan. His capacities for abnegation and charity are
the same as his dreams of brutality and violence: they
spring from an aspiration toward godhead of some kind.
But here and now only the attainment of hell seems possible. *"De profundis Domine,* suis-je bête!" he exclaims
finally with the customary weariness and irony which
terminate his élans toward absoluteness.

The narrator has proposed to follow the Satanic path
of destruction and brutality and consequently we next
find him emulating a hardened criminal:

> Encore tout enfant, j'admirais le forçat intraitable
> sur qui se referme toujours le bagne; je visitais les
> auberges et les garnis qu'il aurait sacrés par son
> séjour; je voyais *avec son idée* le ciel bleu et le travail
> fleuri de la campagne; je flairais sa fatalité dans les
> villes. Il avait plus de force qu'un saint, plus de bon
> sens qu'un voyageur — et lui, lui seul! pour témoin
> de sa gloire et de sa raison.

> [While still a child, I admired the obdurate convict
> on whom the prison gates always close. I visited the
> inns and furnished rooms that he had hallowed by
> his stay; I saw *with his eyes* the blue sky and the
> work of the burgeoning fields. I sniffed his fatality in
> cities. He had more strength than a saint, more good

sense than a traveler—and himself, himself alone to witness his glory and rightness.]

The convict is compared to a saint for his strength, and he "hallows" his places of habitation; the comparability of good and evil is reaffirmed, and the criminal's solitary contemplation of himself suggests the absoluteness of deity. The theme of physical strength is significant, for, as in the previous descriptions of travel and warfare, the body is associated with demonic power. Yet infernal strength is of a special kind: it is committed to destruction and ultimately to self-destruction. We have already seen examples of this curious conception of strength: when proposing to leave Europe and acquire barbaric physical force, the poet mingles together plans of hunting, beating down the underbrush, and other normal affirmations of strength with fantasies of burning his lungs, drinking fiery liquors, and being idle. "I shall be lazy and brutal," he declares, summing up this paradox: strength does not serve any positive end; on the contrary, it exists only to further its own dissipation. The narrator cannot dissociate physical power from the urge to torment one's body, to prove strength by self-destruction: "La vie dure, l'abrutissement simple, — soulever, le poing desséché, le couvercle du cercueil, s'asseoir, s'étouffer." This peculiar notion of force and power now becomes more overt as we reach a further stage in the dialectic of damnation; the narrator's imitation of the convict leads to disincarnation:

> Sur les routes, par des nuits d'hiver, sans gîte, sans habits, sans pain, une voix étreignait mon coeur gelé : "Faiblesse ou force : te voilà, c'est la force. Tu ne sais ni où tu vas ni pourquoi tu vas, entre partout, réponds à tout. On ne te tuera pas plus que si tu étais cadavre." Au matin j'avais le regard si perdu

et la contenance si morte, que ceux que j'ai rencontrés
ne m'ont peut-être pas vu.

[On the roads, in winter nights, homeless, in rags,
breadless, a voice clenched my frozen heart: "Weakness or strength: there you are, it's strength. You
don't know where you're going or why you're going,
go in anyplace, answer everything. They won't kill
you any more than if you were a dead body." In the
morning, I had such a vacant look and so dead an
expression that the people I met *perhaps didn't see
me.*]

The narrator's body dissolves suddenly and ceases to be a
physical object perceptible to the eye. His inner voice
asks whether this test of power is not really weakness and
then reassures him—only to be contradicted by his disembodiment, the symbol of infirmity. His assumption of
the convict's mask of strength turns out to be a form of
death, for, though he may pattern himself after Satan, he
cannot achieve the latter's divinity.

In his solitary, weakened, and ectoplasmatic condition,
the poet has a presage of hell, its hail of fire, and the
precious stones and metals of which Satan is traditionally
the master:

Dans les villes la boue m'apparaissait soudainement
rouge et noire, comme une glace quand la lampe
circule dans la chambre voisine, comme un trésor
dans la forêt! Bonne chance, criais-je, et je voyais
une mer de flammes et de fumée au ciel; et, à gauche,
à droite, toutes les richesses flambant comme un mil-
liard de tonnerres.

[In cities the mud seemed to me suddenly red and
black, like a mirror that reflects a lamp moving about
in the next room, like a treasure in a forest! Good
luck, I cried, and I saw a sea of flames and smoke in

the sky; and on the left, on the right, every kind of wealth flaming like a billion thunderbolts.]

Yet the narrator is not yet ready for damnation; there remain further dialectical ruses to explore.

As the vision of hell fades, the poet's weakness becomes more evident than ever; instead of rejoicing in the convict's proud, god-like solitude he complains of his isolation and weeps at the lack of comprehension on the part of men:

Mais l'orgie et la camaraderie des femmes m'étaient interdites. Pas même un compagnon. Je me voyais devant une foule exaspérée, en face du peloton d'exécution, pleurant du malheur qu'ils n'aient pu comprendre, et pardonnant! — Comme Jeanne d'Arc!

[But debauchery and the companionship of women were forbidden to me. Not even a friend. I saw myself in front of an exasperated mob, facing the firing squad, weeping at the misfortune of not being understood, and forgiving!—Like Joan of Arc!]

The criminal has suddenly become a martyred saint, for in the scheme of *Une Saison en enfer* the two are merely different aspects of election. It suffices to postulate the evil of society for its enemies to achieve sanctity. The terms of good and evil are thus casually inverted as the poet opposes his innocence and capacity for salvation with the populace's certain damnation:

— "Prêtres, professeurs, maîtres, vous vous trompez en me livrant à la justice. Je n'ai jamais été de ce peuple-ci; je n'ai jamais été chrétien; je suis de la race qui chantait dans le supplice; je ne comprends pas les lois; je n'ai pas le sens moral, je suis une brute : vous vous trompez..."

Oui, j'ai les yeux fermés à votre lumière. Je suis

une bête, un nègre. Mais je puis être sauvé. Vous êtes de faux nègres, vous maniaques, féroces, avares. Marchand, tu es nègre; magistrat, tu es nègre; général, tu es nègre; empereur, vieille démangeaison, tu es nègre : tu as bu d'une liqueur non taxée de la fabrique de Satan.

["Priests, teachers, masters, you're making a mistake in handing me over to justice. I've never belonged to this race; I've never been Christian; I come from the breed that sang under torture; I don't understand the laws; I don't have any moral sense, I'm a brute: you're making a mistake . . ." Yes, my eyes are closed to your light. I'm a beast, a savage. But I can be saved. You are false savages, you maniacs, wildmen, skinflints. Merchant, you're a savage; magistrate, you're a savage; general, you're a savage; emperor, old mange, you're a savage: you have drunk of bootleg liquor from Satan's still.]

This complex transition is an excellent example of the dialectic method of *Une Saison en enfer* with its antithetical movement. The narrator proclaims that, not worshipping God, he cannot sin, while the exasperated crowd, being Christian, has damned itself. Even though the criminal or savage follows Satan's law, he cannot be damned like the sinning Christian. Therefore salvation is principally open to the savage. Satanic innocence (if the expression be not too paradoxical) is opposed to Christian damnation. These involved and slightly faulty antitheses are far from being merely Rimbaud's perverse invention, for Christianity has always harbored paradoxes about sin and a fondness for dialectics. Parables like that of the lost sheep (Matthew 18) and works like St. Paul's Epistle to the Romans show the same tendency to play tortuously with moral notions. Rimbaud seizes on this curious characteristic of Christian thought and exploits it for his own purposes.

The complicated opposition of "faux nègres," who would really seem to be the *true* lost souls, to the narrator, a real savage, prepares us for his new departure to Africa, where he will be this time not the colonist but the native. "J'entre au vrai royaume des enfants de Cham," announces the poet as he abandons the sinister damned cities of Europe for the brute-like frenzy of African life, where all concern over matters of the spirit is forgotten in physical excess:

> Connais-je encore la nature? me connais-je? — *Plus de mots.* J'ensevelis les morts dans mon ventre. Cris, tambour, danse, danse, danse, danse! Je ne vois même pas l'heure où, les blancs débarquant, je tomberai au néant.
>
> Faim, soif, cris, danse, danse, danse, danse!

> [Do I yet know nature? Do I know myself?—*No more words.* I'll bury the dead in my belly. Yells, drum, dance, dance, dance, dance! I can't wait for the time when the white men will land and I'll drop into nothingness. Hunger, thirst, yells, dance, dance, dance, dance!]

The arrival of the colonists or missionaries has, however, an unexpected effect; the only shot from the white man's cannon which hits the poet is a blast of grace:

> Les blancs débarquent. Le canon! Il faut se soumettre au baptême, s'habiller, travailler.
>
> J'ai reçu au coeur le coup de la grâce. Ah! je ne l'avais pas prévu.

> [The white men are landing. The cannon! We'll have to be baptized, put on clothes, work. I'm shot in the heart with grace. Ah! I hadn't expected it.]

Unlike the Christian, whose life must be spent in repent-
ance for his inevitable sins since baptism, the savage passes
from ignorance of good to the state of the angels:

> Je n'ai point fait le mal. Les jours vont m'être
> légers, le repentir me sera épargné. Je n'aurai pas eu
> les tourments de l'âme presque morte au bien, où
> remonte la lumière sévère comme les cierges funé-
> raires. . . . Vais-je être enlevé comme un enfant, pour
> jouer au paradis dans l'oubli de tout le malheur!

> [I have not committed evil. The days will weigh
> light upon me, I shall be spared repentance. I shall
> not have suffered the torments of the soul which is
> almost dead to good and from which rises a severe
> flame like that of a funeral taper. . . . I am going
> to be assumed like a child to play in paradise oblivi-
> ous of all misfortune!]

The radical theology implicit in this passage resembles
some early Christian heresy: if grace be received with total
acceptance, the soul is completely purged of evil, for otherwise God's powers would appear to be imperfect and His
goodness but lukewarm. No difference then remains between redeemed man and angel; why therefore should
earth differ from heaven? The narrator pursues this direction of thought, as he refuses to admit that earth's greatest
gift, material wealth, suffices to his aspirations:

> Vite! est-il d'autres vies? — Le sommeil dans la
> richesse est impossible. La richesse a toujours été bien
> public. L'amour divin seul octroie les clefs de la
> science. Je vois que la nature n'est qu'un spectacle
> de bonté. Adieu chimères, idéals, erreurs.

> [Quick! are there other lives? Slumbering in wealth
> is impossible. Wealth has always been public prop-
> erty. Divine love alone grants the keys to knowledge.

I see that all Nature is a spectacle of goodness. Farewell illusions, ideals, errors.]

Nature is transformed, in accordance with the above-
mentioned theological principles, while angels come to
gather him up into their midst. He begs the angels, into
whose boat the white men's vessel seems to have metamor-
phosed, to redeem all mankind:

> Le chant raisonnable des anges s'élève du navire
> sauveur : c'est l'amour divin. — Deux amours! je
> puis mourir de l'amour terrestre, mourir de dévoue-
> ment. J'ai laissé des âmes dont la peine s'accroîtra
> de mon départ! Vous me choisissez parmi les nau-
> fragés, ceux qui restent sont-ils pas mes amis?
> Sauvez-les!

[The reasonable song of the angels rises from the
rescue ship: it's divine love.—Two loves! I could
die of earthly love, die of devotion. I've left behind
souls whose sorrow will increase at my departure!
You choose me among the shipwrecked, aren't those
who remain also my friends? Save them!]

The narrator is assuming Christ's role of intercessor and
envelops all humanity in his "marvelous charity." Christ,
however, did not demand universal salvation of God; the
poet of *Une Saison en enfer* attempts to surpass the foreseen limitations which Christianity imposes on mankind
and matter and has confidence in his ability. "La raison
m'est née. Le monde est bon. . . . Dieu fait ma force, et
je loue Dieu."

The narrator appears to have reached a stable position
of faith and strength with his vision of total redemption
and the benevolence of nature, but there remains a further subtle shift of dialectic which will destroy his state
of grace. The world is good, he has concluded, which

brings to mind the consequent perfection of his own nature in particular:

> L'ennui n'est plus mon amour. Les rages, les débauches, la folie, dont je sais tous les élans et tous les désastres, — tout mon fardeau est déposé. Apprécions sans vertige l'étendue de mon innocence.

> [Ennui is no longer my love. Fury, debauchery, madness—whose every aspiration and disaster I know—all my burden is laid aside. Let's evaluate, without being overwhelmed, the extent of my innocence.]

Innocence is merely a natural phenomenon, and the complexities of Christianity, with its insistence upon atonement, are urbanely mocked in a parodic variation on the traditional metaphor of Jesus wedding the Church: "Je ne serais plus capable de demander le réconfort d'une bastonnade. Je ne me crois pas embarqué pour une noce avec Jésus-Christ pour beau-père." The poet in his state of innocence no longer needs Christianity and its moral scheme.

"Je ne suis pas prisonnier de ma raison," he declares, and the last noun might surprise if we do not recall that he has just spoken of Christianity as the "reason" born to him and alluded to the "reasonable song of the angels." There is a rather special kind of play on words here: the term *raison* has been abused in French since the seventeenth century, and apologists of the faith have not hesitated to claim for Christianity a logical rigor in keeping with their compatriots' prejudices and quite out of harmony with the Church Father's *credo quia absurdum*. The narrator uses *raison* in an antiphrastic, satirical fashion and proceeds to expound a genuinely reasonable faith purged of all sentimentality:

> J'ai dit : Dieu. Je veux la liberté dans le salut : comment la poursuivre? Les goûts frivoles m'ont

quitté. Plus besoin de dévouement ni d'amour divin.
Je ne regrette pas le siècle des coeurs sensibles. Chacun
a sa raison, mépris et charité : je retiens ma place au
sommet de cette angélique échelle de bon sens.

[I said: God. I want freedom in salvation. How to
pursue it? Frivolous tastes have left me. No more
need of devotion or divine love. I don't regret the age
of tender hearts. Each is right, scorn and charity: I
reserve my place at the top of the angelic ladder of
good sense.]

The rejection of Christianity and its conception of sin
entails the dismissal of grace, the manifestation of divine
love to aid our weakness, and charity, the virtue which is
pitted against an evil world. The poet is left with God and
his own perfection of spirit, yet such a state is untenable:
he has not achieved participation in deity, despite his
merit, any more than he was able to attain Satanic godhead by emulating the criminal. The way of the world
remains unchanged, for the tortuous dialectic of salvation
has led him utterly astray, and he can only confess the disparity between it and reality. Instead of the perfect con-
tentment he should feel in the discovery that he and the
world are perfect, he experiences only lassitude:

> Quant au bonheur établi, domestique ou non...
> non, je ne peux pas. Je suis trop dissipé, trop faible.
> La vie fleurit par le travail, vieille vérité : moi, ma
> vie n'est pas assez pesante, elle s'envole et flotte loin
> au-dessus de l'action, ce cher point du monde.

[As for established happiness, domestic or otherwise
. . . no, I can't. I am too exhausted, too weak. Life
flowers through work, an old truth: my life does not
weigh enough, it soars up and floats far above action,
that dear central point of the world.]

The thought of work and domesticity, which the poet scorned at the beginning of "Mauvais sang," recurs, but in a different mode: now he regrets his incapacity for them. His place at the top of the angelic ladder of good sense means nothing for life, and the realization of this inspires the usual fatigue and feeling of corporeal incompleteness. His élan toward God—a matter of pure spirit—produces the same bodily disintegration as the Satanic devotion to strength and brutality. The latter urge comes momentarily to his mind: "Comme je deviens vieille fille, à manquer du courage d'aimer la mort!" The courageous, infernal search for death is at least more decisive than his debilitating dreams of angelic perfection, which fail to provide him with the divine energy he had expected: "Si Dieu m'accordait le calme céleste, aérien, la prière, — comme les anciens saints. — Les saints! des forts! les anachorètes, des artistes comme il n'en faut plus!" We are back at an earlier stage of the dialectic; the poet's innocence makes bestiality impossible to achieve and yet does not suffice to grant him divinity: "Farce continuelle! Mon innocence me ferait pleurer. La vie est la farce à mener par tous." "Mauvais sang" concludes in anger as the poet's longings for a "divine image" lead him around in a futile circle.

There is a brief, ironic coda, in which the Foreign Legion imagery returns:

> Assez, voici la punition. — *En marche!*
>
> Ah! les poumons brûlent, les tempes grondent! la nuit roule dans mes yeux, par ce soleil! le coeur... les membres...
>
> Où va-t-on? au combat? Je suis faible! les autres avancent. Les outils, les armes... le temps!...
>
> Feu! feu sur moi! Là, ou je me rends. — Lâches! — Je me tue! Je me jette aux pieds des chevaux!
>
> Ah!...

— Je m'y habituerai.
Ce serait la vie française, le sentier de l'honneur!

[Enough! Here's your punishment.—"Forward March!" Ah! my lungs burn, my temples pound, I see black in this blinding sunlight! My heart . . . My limbs . . . Where are we going? Into battle? I'm weak. The others are advancing. The tools, the weapons . . . Time . . . Shots! They shooting at me! Stop! or I'll surrender.—"Cowards!"—I'll kill myself! I'll throw myself in front of the horses! Ah! . . . I'll get used to it. It will be the French way of life, the path of honor!]

The punishment is symbolic of all his failures: dreams of power—divine or infernal—lead him ultimately to weakness. He is not the captain but a cowering footsoldier absurdly trying to blackmail the captain with threats of suicide. At the end he is back in the detested world of the nineteenth century and French life, covering his nullity with glorious slogans. There is no escape in this colonized Africa which the European rot has overrun.

"Mauvais sang" serves as a general exposition of the theology of salvation and damnation; as we follow the narrator's metamorphoses, Rimbaud establishes key notions: the spiritual vacuity of nineteenth-century Europe with its false Christianity, the yearnings of the soul for salvation of some sort, the possibility of escape in place if not in time, the inadequacy of grace to transform life, the self-destructiveness of Satanism, and the equal validity of heaven and hell as ideals. These themes have various antithetical relationships which provide the articulations of the chapter; thus its movement is not inductive but dialectic. Constituting as it does an introduction to the thought of *Une Saison en enfer*, "Mauvais sang" reaches no conclusion but rather has an almost futile cyclical motion. Each step in the dialectic leads both forward and backward again to itself. The elaborate parallelisms and contrasts between its parts give an illusion of movement, but essentially the narrative has not progressed.

With "Nuit de l'enfer" we commence the actual descent into hell; the landscape becomes eerie, void of other human figures, and shrouded in darkness. Instead of the erratic turnings and twistings of "Mauvais sang" the chapter consists of a smooth if dense monologue in which the narrator acquaints us with his successive *impressions de damné*. While in "Mauvais sang" he had merely explored the thought of self-damnation as a way of salvaging his soul from the nothingness of nineteenth-century life, here he has definitively committed himself to hell, and its pains and pleasures are such as he had not earlier foreseen. His self-damnation is willful, which he proclaims with satisfaction:

> J'ai avalé une fameuse gorgée de poison. — Trois fois béni soit le conseil qui m'est arrivé! Les entrailles me brûlent. La violence du venin tord mes membres, me rend difforme, me terrasse. Je meurs de soif, j'étouffe, je ne puis crier. C'est l'enfer, l'éternelle peine! Voyez comme le feu se relève! Je brûle comme il faut. Va, démon!

> [I swallowed a terrific mouthful of poison.—Thrice blessed be the notion that came to me! My entrails burn. The violence of the poison twists my limbs, makes me shapeless, flings me to the ground. I'm dying of thirst, I'm choking, I can't cry out. I'm burning the way I should. Come on, demon!]

The way in which he has succeeded in losing his soul remains delicately ambiguous, since the poison he has swallowed is an inexplicit symbol conveying only corporeal destruction. He speaks curiously of an attempted conversion:

J'avais entrevu la conversion au bien et au bonheur, le salut. Puis-je décrire la vision, l'air de l'enfer ne souffre pas les hymnes. C'était des millions de créatures charmantes, un suave concert spirituel, la force et la paix, les nobles ambitions, que sais-je?

[I had glimpsed conversion to good and happiness, salvation. Can I describe the vision?—the air in hell doesn't transmit hymns. It was millions of enchanting creatures, a soft spiritual concert, strength and peace, noble ambitions, how should I know what?]

The rough draft of this passage bears the title "Fausse Conversion," and the expression seems indeed to explain the poet's situation. Yet false conversion is itself an ambiguous notion: it could imply an acceptance of God which somehow failed or a Faustian commitment to Satan in the hope of attaining a happiness which never came about. Rimbaud is carefully creating an equivocal situation which does not fit the usual notions of the discreteness of heaven and hell. This initial ambiguity will become intensified in the course of "Nuit de l'enfer."

At first the narrator is amazed that he remains alive, though in hell, and in possession of his reason, which he employs to analyze his state:

Et c'est encore la vie! — Si la damnation est éternelle! Un homme qui veut se mutiler est bien damné, n'est-ce pas? Je me crois en enfer, donc j'y suis. C'est l'exécution du catéchisme. Je suis esclave de mon baptême. . . . C'est la vie encore! Plus tard, les délices de la damnation seront plus profondes. Un crime, vite, que je tombe au néant, de par la loi humaine.

[And this is still life!—But damnation is eternal! A man who tries to mutilate himself is certainly damned, isn't he? *Cogito in inferis esse, ergo ibi sum.*

It's the effect of the catechism. I'm a slave to my baptism. . . . This is still life! Later, the delights of damnation will be greater. A crime, quick, so I can drop into nothingness according to the law set for man.]

He longs for the *real* hell of the dead, finding the torments of this one too mild; he does not yet understand that his punishment will not consist in mere fire. Satan tempts him to forget he is damned and urbanely offers enchantments to distract him:

> Tais-toi, mais tais-toi!... C'est la honte, le reproche, ici : Satan qui dit que le feu est ignoble, que ma colère est affreusement sotte. — Assez!... Des erreurs qu'on me souffle, magies, parfums faux, musiques puériles.

[Shut up! Will you shut up! . . . Here there's supposed to be shame, reproof; Satan says the fire is ignoble, that my anger is terribly silly.—Enough! . . . They are urging hallucinations upon me: magic sights, odd perfumes, puerile melodies.]

The poet angrily and suspiciously refuses the delights which are being pressed on him, not realizing that he is already succumbing to his true punishment, the illusion of his own perfection: "— Et dire que je tiens la vérité, que je vois la justice : j'ai un jugement sain et arrêté, je suis prêt pour la perfection... " Fear overcomes him, as he suddenly recognizes in what way hell is overpowering him and he recalls the earth in a violent outburst:

> Orgueil. — La peau de ma tête se dessèche. Pitié! Seigneur, j'ai peur. J'ai soif, si soif! Ah! l'enfance, l'herbe, la pluie, le lac sur les pierres, *le clair de lune quand le clocher sonnait douze...* le diable est au

clocher, à cette heure. Marie! Sainte-Vierge!... —
Horreur de ma bêtise.

[Pride.—My scalp is drying up. Pity! Lord, I'm afraid.
I'm thirsty, so thirsty! Ah! childhood, grass, rain, the
lake water on the stones, *the moonlight when the bell-
tower rang twelve* . . . The devil is in the tower now.
Mary! Holy Virgin! . . . The horror of my stupidity.]

The last word sums up his reactions to the ambivalence
of his feelings: the narrator has chosen to damn himself,
yet prays to God; he feels certain of his own perfection
but knows that only the hopelessly vitiated belong to hell.
After this point, however, his last awareness of his situation vanishes and true damnation begins.

"Les hallucinations sont innombrables," he announces
as he sinks into the lower depths of hell—the hell of the
truly dead for which he had earlier longed:

> Ah çà! l'horloge de la vie s'est arrêtée tout à l'heure.
> Je ne suis plus au monde. — La théologie est sérieuse,
> l'enfer est certainement *en bas* — et le ciel en haut. —
> Extase, cauchemar, sommeil dans un nid de flammes.

[Ah! there! The clock of life stopped just now. I
am no longer in the world.—Theology is serious:
hell is certainly *down below*—and heaven up there.—
Ecstasy, nightmare, slumber in a nest of flames.]

The peculiarity of the poet's hell is its sporadic semblance
of beatitude: "hell is certainly *down below*" is a query,
for visions of divinity and power are stealing on the narrator. First Jesus appears to the poet, who seems to have
taken a seat among the disciples in the boat on the Sea of
Galilee (John 6; Matthew 14):

> Jésus marche sur les ronces purpurines, sans les
> courber... Jésus marchait sur les eaux irritées. La

lanterne nous le montra debout, blanc et des tresses brunes, au flanc d'une vague d'émeraude...

[Jesus is walking on the scarlet brambles, without bending them down . . . Jesus was walking on the angry waters. The lantern showed him to us, pale with dark locks, beside an emerald wave.]

The omniscience of deity then possesses the narrator: "Je vais dévoiler tous les mystères : mystères religieux ou naturels, mort, naissance, avenir, passé, cosmogonie, néant." He presents himself as the supreme magician, a role which Satan traditionally enjoys:

Ecoutez!...

J'ai tous les talents! . . . Veut-on des chants nègres, des danses de houris? Veut-on que je disparaisse, que je plonge à la recherche de l'*anneau?* Veut-on? Je ferai de l'or, des remèdes.

[Listen! . . . I have every talent! . . . Do you want songs of savages, houri dances? Do you want me to plunge in search of the *ring?* Do you? I'll make gold, remedies.]

The narrator has been uncertain up to this point whether there are other people around him: "Il n'y a personne ici et il y a quelqu'un : je ne voudrais pas ré- pandre mon trésor." This eerie, paranoid mood vanishes however at the height of his delirium, where he is no longer simply Satan but Christ as well, come to redeem the waiting throngs:

Fiez-vous donc à moi, la foi soulage, guide, guérit. Tous, venez, — même les petits enfants, — que je vous console, qu'on répande pour vous son coeur, — le coeur merveilleux!

[Trust yourselves to me, faith relieves, guides, cures. Come all, even little children, so that I can console you, pour out for you my heart—my marvelous heart!]

This passage contains reminiscences from Matthew 11 and 19, and as usual charity symbolizes Christianity for Rimbaud. The false conversion is complete in all its divine and infernal ambiguity; heaven and hell are united, and the poet imagines himself the master of both. His conversion is thus false not only in the sense that the two eschatological realms are brought together, but also because it represents not so much a conversion as an attempted usurpation of superhuman power.

The price of attaining godhead, however, is dissolution: in the course of his unreal visions the poet himself has become unreal and disincarnate. Lassitude steals on him as he has a last vertiginous vision of a castle and eternity, the themes Rimbaud exploited in his last verse poems:

Décidément, nous sommes hors du monde. Plus aucun son. Mon tact a disparu. Ah! mon château, ma Saxe, mon bois de saules. Les soirs, les matins, les nuits, les jours... Suis-je las! . . . Satan, farceur, tu veux me dissoudre, avec tes charmes. Je réclame. Je réclame! un coup de fourche, une goutte de feu.

[Decidedly we are out of the world. No more sound. My touch has vanished. Ah! my castle, my Saxony, my willow grove. The evenings, mornings, nights, days . . . How tired I am! . . . Satan, joker, you're trying to dissolve me with your charms. I object. I object! A poke with the pitchfork! A drop of fire!]

The real hell is not the medieval apparatus of fires and devils but the fatal ecstasies of salvation and the terror of losing all materiality. In "Mauvais sang," God and Satan were discovered to be equally possible masters: the abandoned soul turns alternately to one or the other for spiritual satisfaction. Both offer an escape from the aridity of this life, and the choice between them is a matter of circumstances. "Nuit de l'enfer," however, carries a more sinister implication: that God and Satan are somehow inseparable and indistinguishable. Each is capable of assuming the other's mask, and how then can either really be identified? Where such ambiguities exist, there is ultimately no difference between heaven and hell: the former is merely a variant of the latter. With this new discovery in the dialectics of damnation, we approach the bottom of the pit.

The two "Délires," which form the lowest circle in Rimbaud's hell, have a distinctly autobiographical coloring—in "Vierge folle" the speaker has some resemblance to Verlaine, and "Alchimie du verbe" makes use of Rimbaud's last verse poems—but, as should be the case, poetry has altered and distorted autobiographical facts to its own ends. It is difficult to refrain from maliciously enjoying "Vierge folle" as a deadly portrait of Verlaine's mawkish character, but the interest of the episode comes, perhaps more than is usually realized, from sheer verbal brilliance and does not really depend on reading into it references to Verlaine's foibles. The elements of satire and caricature are pushed to such grotesque limits that we see in the Foolish Virgin more a spiritual type than a real person. The very title of the chapter belongs to Biblical typology, although Rimbaud alters considerably the parable of the Wise and Foolish Virgins (Matthew 25) in order to provide them with an Infernal Spouse. The text of the Gospel merely says that they did not fill their lamps with oil in time to receive the Bridegroom, who is symbolic of salvation, but Rimbaud was doubtless inspired by the utterly non-Biblical sense which *vierge folle* had acquired in French, where the term designates quite the opposite of a virgin.

"Ecoutons la confession d'un compagnon d'enfer," announces the narrator, as he presents his ambiguously
gendered friend. The Foolish Virgin's language is a nice
combination of pious rhetoric and bathos: "O divin
Epoux, mon Seigneur, ne refusez pas la confession de la
plus triste de vos servantes. Je suis perdue. Je suis soûle.
Je suis impure. Quelle vie!" The ridiculous "quelle vie"
coming after a hysterical series of self-accusations gives
the measure of her abuse of language. Throughout this
section there is an implicit contrast with the style of the
narrator of "Mauvais sang" and "Nuit de l'enfer," whose
self-irony never permits him so complacently tearful an
outburst. The tone of confessional hysteria, with its
choppy little phrases and drolly blasphemous sexual metaphor, is further developed:

> Pardon, divin Seigneur, pardon! Ah! pardon!
> Que de larmes! Et que de larmes encore plus tard,
> j'espère!
> Plus tard, je connaîtrai le divin Epoux! Je suis
> née soumise à Lui. — L'autre peut me battre
> maintenant!

> [Pardon, divine Lord, pardon! Ah! pardon! So many
> tears! And so many more tears later, I hope! Later
> I will know the divine Spouse! I was born His servant.
> —The other one can beat me now!]

For one so forlorn the Foolish Virgin is, however, singularly sure of her redemption. An absurdly ill-graduated trio
of phrases ushers in a curious avowal of superiority: "Ah!
je souffre, je crie. Je souffre vraiment. Tout pourtant
m'est permis, chargée du mépris des plus méprisables
coeurs." The casuistry by which the amount of scorn
heaped on her assures forgiveness for everything remains
rationally obscure yet psychologically all too comprehen-
sible: this cringing yet arrogant attitude epitomizes the

Foolish Virgin's bad faith. She has none of her Infernal Spouse's passion for absolute sanctity or damnation but rather seems intent on bargaining with heaven: "j'ai été bien sérieuse jadis, et je ne suis pas née pour devenir squelette."

"Je suis esclave de l'Epoux infernal, celui qui a perdu les vierges folles. C'est bien ce démon-là." The narrator of "Mauvais sang" and "Nuit de l'enfer" is suddenly put into a new perspective as we see him through the eyes of the Foolish Virgin. No longer is he merely a damned soul but the active agent of hell, who exists on another plane than that of men and earth:

> Lui était presque un enfant... Ses délicatesses mystérieuses m'avaient séduite. J'ai oublié tout mon devoir humain pour le suivre. Quelle vie! La vraie vie est absente. Nous ne sommes pas au monde. Je vais où il va, il le faut. Et souvent il s'emporte contre moi, *moi, la pauvre âme*. Le Démon! — C'est un Démon, vous savez, *ce n'est pas un homme*.

> [He was almost a child . . . His mysteriously delicate ways had seduced me. I forgot all my human duty to follow him. What a life! Real life is absent. We're not in the world. I go where he goes, I have to. And often he gets angry at *me, poor me*. The Demon!— He's a Demon, you know, *he's not a man*.]

As his slave the Foolish Virgin accepts the hallucinations which overcame the narrator in "Nuit de l'enfer": she believes him to be an infernal deity existing *out of this world* in the eschatological realms of godhead, where time and space are meaningless. At the same time she attempts feeble apologies for her own conduct with exclamations like "quelle vie," "moi, la pauvre âme," "il le faut," and "le Démon." She is moved somewhat incongruously to moral indignation at the devil for having seduced her and not having treated her better: one senses that she has, however, no objections to him merely because he is a devil. The Foolish Virgin's monologue is a masterful exercise in the language of self-deception, the testimony of one eager to give both God and Satan their due and to profit fully from both of them.

As the Foolish Virgin describes her lover, he comes to assume more than the simple role of tormenting devil: there is something in him of a demonic Christ come to transform the world in some strange way. He makes ambiguous declarations: "Je n'aime pas les femmes. L'amour est à réinventer, on le sait." Whether he alludes to the triumph of Sodom or a new era of universal love remains unclear, especially given the precarious sex of his companion. At times he appears to aspire solely to violence; then love of humanity overcomes him:

> Je l'écoute faisant de l'infamie une gloire, de la cruauté un charme. "Je suis de race lointaine : mes pères étaient Scandinaves : ils se perçaient les côtes, buvaient leur sang. . . . Ma richesse, je la voudrais tachée de sang partout. . . ."
>
> Parfois il parle, en une façon de patois attendri, de la mort qui fait repentir, des malheureux qui existent certainement, des travaux pénibles, des départs qui déchirent les coeurs. Dans les bouges où nous nous enivrions, il pleurait en considérant ceux qui nous entouraient, bétail de la misère. . . .

> [I listen to him making infamy into a glory, cruelty into a charm. "I'm from a distant race: my ancestors were Scandinavians, they pierced their sides, drank their own blood. . . . My wealth I would like spattered with blood all over. . . . " Sometimes he talks in a kind of tender patois of death bringing repentance, of the wretchedness which must exist for many, of heart-breaking farewells. In the hovels where we got drunk,

he would weep as he contemplated our companions,
poverty's herd. . . .]

The contrast between beast and saint is merely superficial,
however: just as hell sometimes resembles heaven in "Nuit
de l'enfer," so here the Infernal Spouse's redeeming mission, his love, and his charity are actually death-giving:

A côté de son cher corps endormi, que d'heures des
nuits j'ai veillé, cherchant pourquoi il voulait tant
s'évader de la réalité. Jamais homme n'eut pareil
vœu. Je reconnaissais, — sans craindre pour lui, —
qu'il pouvait être un sérieux danger dans la société.
— Il a peut-être des secrets pour *changer la vie?* Non,
il ne fait qu'en chercher, me répliquais-je. Enfin sa
charité est ensorcelée, et j'en suis la prisonnière.

[How many night hours I have lain awake beside his
dear sleeping body, wondering why he so wanted to
escape from reality. Never has a man had such a wish.
I recognized—without fearing for him—that he could
be a serious danger for society.—Does he perhaps have
secrets for *changing life?* No, he's only looking for
them, I told myself. In any case, his charity is bewitched and I am the prisoner of it.]

The escape from reality and the transformation of life
are infernal counterparts of Christ's offer of a new life.
The phrase "bewitched charity" epitomizes the sinister
character of the Infernal Spouse's benevolence: real charity is a disinterested love like God's and does not imprison
or destroy. We thus realize what demonic nuance the
word "charity" has in the prologue to *Une Saison en enfer,*
where the poet dismisses it as a means of salvation from
hell. The language of "Vierge folle" is inspired by the
old myth that heaven and hell are mirror-images of each
other: each has its king, its virtues, and its redemption to

offer. Thus all the concepts of theology can be interpreted in a divine or demonic sense. Such is the theory behind the Black Mass and similar phenomena: the worship of Satan need not necessarily differ in structure from that of God. Infernal charity exists as well as Christ's charity and can at times be mistaken for the latter, although their goals are distinct. The Foolish Virgin speaks of the "heaven, a dark heaven," into which the Infernal Spouse leads her and expects him one day to be assumed miraculously, like the demonic Saviour that he is, into "a heaven." Likewise the martyr's sentiments can be echoed by the demon with his own particular shade of meaning: when the Infernal Spouse speaks of eventually abandoning the Foolish Virgin (with a reminiscence perhaps of a passage in John 7), he declares, Christ-like, that "il faut que j'en aide d'autres : c'est mon devoir." "Tu me feras mourir . . . C'est notre sort, à nous, coeurs charitables... " he sighs in an ultimate inversion of good and evil. As the Christ of hell he appropriates indiscriminately the signs of either force and presents himself as a lamb as well as a serpent. Perfidy is an essential demonic virtue.

The "Vierge folle" episode not only provides the variety of a new voice in *Une Saison en enfer;* it also underscores by contrast one aspect of the narrator: he aspires toward infernal sanctity, whereas the Foolish Virgin merely submits to heavenly and Satanic forces and makes the best of both. Her passivity grotesquely parodies the assembly of the faithful, the Church, who, in the traditional metaphor, awaits her Spouse—while perhaps beguiling herself with other temptations. The Foolish Virgin is not so much in hell as in limbo, the *patrie de coeur* of the self-seeking and the spiritually indecisive. The narrator, on the other hand, will be satisfied with nothing short of conquering the actual condition of deity. It remains for him, however, to show a sign, as Christ was asked to do, to initiate that transformation of life which the Foolish Virgin fears he is incapable of. The second "Délires," "Alchimie du verbe," describes his assault on reality through the medium of language.

A problem which "Alchimie du verbe" brings up is the autobiographical one: it is his own poems of 1872 that, in slightly altered or truncated forms, Rimbaud uses as examples of the verbal magic with which the narrator hopes to alter reality. The commentators who read *Une Saison en enfer* simply as a cryptographic account of Rimbaud's life have been somewhat embarrassed in explaining whether Rimbaud was actually a magician or merely thought he was. The narrator's "pouvoir magique," which the Foolish Virgin speaks of, has been sometimes taken to indicate that Rimbaud believed in and practiced magic. The question remains open—although historical considerations, as we shall eventually see, militate against such a theory. However, such hypotheses need not affect our reading of the poem, which is of far more than biographical import. *Une Saison en enfer* by its very subject demands the imagery of the supernatural. The mythic mode in which it is written simultaneously reduces all autobiographical allusions to as tangential a position as they have in Dante's poem. The "identity" of the Foolish Virgin matters no more than that of the "real" Beatrice. Similarly the fact that "Larme," "L'Eternité," and other poems of 1872 are quoted as examples of "alchemy" should not lead us into unwarranted speculations about the circumstances of their composition. Rimbaud is making use of his earlier poems for the purposes of *Une Saison en enfer* rather than writing a treatise on them.

"A moi. L'histoire d'une de mes folies," exclaims the narrator at the beginning of "Alchimie du verbe," bringing attention from the Foolish Virgin back to himself. What follows is an account of his discovery that imagination and poetry are literally supernatural and can displace reality. The realistic art of the mid-nineteenth century, whose ideal was mere mimesis, is rejected in favor of crude, discredited, or more stylized traditions:

> Depuis longtemps je me vantais de posséder tous les paysages possibles, et trouvais dérisoires les célébrités de la peinture et de la poésie moderne.
> J'aimais les peintures idiotes, dessus de portes, décors, toiles de saltimbanques, enseignes, enluminures populaires; la littérature démodée, latin d'église, livres érotiques sans orthographe, romans de nos aïeules, contes de fées, petits livres de l'enfance, opéras vieux, refrains niais, rhythmes naïfs.

> [For a long time I had boasted having all possible landscapes and found laughable the great names of modern poetry and painting. I liked stupid paintings, dessus de porte, stage settings, acrobats' backdrops, signs, popular engravings, old-fashioned literature, Church Latin, erotic books with bad spelling, our grandmothers' romances, fairy tales, little books from childhood, old operas, silly refrains, naïve rhythms.]

The narrator prepares us for the poems he will quote by listing various old-fashioned conventions: fairy tale, pastoral, folk song, and naïve religious art. Along with what appear to be literal and autobiographical allusions to Favart and other outmoded literary models, he suggests corresponding works of visual art.

Parallel to the dismissal of contemporary literature is a channeling of the imagination toward the unknown and the improbable: "Je rêvais croisades, voyages de découvertes dont on n'a pas de relations, républiques sans histoires, guerres de religion étouffées . . . " His own poetry he conceives of as a perfectly responsive instrument for creating a new reality:

> J'inventai la couleur des voyelles! — *A* noir, *E* blanc, *I* rouge, *O* bleu, *U* vert. — Je réglai la forme

et le mouvement de chaque consonne, et, avec des rhythmes instinctifs, je me flattai d'inventer un verbe poétique accessible, un jour ou un autre, à tous les sens. Je réservais la traduction.

[I invented the colors of the vowels!—A black, E white, I red, O blue, U green.—I fixed the form and movement of each consonant, and, with instinctive rhythms, I prided myself on inventing a poetic language accessible, at some time or another, to all the senses. I reserved translation rights.]

The allusion to the vowel sonnet is characteristic of Rimbaud's use of his own work in *Une Saison en enfer* for new ends: he here implies that "Voyelles" contains an esthetic doctrine, which it does not, and that even the use of consonants has been subjected to codification! These "enchantments" belong to the supernatural and mythic world of *Une Saison en enfer* and have no literal meaning for Rimbaud's poetic practice. His sly comment on translation rights, with its intrusion of another world of ideas and activities, is typical of the irony which his own mythopoeic inventions occasionally inspire in the poet and which is so characteristic an element of the tone of *Une Saison en enfer*.

"Ce fut d'abord une étude." The narrator's language is at first that of the classic magician whose art demands patient discipline, as opposed to the vulgar witch with her simple charms. Superhuman powers, however, risk getting out of control; as the poet continues the tale of his verbal alchemy, it becomes apparent that he has gradually become the prisoner of his own experiments:

Je m'habituai à l'hallucination simple : je voyais très franchement une mosquée à la place d'une usine, une école de tambours faite par des anges, des calèches sur les routes du ciel, un salon au fond d'un lac; les monstres, les mystères; un titre de vaudeville dressait des épouvantes devant moi.

[I accustomed myself to pure hallucination: I saw quite frankly a mosque in place of a factory, a school for drummers attended by angels, carriages on the roads in the sky, a living-room at the bottom of a lake, monsters, mysteries. The title of a vaudeville would conjure up horrors before my eyes.]

Being a prey to hallucinations differs considerably from inventing and exploiting a new language. The latter indeed becomes subsidiary to the poet's mental disorder: "Puis j'expliquai mes sophismes magiques avec l'hallucination des mots!" Language is no longer the means by which reality is transformed; it has become merely an instrument for communicating madness. As in "Nuit de l'enfer" the price due Satan for granting superhuman visions is weakness and physical death: "J'étais oisif, en proie à une lourde fièvre . . ." "Je disais adieu au monde dans d'espèces de romances . . ."

The poems of 1872 which Rimbaud now quotes are those dealing with aspirations toward divinity and bodily dissolution. Their summer imagery is taken up in the prose passages which serve as bridges between them:

J'aimai le désert, les vergers brûlés, les boutiques fanées, les boissons tiédies. Je me traînais dans les ruelles puantes et, les yeux fermés, je m'offrais au soleil, dieu de feu.

.   .   .   .

Oh! le moucheron enivré à la pissotière de l'auberge, amoureux de la bourrache, et que dissout un rayon!

[I loved the desert, burnt orchards, musty shops, warmish drinks. I dragged myself through the stink-

ing little streets and, my eyes closed, offered myself
to the sun, the god of fire. . . . Oh! the drunken gnat
by the inn's urinal, enamored of diuretic borage and
dissolved by a sunbeam.]

Summer is a common symbol of growth, vigor, and godhead, but the summer of *Une Saison en enfer* must be
seen as a false symbol of divinity, the grace of a mendacious god who is Satan in disguise. It is associated not
with fecundity but with destruction and drought. The
narrator believes himself a magician and actually partici-
pates in a supernatural power but a demonic one. He
finds himself in a landscape which is a mockery of summer's fertility, under a sun that dissolves rather than
regenerates. Yet he is still unaware of the sinister character
of his experience. At the height of his ecstasy the poet
turns into pure light:

Enfin, ô bonheur, ô raison, j'écartai du ciel l'azur,
qui est du noir, et je vécus, étincelle d'or de la
lumière *nature*. De joie, je prenais une expression
bouffonne et égarée au possible :

Elle est retrouvée!
Quoi? l'éternité.
C'est la mer mêlée
Au soleil.

[Finally, O happiness, O reason, I removed from the
sky the blue, which is black, and I lived like a spark
of gold of *pure* light. From joy I assumed as weird and
buffoonish a tone as possible: It is found again. What?
Eternity. It's the sea mixed with the sun.]

For the moment he has achieved the fulfillment of his
longings but at a price that he does not yet realize. Since
this summer which Rimbaud places in the lowest depths
of hell is unnatural, a demonic artifice, it must yield again

to darkness. Sleep, shadow, and winds overcome the exhausted poet: "J'étais mûr pour le trépas, et par une route de dangers ma faiblesse me menait aux confins du monde et de la Cimmérie, patrie de l'ombre et des tourbillons."

In a sudden dramatic shift of imagery the narrator realizes that his whole experience in hell has been a false conversion, a fatal worship of Satanic strength and beauty:

> Je dus voyager, distraire les enchantements assemblés sur mon cerveau. Sur la mer, que j'aimais comme si elle eût dû me laver d'une souillure, je voyais se lever la croix consolatrice. J'avais été damné par l'arc-en-ciel. Le Bonheur était ma fatalité, mon remords, mon vers : ma vie serait toujours trop immense pour être dévouée à la force et à la beauté.

> [I had to travel, to remove the enchantments assembled over my head. Over the sea, which I loved as if it were washing me clean of a stain, I saw the consoling cross rise. I had been damned by the rainbow. Happiness was my fatality, my regret, my worm: my life would always be too immense to be devoted to strength and beauty.]

The elusive rainbow represents his experiments with verbal alchemy, while the Southern Cross rising over the water recalls true salvation and the possibility of happiness which does not weaken and destroy.[6] The poet is incapable of willfully giving his life up to strength, with its paradoxical connotation of self-destruction, and to beauty, which leads to disintegration. He is torn between two promises of happiness—divine and infernal—and fears

6. My interpretation of this passage is supported by a study of the *ébauche*. The symbolism of the rainbow as well as the sense of "bonheur," "fatalité," and certain other words is clarified by the draft, for the style of the latter is less dense than that of the finished version and sometimes shows more clearly the direction of Rimbaud's thought.

he has lost both, for, as Easter morning dawns and the night of hell draws to its close, he realizes that it is too late to extricate himself from the throes of death: "Le Bonheur! Sa dent, douce à la mort, m'avertissait au chant du coq, — *ad matutinum,* au *Christus venit,* — dans les plus sombres villes." The Latin phrases are not quotations but merely evoke the passage from St. Mark which is read during the Easter Mass, while the identification of Christ and the sun is part of liturgical tradition. In his anguish the narrator quotes "O saisons, ô châteaux . . . ," the poem which sums up his demonic and magical search for happiness and the annihilation which will result from it:

> O saisons, ô châteaux!
> Quelle âme est sans défauts?
>
> J'ai fait la magique étude
> Du bonheur, qu'aucun n'élude.
>
> Salut à lui, chaque fois
> Que chante le coq gaulois.
>
> Ah! je n'aurai plus d'envie :
> Il s'est chargé de ma vie.
>
> Ce charme a pris âme et corps
> Et dispersé les efforts.
>
> O saisons, ô châteaux!
>
> L'heure de sa fuite, hélas!
> Sera l'heure du trépas.
>
> O saisons, ô châteaux!

[O seasons, O castles! What soul is without flaws? I have made the magic study of happiness, which no one can avoid. A salute to him every time the Gallic cock sings. Ah, I will have no more desires: he has taken charge of my life. This charm has taken body

and soul and dispelled all effort. O seasons, O castles!
The hour of its vanishing, alas, will be my hour of
death.]

The seasons are the infernal summer of hell with its de-
ceptive vision of the castle of spiritual attainment. The
Gallic cock is here not a Revolutionary patriotic symbol,
as it is usually, but the emblem of the poet's dangerous
initiation; Gaul was a country of strange magic rites. The
words "bonheur," "coq," and "charme" form an associated
group to which the pronouns ambiguously refer; the
effect is highly evocative if not rationally precise. The
cock's crow becomes a poignant symbol suggesting at once
the height of ecstasy after the night's vigil and the disper-
sion of the charm which day will shortly bring. The morning of salvation for mankind will be the hour of the poet's
death, for he has beguiled himself with false hopes and
fatal visions.

A sudden shift in temporal perspective occurs at the
conclusion of "Alchimie du verbe." The latter is the only
part of *Une Saison en enfer* written predominantly in the
passé simple, and at the end of it the narrator exclaims:
"Cela s'est passé. Je sais aujourd'hui saluer la beauté."
His hell is suddenly pushed back in time; the following
chapters are based on the present tense and relate his
search for a way out. At this point we pass beyond the
boundary set by the prologue, which foresees no release
for the poet; however, *Une Saison en enfer* is not a prayer
de profundis, but a recollection of hell. With the "Alchimie du verbe" he has passed beyond the lowest point
in hell; as in the medieval poet's inferno, there is a path
upward on the far side of the pit, and the next sections
record his struggle to free himself from God and Satan
and their inseparable toils. For the hell of Rimbaud's
poem is the Christian one and can exist only so long as
Christianity does: "C'était bien l'enfer; l'ancien, celui

dont le fils de l'homme ouvrit les portes." Rimbaud refers not only to the Harrowing of Hell but also to the necessary coexistence of good and evil in the Christian scheme of things. Christianity is dualistic in Rimbaud's conception, and any real aspiration toward godhead must be double, at once divine and Satanic. Hence the constant confusion of the two eschatological realms in *Une Saison en enfer*. An extraordinary instance of this inevitable union of opposites occurs in the chapter "L'Eclair," where, discouraged momentarily at finding any escape from his dilemma, the narrator resolves to fall back into his old life:

> Ma vie est usée. Allons! feignons, fainéantons, ô pitié! Et nous existerons en nous amusant, en rêvant amours monstres et univers fantastiques, en nous plaignant et en querellant les apparences du monde, saltimbanque, mendiant, artiste, bandit, — prêtre! Sur mon lit d'hôpital, l'odeur de l'encens m'est revenue si puissante; gardien des aromates sacrés, confesseur, martyr...

> [My life is worn out. Come on, let's pretend, be idle, O pity! And we shall exist on amusing ourselves, dreaming of monstrous loves and fantastic universes, complaining and railing against the outward appearances of the world—a clown, beggar, artist, bandit, priest! On my hospital bed the odor of incense comes back to me so strong—keeper of the sacred aromatics, confessor, martyr . . .]

No sooner do dreams of perversion, escape, debasement, and violence come to the poet's mind than he is surrounded by priests, incense, and holiness. "Je reconnais là ma sale éducation d'enfance," he remarks. The only issue from this constant futile oscillation between sanctity and bestiality must lie in the repudiation of both.

In "L'Impossible" and "L'Eclair," the two chapters

which follow "Alchimie du verbe," the narrator examines various philosophies current among nineteenth-century intellectuals in the hope of finding some substitute for his perverted Christianity. A drier, more discursive style replaces the febrile lyricism of "Alchimie du verbe," and the poet begins again to discuss history and peoples as he did earlier in "Mauvais sang." *Une Saison en enfer* is thus constructed symmetrically, so that the stages of the descent into hell correspond to those of the climb upward. Similarly, a band of darkness lies both before and beyond the summer light of "Alchimie du verbe."

In "L'Impossible" the narrator announces, "J'ai eu raison dans tous mes dédains : puisque je m'évade!" First he suggests Oriental philosophy as a refuge from Christianity:

> M'étant retrouvé deux sous de raison — ça passe vite! — je vois que mes malaises viennent de ne m'être pas figuré assez tôt que nous sommes à l'Occident. . . . Bon! voici que mon esprit veut absolument se charger de tous les développements cruels qu'a subis l'esprit depuis la fin de l'Orient... Il en veut, mon esprit!
>
> ...Mes deux sous de raison sont finis! — L'esprit est autorité, il veut que je sois en Occident. Il faudrait le faire taire pour conclure comme je voulais.

> [Finding I have two cents' worth of reason—it's quickly spent—I decide that my malaises come from the fact that I hadn't realized soon enough that we're in the West. . . . All right! Now my spirit wants to take upon itself all the cruel developments that the human spirit has undergone since the end of the East. My spirit insists on it! My two cents' worth of reason are finished!—My spirit is authoritarian, it wants me to be in the West. I would have to make it keep quiet in order to conclude my thought as I intended to.]

Reason is useless against spiritual demands: circumstances of place and history make it idle to hope to escape "modern sufferings" through a bookish cult of the East. The *temporal* aspect of religious feeling is such that no vanished form of spiritual aspiration can be revived. Thus Christianity itself has been dead and ossified since the rise of science, and its remains can offer no satisfaction:

> Mais n'y a-t-il pas un supplice réel en ce que, depuis cette déclaration de la science, le christianisme, l'homme *se joue,* se prouve les évidences, se gonfle du plaisir de répéter des preuves et ne vit que comme cela!

> [But isn't there a real torment in the fact that since the advent of science, Christianity and man are *playing games with themselves,* proving self-evident truths, puffing up with the pleasure of repeating proofs, and living only through that!]

Yet since Christianity became a sterile game of exchanging the same old theological counters, no new religion has arisen to replace it. The most the nineteenth century has invented is philosophical idealism, whose subjective bent Rimbaud parodies: "Vous êtes en Occident, mais libre d'habiter dans votre Orient, quelque ancien qu'il vous le faille, — et d'y habiter bien. Ne soyez pas un vaincu." However, idealism is again merely a product of reason and does not correspond to spiritual needs.

"L'Impossible" is entirely concerned with salvation as an immaterial thing, and the key word of the section is "esprit." Yet the body's place in time determines the spirit's possibilities, and, a further difficulty, man is not spirit alone. The latter alternates with body as the dominating force in life. Thus in conclusion the narrator discovers his dreams of redemption to be impossible—whence the title of the chapter:

Mon esprit, prends garde. Pas de partis de salut violents. . . .

— Mais je m'aperçois que mon esprit dort.

S'il était bien éveillé toujours à partir de ce moment, nous serions bientôt à la vérité, qui peut-être nous entoure avec ses anges pleurant!... — S'il avait été éveillé jusqu'à ce moment-ci, c'est que je n'aurais jamais cédé aux instincts délétères, à une époque immémoriale! . . .

C'est cette minute d'éveil qui m'a donné la vision de la pureté! — Par l'esprit on va à Dieu!

Déchirante infortune!

[Watch out, my spirit. No violent enterprises of salvation! . . . —But I notice that my spirit is sleeping. If it were always wide awake from now on, we would soon arrive at truth, who perhaps at this minute surrounds us with her weeping angels!—If my spirit had been awake up to now, I would never have yielded to deleterious instincts at an immemorial time! . . . It's this moment of awakening which has given me a vision of purity! Through spirit you arrive at God! What a heartbreaking misfortune!]

The tendency of religious philosophies to consider man as disembodied spirit brings only feelings of futility and perdition. Realizing the hopelessness of purely spiritual effort, the narrator then turns to another kind of philosophy current in the nineteenth century: scientism, which conceives of redemption in material terms. In "L'Eclair" he no sooner considers it than he rejects it:

Le travail humain! c'est l'explosion qui éclaire mon abîme de temps en temps.

"Rien n'est vanité; à la science, et en avant!" crie l'Ecclésiaste moderne, c'est-à-dire *Tout le monde*. Et pourtant les cadavres des méchants et des fainéants

tombent sur le coeur des autres... Ah! vite, vite un
peu; là-bas, par delà la nuit, ces récompenses futures,
éternelles... les échappons-nous?...

[Human work! This is the explosion which from time
to time lights up my abyss. "Nothing is vanity; science
and onward!" cries the modern Ecclesiastes, that is,
everyone. And yet the bodies of the wicked and idle
fall on the hearts of others . . . Ah! quick, quick now!
Over there, beyond the night, those future and eternal rewards—will we miss them?]

The idea of progress is disappointing because it promises
no real salvation for the individual but merely a hazy
future one for the race; it cannot satisfy the need for
absolute, metaphysical change. "Qu'y puis-je? Je connais
le travail; et la science est trop lente." As at the end of
"L'Impossible," where spirit appears too weak to effect
alone the poet's salvation, attempts at redemption through
material means also prove vain: "Alors, — oh! — pauvre
chère âme, l'éternité serait-elle pas perdue pour nous!"

After the dark abyss of "L'Eclair" comes the promise of
approaching light in "Matin," which opens with a recollection of the prologue: "N'eus-je pas *une fois* une jeunesse
aimable, héroïque, fabuleuse, à écrire sur des feuilles d'or,
— trop de chance!" The cycle is coming full swing:
"Pourtant, aujourd'hui, je crois avoir fini la relation de
mon enfer." A sudden faith in the future invades the poet,
who has a tentative vision of salvation:

Du même désert, à la même nuit, toujours mes
yeux las se réveillent à l'étoile d'argent, toujours,
sans que s'émeuvent les Rois de la vie, les trois mages,
le coeur, l'âme, l'esprit. Quand irons-nous par delà
les grèves et les monts, saluer la naissance du travail
nouveau, la sagesse nouvelle, la fuite des tyrans et

des démons, la fin de la superstition, adorer — les
premiers! — Noël sur la terre!

[From the same wilderness, in the same night, my
weary eyes always awaken to the silver star—always,
though the Kings of life, the three magi, the heart,
the soul, the spirit, never quicken. When will we go
beyond the strands and hills to salute the birth of
the new work, and the new wisdom, the flight of
tyrants and demons, the end of superstition, and be
the first to worship renascence here on earth!]

This imagery of stars and Nativity belongs to the Christian
epiphanic tradition, but, as Christian imagery must not
be taken at its face value in "Nuit de l'enfer" or "Vierge
folle," where it represents a demonic artifice, here also we
must distinguish the peculiar nuance of Rimbaud's regeneration symbols. Like Hugo, Michelet, and other
writers of the nineteenth century who believed that Christianity was shortly to be modified or replaced, Rimbaud
tended to keep a certain body of Christian symbols when
speaking of the future spiritual regeneration. Consequently we must be on our guard against misunderstanding
such images as the star and the Nativity, which have been
purged of all theological reference. The "travail nouveau"
and "sagesse nouvelle" which they herald seem to describe
a world in which both physical and spiritual conditions
have changed, where nineteenth-century scientific ma-
terialism as well as Christian otherworldliness will be outmoded, but, given the symbolic nature of prophetic poetry, we must not push our interpretation too far.

"L'Automne déjà!" As "Adieu," the last chapter of *Une
Saison en enfer,* begins, we become finally aware of the
seasonal pattern of the work, which starts with a reference
to spring in the prologue ("Et le printemps m'a apporté
l'affreux rire de l'idiot"), continues through the summer
of "Alchimie du verbe"—the season in hell—and con-

cludes with the return of autumn. Just as the prologue is
a brief presage of the content of the opening chapters, so
in "Adieu" the narrator recollects and summarizes his
sojourn in hell. First his attempts at physical degradation,
at salvation through violence:

> L'automne. Notre barque élevée dans les brumes
> immobiles tourne vers le port de la misère, la cité
> énorme au ciel taché de feu et de boue. Ah! les
> haillons pourris, le pain trempé de pluie, l'ivresse,
> les mille amours qui m'ont crucifié!

> [Autumn. Our boat, high in the motionless mist,
> turns toward the harbor of wretchedness, the enor-
> mous city under a sky stained with fire and mud. Ah!
> the rotten rags, the rain-soaked bread, the drunken-
> ness, the thousand loves which have crucified me!]

The image of the city recalls the "sombres villes" of "Alchimie du verbe" and the red and black urban landscape
in "Mauvais sang," while the experiences alluded to echo
the Foolish Virgin's account of life with her Infernal
Spouse. "J'aurais pu y mourir... L'affreuse évocation!
J'exècre la misère. Et je redoute l'hiver parce que c'est la
saison du comfort!" The thought of physical wretchedness
brings to the narrator's mind the test to which he is about
to be put in his search for "divine light" and the necessity
of resisting the drowsy complacency which winter hearths
urge. Physical trials yield to spiritual ones, in an ellipsis
characteristic of Rimbaud's style.

Sky imagery recurs, with its implicit contrast to the pit
of hell. The boat here symmetrically balances the "navire
sauveur" glimpsed in "Mauvais sang": "— Quelquefois
je vois au ciel des plages sans fin couvertes de blanches
nations en joie. Un grand vaisseau d'or, au-dessus de moi,
agite ses pavillons multicolores sous les brises du matin."
This vision, though seemingly one of promise, recalls to

the narrator his experiments in verbal alchemy and his own supernatural fabrications:

> J'ai créé toutes les fêtes, tous les triomphes, tous les drames. J'ai essayé d'inventer de nouvelles fleurs, de nouveaux astres, de nouvelles chairs, de nouvelles langues. J'ai cru acquérir des pouvoirs surnaturels. Eh bien! je dois enterrer mon imagination et mes souvenirs! Une belle gloire d'artiste et de conteur emportée!

> [I have created all celebrations, all triumphs, all dramas. I have tried to invent new flowers, new stars, new flesh, new tongues. I thought I had acquired supernatural powers. Well! I must bury my imagination and memories! A nice reputation as an artist and story-teller lost!]

This famous passage has occasioned much concern among those who attempt to read *Une Saison en enfer* as a literal and autobiographical document, since it now seems likely that Rimbaud did not end his poetic career with this work. It has even been suggested that the poem is considerably weakened if the narrator-Rimbaud was either lying or later changed his mind about ceasing to write. However, aside from the fact that *Une Saison en enfer* is not in any way conceived according to the conventions of autobiography or literalism, the shape and dialectic of the poem here require a repudiation of Christian-Satanic aspirations, poetic or otherwise, such as they are seen in "Délires." The whole experience of "Délires" is summed up and dismissed in a brief paragraph:

> Moi! moi qui me suis dit mage ou ange, dispensé de toute morale, je suis rendu au sol, avec un devoir à chercher, et la réalité rugueuse à étreindre! Paysan!
> Suis-je trompé? la charité serait-elle soeur de la mort, pour moi?

> [I! I who called myself a magician or angel, dispensed
> from all morality, I am cast back to the earth, with
> a duty to find and rough reality to embrace! Peasant!
> Was I wrong? Could charity be for me the sister of
> death?]

The dualistic and ambivalent character of the narrator's
false conversion is expressed by the juxtapositions "mage"
and "ange," "charité" and "mort." In his perverse Christianity no distinction is made between the supernatural
emanating from God or Satan, and the virtue of charity
can be as fatal as vice.

"Mais pas une main amie! et où puiser le secours?" The
narrator is again alone, just as in the depths of hell, where
even the Foolish Virgin admits to being cut off from him.
His salvation, like his damnation, is solitary: the lives of
others belong to an intermediary limbo and have no
relevance to the state into which he is about to enter. As
for help, it will come from within himself: new vitality
is suggested by the narrator's search for a "devoir" (implying both a task and responsibility) and his embracing
of "rough reality." "Oui, l'heure nouvelle est au moins
très sévère," he declares with a wry pleasure in hardship.
The memory of damnation, his last urges toward destruction of self and others vanish:

> Car je puis dire que la victoire m'est acquise : les
> grincements de dents, les sifflements de feu, les soupirs
> empestés se modèrent. Tous les souvenirs immondes
> s'effacent. Mes derniers regrets détalent, — des
> jalousies pour les mendiants, les brigands, les amis
> de la mort, les arriérés de toutes sortes. . . .
> Il faut être absolument moderne.

> [For I can say that victory is mine: the gnashing of
> teeth, the whistle of fire, the reeking sighs diminish.
> All the filthy memories grow dim. My last regrets

clear out: envy of beggars, brigands, friends of death, backward people of all sorts. . . . We must be absolutely modern.]

Being "modern" is opposed to the state of those who accept the worship of death, which is the evil implicit in Christian thought. The poet's rejection of Christianity implies in no way, however, the denial of deity, but merely a further movement in the dialectic of religious history: "Point de cantiques : tenir le pas gagné. Dure nuit! le sang séché fume sur ma face, et je n'ai rien derrière moi, que cet horrible arbrisseau!..." The withered and stunted bush beyond which the poet has succeeded in fighting is assumed by some critics—and rightly, I think—to be the Edenic tree, for the conclusion of *Une Saison en enfer* is based on the refusal to accept the dualism of good and evil.[7] Beyond lies the realm of real conquest: "Le combat spirituel est aussi brutal que la bataille d'hommes." The energetic warfare imagery contrasts with the weary feeling of dissolution which characterized the narrator's ventures into Christianity and Satanism. The poet's ultimate vision, the taking of a heavenly citadel at dawn, unites his twin longings for light and strength: "Cependant, c'est la veille. Recevons tous les influx de vigueur et de tendresse réelle. Et à l'aurore, armés d'une ardente patience, nous entrerons aux splendides villes." The vaporous, dark city which he faced at the beginning of "Adieu" has given way to a glorious, celestial one.

The final paragraph of *Une Saison en enfer* acquires all its force from an implied contrast with Christian thought and the dialectics of damnation:

> Que parlais-je de main amie! Un bel avantage, c'est que je puis rire des vieilles amours mensongères, et frapper de honte ces couples menteurs, — j'ai vu

7. See, for example, Y. Bonnefoy, *Rimbaud par lui-même* (Paris, 1961), p. 133.

l'enfer des femmes là-bas; — et il me sera loisible de *posséder la vérité dans une âme et un corps.*

[What was I saying about a helping hand! One great advantage is that I can laugh about my old mendacious loves and strike with shame those lying couples —I saw the hell of women down there—and I shall be allowed to *possess truth in one body and soul.*]

The rejection of all aid and community with others is a denial of the value of charity, ever the chief ideal of Christianity for Rimbaud, while the italicized last words indicate that the ancient opposition of body and spirit no longer exists for the narrator. Body and spirit are constantly at variance in the course of the poem, thus the importance of images of physical brutality and disembodiment. The poet's adventures in damnation have constantly taken the form of bodily violence or aspirations to ethereality, both of which are forms of death. The otherworldliness of Christianity—including both the divine and infernal realms—is untenable: the poet insists on the abolishment of distinctions between here and the beyond. The synthesis of body and spirit, the material and immaterial, is the essence of the "modern" conception of salvation, and it stands in total contrast to the devious and painful scruples of Christianity about the value of the *saeculum* or physical world.

While *Une Saison en enfer* is a very personal and distinctive work, we should nevertheless not forget that Rimbaud is not an isolated case of a nineteenth-century French writer attempting to work out his own solution to major religious problems. Indeed, we must see *Une Saison en enfer* in the perspective of a whole tradition of French romantic literature. Rimbaud is so commonly held up as a great innovator that one runs the danger of forgetting that certain aspects of his work reflect characteristic nineteenth-century concerns. Such is certainly the case with his religious notions: we can find many elements of them in other romantic writers.

The most typical feeling of heterodox writers of the period—aside from a pantheistic view of nature—is that their epoch marks a great turning point in the history of religious beliefs. Evolutionary changes in religion were foreseen, and many thinkers considered that a new era of spiritual life was drawing near. Thus Michelet once wrote to Hugo that the latter's *Légende des siècles* would certainly become a basic text of "the new religion." Neither writer found it at all unlikely that Christianity would shortly be replaced by a much more universal form of worship, or that their writings might count among its prophetic works. Both felt it logical that humanity, having outworn feudalism and having abolished it with the Revolution, would create a new spiritual order in keeping with the new social one.

There were many valid reasons why Christianity seemed doomed to men like Hugo and Michelet: the Church had ceased to be a dominant intellectual force in the eighteenth century; it had become excessively identified with the ruling classes, and its dogmatic rigidity took no account of the great realms of knowledge—both historical and scientific—which had opened up for the nineteenth century. Indeed, the Church, with its new affirmations of the Immaculate Conception, Papal Infallibility, and the pre-excellence of Thomistic philosophy, appeared bent on retreating into a quaint medievalism. What liberalizing and modernizing forces existed within the ranks of Catholicism were largely repressed. But above all Christianity failed for Hugo and Michelet by giving an unsatisfactory account of evil. (Here we must do some injustice to the subtleties of orthodox theology in order to describe the point of view of its critics.) In principle, Christianity is not dualistic and does not recognize evil as metaphysically comparable to good as a force. In St. Augustine's classical definition of evil, "nomenque hoc non sit nisi privationis boni."[8] The "non . . . nisi" is a persuasive rhetorical device; to describe evil as "merely" the absence of good somehow relegates it to a position of relative insignificance. The rhetoric, however, convinces only for a moment; on reflection we know that evil, as it is *experienced,* is not simply nothingness but the visitation of Satan. In short, there cannot be a real antithesis without both terms being equal in strength. Furthermore, the two terms of an antithesis cannot exist without each other: good is a meaningless notion unless complemented by that of evil.[9] The dualistic universe of Baudelaire's poetry is an excellent example of the power which this conception had over certain nineteenth-century minds.[10]

An escape from this dilemma is to introduce the element of time into the dualism of good and evil. Since world history seemed for Hugo and Michelet to consist of progress in all domains, it was natural for them to apply the same notion to the realms of God and Satan and to assume that the devil's was diminishing to make place for divine omnipotence. As Satan says to God in Hugo's *Fin de Satan:*

> Grâce, ô Dieu! Pour toi-même il faut que je l'obtienne.
> Ma perpétuité fait ombre sur la tienne.
> Devant ton oeil flambeau rien ne doit demeurer,
> Tout doit changer, vieillir et se transformer.
> Toi seul es. Devant toi tout doit avoir un âge.
> Et c'est pour ta splendeur un importun nuage
> Qu'on voie un spectre assis au fond de ton ciel bleu,
> Et l'éternel Satan devant l'éternel Dieu!

8. *De Civitate Dei,* XI. 22.

9. The psychology of the antithesis is thoroughly explored in J.-P. Sartre, *Saint Genet, comédien et martyr* (Paris, 1952).

10. See J. Duron, "Destin de Baudelaire," *Revue des Sciences Humaines, 89* (1958), 64–73.

The redemption of Satan and all evil thus constituted the next stage in the dialectic of history. In *Une Saison en enfer* Rimbaud's rejection of the antithesis of good and evil is another variation on the same process of putting Christianity into a temporal perspective and then moving one step beyond it.

The importance accorded to Satan in these notions is not entirely commensurate with his ancient role as adversary of God and man, for the romantics had become interested in the conception of Satan as mankind's benefactor. The devil is, according to certain traditions, a deity of knowledge, and Michelet in his historical studies emphasized the bond between early scientific research and diabolism. By 1871, Rimbaud had enthusiastically appropriated the idea that knowledge is a gift of infernal powers; already in the "Lettre du voyant" he had sketched out a first version of his myth of the Satanic poet:

> Toutes les formes d'amour, de souffrance, de folie; il cherche lui-même, il épuise en lui tous les poisons, pour n'en garder que les quintessences. Ineffable torture où il a besoin de toute la foi, de toute la force surhumaine, où il devient entre tous le grand malade, le grand criminel, le grand maudit, — et le suprême Savant! — Car il arrive à l'*inconnu!* . . . Qu'il crève dans son bondissement par les choses inouïes et innommables : viendront d'autres horribles travailleurs . . .

> [All forms of love, suffering, madness; he searches himself, he exhausts on himself all poisons in order to keep only the quintessence of them. An unspeakable torture in which he needs all his faith and superhuman strength, in which he becomes above all others the great diseased one, the great criminal, the great accursed—and the supreme Savant!—For he arrives at the *unknown!* . . . Even if he dies in his

> leap into the unheard of and the unnamable, other
> horrible workers will come along . . .]

Fortunately Rimbaud was to transform this none too
original Satanism into something more personal and
artistically more persuasive. This passage, with its second-
hand Baudelairean sentiments, is not nearly the important
esthetic doctrine it is usually said to be, for it remains
vague and remote from the real practice of poetry. On
the other hand, these lines are interesting insofar as they
reveal some distant origins of *Une Saison en enfer*. The
theme of damnation and physical annihilation is already
associated with the creation of poetry, yet without the
theological framework of *Une Saison en enfer*, Rimbaud's
phrases about "le grand maudit" seem puerile and lacking in reference. The difference is immense between this
juvenile dithyramb and the splendors of "Alchimie du
verbe."

The terms of nineteenth-century religious thought were
also influenced by a vast revival of interest in occultism
and hermetic philosophy, so vast, indeed, that its magnitude is difficult to conceive of today. This body of esoteric
theology is, at its best, much more sophisticated than the
modern reader might imagine, and deals not with magic
hocus-pocus but with the progress of the individual and
the world toward spiritual perfection and the reunion
of man and God. Its sources lie to a large extent in late
antiquity, and it can be considered an offshoot of Greek
and Hebrew philosophy. Given the profusion of more or
less "hermetic" texts in the nineteenth century, it is difficult to assert that Rimbaud was influenced by any one of
them in particular, but the general tenor of his thought
suggests acquaintance with this material.[11] In particular
his conception of language as molding reality—"changing

11. An excellent short survey of occult thought and its parallels in
Rimbaud's work can be found in Starkie, *Rimbaud*, pp. 95–128.

life"—is typically occultist. To words, names, and letters esoteric philosophy tends to grant an enormous power, and poetry is often held to be a prime moving force in the world. Rimbaud also could have absorbed such notions from other poets, principally Hugo, for the latter's work is permeated with the idea that poetry has a prophetic power. Whatever the case may have been, Rimbaud had ample opportunities to come into contact with occult theologies and metaphysics.

Finally, something must be said further about the meaning of magic and related words in Rimbaud's poetry. The serious practice of magic having largely vanished, nineteenth-century writers were free to embroider at will upon the idea of it, and they tended to confuse the matter with all sorts of theological and moral connotations, from which the tradition of ritual magic had, on the whole, been free. Michelet, and most of all the famous "Eliphas Lévi" (Alphonse Constant, 1810–75), whose works Rimbaud may well have known, typically obscured the theory of magic with romantic Satanist conceptions. One cannot stress too much the fact that devil worship is primarily a nineteenth-century literary addition to magical lore; for example, while pretending to write a history of magic, Eliphas Lévi satisfied the taste of his contemporaries by shrouding the subject in piquant, blasphemous conceptions of his own invention.[12] Rimbaud absorbed the romantic notion of magic and embellished it even further: in *Une Saison en enfer* and in the *Illuminations,* magic becomes associated with apocalyptics, visions of metaphysical truth, and other para-religious phenomena. All this is a long way from the classical magicians' simple attempts to enslave devils and get a bit of work out of them. The difference arises because magic was not, for the nineteenth century, a practical activity but a vast myth

12. See E. M. Butler, *Ritual Magic* (New York, 1959), pp. 95–99, 295–317.

with religious and philosophical implications, all the more unbounded in that it was infinitely remote from reality.

When we attempt to examine conceptions like the surpassing of Christianity, the end of evil, changing life, and verbal magic in relation to other nineteenth-century writers' ideas, some of the obscurity of Rimbaud's work is dissipated, and his preoccupations seem less idiosyncratic. There are characteristic kinds of nineteenth-century thought which, taken out of context, are peculiar and hermetic, but which are neither unusual nor erratic when seen in a proper historical perspective. Rimbaud's critics have sometimes done him the disservice of treating his thought as if it were unique, thereby making him seem more eccentric than anything else. An unfortunate result of this is that his poems have been assumed to be susceptible of any interpretation whatsoever. Only when we become conscious of the character and direction of romantic myth-making can we begin to discern the nature of Rimbaud's imagination and the themology of his work. It is important to insist on this fact here, for we must now turn to the *Illuminations,* whose uncertain date and origins and whose density of texture have given rise to the most divergent readings.

6. *Illuminations* I: The Changing of Life

R IMBAUD'S early biographers usually stated that the *Illuminations* were the poems that Rimbaud wrote in Verlaine's company in 1872–73 before their quarrel in Brussels and the repudiation of literature which Rimbaud announced in *Une Saison en enfer*. Some of these biographers were serious scholars, but handicapped in their undertaking by lack of adequate and reliable documentation; more of them, however, were enthusiasts only too happy to embroider at will upon what has been scourged as the "myth of Rimbaud": the story of the God-Demon-Poet who, after exhausting all forms of experience and literature, cast his achievement aside and abruptly retreated into an unparalleled silence. To be fair, one must admit that Rimbaud himself was instrumental in creating this legend; he was apparently what the French call a *mythomane* and seldom attempted to make other than a forbidding and fantastic impression on those he encountered. Modern biographers, however, have attempted with some success to pierce the screen of hearsay and hagiography which earlier writers unwittingly erected about the poet. The most important recent discovery has been that Rimbaud's famous renunciation of literature in August 1873 either did not take place or did not last and that at least some of the *Illuminations* are posterior to *Une Saison en enfer*.

Verlaine had declared, in his preface to the first edition of the *Illuminations* (1886), that they were composed between 1873 and 1875 during stays in Charleville, Paris, England, and Germany, but this claim was long ignored. By now, however, a number of arguments other than Verlaine's testimony have been advanced for dating the *Illuminations* after *Une Saison en enfer*.[1] They are all interesting if not completely irrefutable, and we shall classify them with appropriate observations:

1. Graphological study of the manuscripts apparently suggests that they were written at a different time from the poems of 1872 and the drafts of *Une Saison en enfer*. One may object, however, that graphology is an uncertain science and that, in any case, the date of a manuscript is not necessarily that of the poem's composition. Rimbaud may have simply copied earlier poems in 1873–75; yet, on the other hand, such an occupation would be strange for someone who had repudiated literature.

2. Allusions and influences have been invoked in order to establish the most divergent dates for the *Illuminations*. Thus, Rimbaud's use of the word *Wasserfall* (in "Aube") supposedly indicates that the poem was written in 1875 when he was studying German. This argument is weakened, however, when we reflect that nothing is simpler than to acquire odd words of a neighboring language— particularly when one has lived in territory occupied by people speaking it, as was the case of Rimbaud during

1. The principal writings on this question are H. de Bouillane de Lacoste, *Rimbaud et le problème des Illuminations* (Paris, 1949); D. De Graaf, *Arthur Rimbaud, homme de lettres* (Assen, 1948); P. Guirard, "L'Evolution stylistique de Rimbaud et le problème des *Illuminations*," *Mercure de France*, 322 (1954), 201–34; and Adam, "L'Enigme des Illuminations." A thorough-going refutation of all these theses can be found in Chadwick, *Etudes*, pp. 74–132.

the Franco-Prussian War. An even more fragile kind of
contention rests on supposed biographical references: a
mention of the Indies inclines one critic to date "Enfance"
from after Rimbaud's trip to Java in 1876. Attempts to
date the *Illuminations* in this fashion depend, however,
on untenable presuppositions: that the so-called biographical references are unambiguous, that poets allude only
to strictly contemporary events, or that they are incapable
of speaking of places and things they have not seen.

3. The rare attempts to date the *Illuminations* by
general stylistic evidence are vitiated by debatable assump-
tions that a writer's style must evolve in such and such a
manner, that he will not experiment with more than one
style at a time, and that he will never return to a previous
manner.

I have pointed out weaknesses in the main methods
used for dating the *Illuminations* after *Une Saison en
enfer* because, although I favor the newer theory, one
should not ignore the objections to it. The old dating of
the *Illuminations* from 1872–73 has, however, two grave
defects. First of all, there is Verlaine's claim that they
were composed later. Verlaine had visited Rimbaud in
1875 on his release from prison (when apparently he was
given the manuscript of the *Illuminations*), and he was
almost the only contemporary whom Rimbaud respected
enough for his intelligence in matters of poetry to confide
in him about work in progress. Furthermore, and this
brings us to our second point, Verlaine knew Rimbaud
too well to credit him with the melodramatic and sudden
renunciation of literature which inspired later biographers
to wax metaphysical. The story of Rimbaud's burning his
manuscripts, and uttering (doubtless with gestures) a vow
of eternal silence, is suspect and distasteful on psychological grounds; it smacks altogether too much of "literature" and the romantic imagination. That Rimbaud himself was not an enemy of romantic myth should not

encourage us to perpetuate legends about his work; on the contrary, it behooves us to absorb some of the irony about his own myth-making which he displays in the *Illuminations*.

Though it seems to me not unnatural that Rimbaud continued his literary activities for some time after his break with Verlaine, I can find few incontestable arguments for dating any specific *Illuminations* from any precise period. The apparently irregular rhythm of Rimbaud's production in 1870–72, his presumably regular inactivity during winter, suggests that the composition of such a large number of poems (42) may have spanned several years. Thus we are in the presence of a truly enigmatic collection as regards any attempt to study the evolution of Rimbaud's style or the influences on it. Nor is the matter clarified by any design within the work: its first editor stated that the manuscripts of the poems were not classified in any order, and no one since has found any cogent sequence for them.[2] Finally, the title itself seems haphazard and unenlightening. Verlaine claimed it to be an English word meaning "painted plates" (whatever they might be), while others have taken it in the French sense of a God-given higher state of spiritual perception. Neither definition applies to all the poems, which are variously descriptive, narrative, lyrical, literal, and metaphoric.

With these indications that the *Illuminations* is a composite work, it seems to me futile and factitious to seek any general unity or pattern in the collection; though many poems are obviously related in vocabulary and theme, any attempt to make them all fit a common scheme is belied by one's actual experience of them. I have therefore chosen to discuss the *Illuminations* from two points of view: first, by an analysis of several pieces bound to-

2. See the "Notice" about the *Illuminations* in the Garnier edition, p. 247.

gether by cross-references, second, in a study of certain ones as individual experiments in prose poetry. Hopefully, the *Illuminations* will thus seem neither totally unrelated to each other nor falsely complementary.

Ten or fifteen of the *Illuminations* are reminiscent of certain themes in *Une Saison en enfer*. They deal with transformations of reality, with enormous projects to be undertaken, and with strange new domains of knowledge. The order in which we shall examine them is purely a matter of expository convenience, for they do not form a sequence but rather constitute variations—lyrical, ironic, sinister, grandiloquent—on the subject of the poet endowed with magical powers and the metamorphosis of the world which his presence will excite. As we shall have ample occasion to observe, the magic Rimbaud writes of is, like the "alchimie du verbe," a greater mythic conception than the word ordinarily suggests, and resembles more a kind of epiphany. Although these poems recall *Une Saison en enfer,* we must not simply interpret them as if they were part of that poem, but examine them as separate works. At the same time, however, our first example, "Vagabonds," cannot help but seem like a parallel to "Vierge folle":

Pitoyable frère! Que d'atroces veillées je lui dus! "Je ne me saisissais pas fervemment de cette entreprise. Je m'étais joué de son infirmité. Par ma faute nous retournerions en exil, en esclavage." Il me supposait un guignon et une innocence très bizarres, et il ajoutait des raisons inquiétantes.

Je répondais en ricanant à ce satanique docteur, et finissais par gagner la fenêtre. Je créais, par delà la campagne traversée par des bandes de musique rare, les fantômes du futur luxe nocturne.

Après cette distraction vaguement hygiénique, je

m'étendais sur une paillasse. Et, presque chaque nuit,
aussitôt endormi, le pauvre frère se levait, la bouche
pourrie, les yeux arrachés, — tel qu'il se rêvait! —
et me tirait dans la salle en hurlant son songe de
chagrin idiot.

J'avais en effet, en toute sincérité d'esprit, pris
l'engagement de le rendre à son état primitif de fils
du Soleil, — et nous errions, nourris du vin des
cavernes et du biscuit de la route, moi pressé de
trouver le lieu et la formule.

[Pitiful brother! How many dreadful sleepless nights
I owed him! He said I wasn't seriously involved in
this undertaking. I had taken advantage of his weakness. Through my fault we would go back into exile,
slavery. He imagined I had a very strange innocence
and jinx, and proffered disquieting reasons. I answered this Satanic doctor with a sneer and turned
away to the window. Beyond the countryside streaked
with rare music I created the phantoms of the future
nocturnal luxury. After this vaguely hygienic distraction I stretched out on a pallet, and, almost every
night, as soon as he fell asleep, my poor brother got
up, his mouth stinking and eyes rolling—just as he
dreamed he looked!—and dragged me into the room,
screaming his sorrowful idiot's dream. For I had, in
all sincerity of intention, undertaken to return him
to his original state of Sun Child—and we were wandering, living on cave wine and roadside crackers, as
I strove to find the place and formula.]

The outlines of the situation are the same as in "Vierge
folle": a weak and tormented soul has been led by a
stronger one into a hazardous enterprise of uncertain out-
come—the transformation of life by the breaking of an
enchantment. Yet the prose of this passage is of an alto-

gether different sort from that of *Une Saison en enfer*. Rather than a succession of short, nervous sentences, "Vagabonds" consists of varied sentence structures with the periodic flow of normal literary French. The last two paragraphs in particular are models of rhythmic elegance, with their numerous pauses and rounded final cadences. The language is concise—as in the elliptic indirect discourse of the first paragraph—but free from obscurity of phrasing. The convention of magic suffices to explain the spell cast over the land which the narrator seeks to break. The choice of a propitious spot and the correct ritual are essential aspects of the traditional practice of magic. The sun is associated, as in the last verse poems and "Alchimie du verbe," with an essential, pure form of life unblemished by human needs and restrictions. However, a certain note of detachment created by the polished language contrasts oddly with the esoteric subject; an element of irony is present which qualifies the supernatural situation. Expressions like "raisons inquiétantes," "distraction vaguement hygiénique," and "en toute sincérité d'esprit" belong to the reasonable vocabulary of polite intercourse and provide a mild undercurrent of mockery. This is not the crushing and desperate self-irony we have encountered so often in *Une Saison en enfer* but a delicate tension between the poet and his chosen conventions. We have had occasion to remark on this playful tone in regard to "Alchimie du verbe" ("Je réservais la traduction!"), but only in certain *Illuminations* does it become of the first importance and modify the poem's meaning.

"Vagabonds" looks back toward the past and an original higher state, but it also contains an allusion to "future nocturnal luxury" which connects it with a whole series of *Illuminations* where the theme of creating a new world by magic is reworked and explored in sometimes complicated ways. The long piece "Jeunesse" is interesting for its ambiguities in this respect. The opening part is entitled

"Dimanche"—the symbol of interim boredom, a tedious state between two higher moments:

> Les calculs de côté, l'inévitable descente du ciel, et la visite des souvenirs et la séance des rhythmes occupent la demeure, la tête et le monde de l'esprit.
>
> — Un cheval détale sur le turf suburbain, et le long des cultures et des boisements, percé par la peste carbonique. Une misérable femme de drame, quelque part dans le monde, soupire après des abandons improbables. Les desperadoes languissent après l'orage, l'ivresse et les blessures. De petits enfants étouffent des malédictions le long des rivières. —
>
> Reprenons l'étude au bruit de l'oeuvre dévorante qui se rassemble et remonte dans les masses.

[Calculations put aside, the inevitable descent from heaven, and the visit of memories and a session of rhythms occupy the dwelling, the head and world of the mind. A horse darts off on the suburban lawn, and along the fields and woods, struck with carbonic plague. A wretched woman out of a play, somewhere in the world, sighs after unlikely abandonments. Desperadoes languish after storms, drunkenness, and wounds. Little children choke back curses along the river banks. Let us take up again our studies with the noise of the devouring opus that draws itself together and rises in the masses.]

The central paragraph is the clearest: its four images—the dingy landscape with the fleeing horse, the absurd woman recalling the dreariness of love as it now exists ("l'enfer des femmes"), criminals longing for destruction, and wretched children—symbolize the present world and have analogues in *Une Saison en enfer* and earlier poems. The first sentence suggests a moment of weariness, a return to this world from a superior one, but contains unsolvable grammatical ambiguities: the relation of "souvenirs" and "séances des rhythmes" to the descent from heaven remains uncertain. Finally the "masses" who are touched by the poet's work bring up another question of relationship, though one which will be clarified later on in the poem. These obscurities, like the unvaried sentence patterns of the middle paragraph (each sentence begins with a noun subject), are quite unlike the elegant style of "Vagabonds," and such differences should come to mind if we are tempted to assimilate one *Illumination* to another too closely. In "Sonnet,"[3] the second part of "Jeunesse," the language breaks down almost entirely as the poet attempts to explain at what point he has arrived in his *œuvre*—a rich term designating both the poet's and the alchemist's work:

> *Homme* de constitution ordinaire, la chair n'était-
> elle pas un fruit pendu dans le verger, ô journées
> enfantes! le corps un trésor à prodiguer; ô aimer, le
> péril ou la force de Psyché? La terre avait des versants
> fertiles en princes et en artistes, et la descendance
> et la race nous poussaient aux crimes et aux deuils :
> le monde votre fortune et votre péril. Mais à présent,
> ce labeur comblé, toi, tes calculs, toi, tes impatiences,
> ne sont plus que votre danse et votre voix, non fixées
> et point forcées, quoique d'un double événement
> d'invention et de succès une raison, en l'humanité
> fraternelle et discrète par l'univers sans images; —
> la force et le droit réfléchissent la danse et la voix à
> présent seulement appréciées.

> [*Man* of ordinary constitution, wasn't the flesh a fruit
> hanging in the orchard, oh childhood days! the body

---

3. The title of this section apparently derives from the fact that it contains phrases reminiscent of a sonnet of Verlaine's. See V. P. Underwood, "Rimbaud et l'Angleterre," *Revue de Littérature Comparée,* *29* (1955), 34, n. 1.

a treasure to spend extravagantly, oh love! the peril or the strength of Spirit? The earth had slopes rich in princes and artists, and heredity and race inclined us toward crimes and mourning: the world, your fortune and peril. But at present, this task accomplished, you, your calculations, you, your fits of impatience, are nothing but your dance and voice, not fixed and not forced, although a reason for a double event of invention and success amid mankind fraternal and discrete throughout the imageless universe;—strength and right reflect the dance and voice, which are only estimated at present.]

The poet, like the narrator of *Une Saison en enfer,* hovers between his past undertakings, which have an erotic and criminal as well as an artistic connotation, and the future achievement of his "dance and voice." The last sentence is hopelessly garbled with the oscillation between *tutoiement* and *vousoiement,* the inversion before "raison," the elliptic use of *par* (the preposition whose meaning Rimbaud most often strains beyond normal intelligibility), and the dense accumulation of abstract nouns. Yet though this sentence is somewhat unsatisfactory—and perhaps only a rough draft—it interests us by the association of certain words: the poet's future *œuvre* is related to success, invention, humanity, and strength. This enterprise suggests not only a total art, inclusive of dance, but something even greater. We encounter here words that will return incessantly in other *Illuminations,* but in somewhat clearer contexts. "Sonnet" is interesting to the extent that it provides us with an important complex of terms.

In the third part of "Jeunesse" ("Vingt ans"[4]), the

4. It should be remembered, of course, that "vingt ans" in French most often designates a general period of life and not a specific age. This title is of no more help in dating the poem from 1874 than is the expression "aller mes vingt ans" ("L'Eclair") in dating *Une Saison en enfer* from this same year.

erotic theme and garden imagery return in a loosely constructed passage expressive, like Part I, of abandonment,
of inability to achieve the *œuvre:*

> Les voix instructives exilées... L'ingénuité physique
> amèrement rassise... Adagio. Ah! l'égoïsme infini de
> l'adolescence, l'optimisme studieux : que le monde
> était plein de fleurs cet été! Les airs et les formes
> mourant... Un choeur, pour calmer l'impuissance et
> l'absence! Un choeur de verres de mélodies noc-
> turnes... En effet les nerfs vont vite chasser.

> [The instructive voices exiled . . . Physical ingenuous-
> ness bitterly satisfied . . . Adagio. Ah! the infinite ego-
> tism of adolescence, studious optimism: how full of
> flowers the world was last summer! Airs and forms
> dying . . . A chorus, to calm impotence and absence!
> A chorus of glasses making nocturnal melodies . . .
> Indeed, our senses are off again on their hunt.]

The musical vocabulary is of capital importance: the
poet's work and the world's transformation are continually associated with it in the *Illuminations*. The final sentence of the passage, with its erotic overtones (which as
before have some relation to the poet's *œuvre*), makes a
nice transition to Part IV:

> Tu en es encore à la tentation d'Antoine. L'ébat
> du zèle écourté, les tics d'orgueil puéril, l'affaisse-
> ment et l'effroi. Mais tu te mettras à ce travail : toutes
> les possibilités harmoniques et architecturales
> s'émouvront autour de ton siège. Des êtres parfaits,
> imprévus, s'offriront à tes expériences. Dans tes
> environs affluera rêveusement la curiosité d'anciennes
> foules et de luxes oisifs. Ta mémoire et tes sens ne
> seront que la nourriture de ton impulsion créatrice.
> Quant au monde, quand tu sortiras, que sera-t-il
> devenu? En tout cas, rien des apparences actuelles.

[You are still at the stage of Saint Anthony's Temptation. The burst of zeal cut short, the twitches of childish pride, discouragement and fear. But you will put yourself to this task: all harmonic and architectural possibilities will stir about your seat. Perfect, unforeseen beings will offer themselves for your experiments. Around you will flow dreamily the curiosity of ancient crowds and idle luxury. Your memory and senses will merely be the food of your creative impulse. As for the world, when you go out, what will have become of it? In any case, none of its present look.]

With the return of the poet's confidence in himself, the fragmentary and meandering language suddenly gives way to normal prose sentence structures and rhythms. His future accomplishment is now described in concrete rather than abstract terms: new buildings, new beings. The nature of his *œuvre* has gradually become more complex: it is not simply poetry, art, erotic fulfillment, personal triumph, and the amelioration of mankind, but extends even to the metamorphosis of the existent physical world. Yet a muted note of irony closes this sanguine prophecy: the poet's visions will have taken place in the privacy of his room, but how will they affect life outside? The reply is boastful and flippant: its familiarity of tone implies a certain doubt about the correspondence of the change to the poet's wishes.

"Jeunesse" is not a very perfect poem in structure or detail, but perhaps exactly because of its rough-hewn, seemingly unfinished character, it provides us with many of the key terms which Rimbaud works and reworks in the *Illuminations.* Aside from the persistent musical imagery there are three things we should note that are associated with the narrator's work: success, with an almost worldly connotation; new beings and visions, with erotic and esthetic overtones; and the fraternal redemption of mankind. These three aspects of the poet's enterprise, however curious a combination they make, return in other poems and constitute the fundamental themology of a large number of the *Illuminations*. "Angoisse" will serve as a convenient example of how Rimbaud uses the same thematic materials and words in more than one poem without seeming to repeat or imitate himself. Here again the poet despairs of his future accomplishment:

Se peut-il qu'Elle me fasse pardonner les ambitions continuellement écrasées, — qu'une fin aisée répare les âges d'indigence, — qu'un jour de succès nous endorme sur la honte de notre inhabileté fatale?

(O palmes! diamant! — Amour, force! — plus haut que toutes joies et gloires! — de toutes façons, partout, — démon, dieu, — Jeunesse de cet être-ci : moi!)

Que des accidents de féerie scientifique et des mouvements de fraternité sociale soient chéris comme restitution progressive de la franchise première?...

Mais la Vampire qui nous rend gentils commande que nous nous amusions avec ce qu'elle nous laisse, ou qu'autrement nous soyons plus drôles.

Rouler aux blessures, par l'air lassant et la mer; aux supplices, par le silence des eaux et de l'air meurtriers; aux tortures qui rient, dans leur silence atrocement houleux.

[Can it be that It will make me pardoned for my continually crushed ambitions, that a wealthy end will make up for the periods of poverty, that a day of success will make us forget the shame of our fatal inability? (Oh Palms, diamonds, love, strength!— higher than all joys and glories—in every way, everywhere—demon, god—youth of this being: me.) That accidents of scientific magic and movements of social

fraternity will be cherished as a progressive restitution of original freedom? But the Vampire who makes
us good orders us to amuse ourselves with what she
leaves us or otherwise be more foolish. Roll in
wounds, through the wearying air and the sea; in
torments through the silence of the murderous air
and water; in tortures laughing in the atrocious
swell of their silence.]

The use of "Elle" first deserves some comment since it does
not seem to refer to any noun in the text (I prefer to dissociate it from "Vampire"). We have noted before the
ambiguity which pronouns can have in French by referring either to people or things, and I tend to connect this
"Elle" with the poet's undertaking, his *œuvre*. Since the
verb is "fasse pardonner" and not "pardonne" I find this
reading more simple and satisfactory than to interpret
"Elle" as a person and, necessarily, an intercessor. The
capital letter of the pronoun adds a curious feeling of
personification which is not uncharacteristic of Rimbaud's
style: a similar lack of distinction between the animate
and the inanimate, the concrete and the abstract, can be
found in "Métropolitain," "H," "A une raison," and
"Mémoire."

The first three paragraphs present the three themes we
have picked out in "Jeunesse." The mundane character
of the expression "fin aisée" emphasizes the almost commercial sense which "success" sometimes has in the *Illuminations* and which we shall come across again. The second
paragraph associates visual beauty—diamonds—with love
and strength. "Démon" and "dieu" do not have clear
theological implications as in *Une Saison en enfer*—the
point is important to make for the general intelligence of
the *Illuminations*—but designate together the extent of
the poet's aspirations, which break off in irony about his
own youth. Finally magical science and the redemption

of humanity, the return to its original state of *fils du soleil,* are restated as part of the poet's task.

The vampire who prevents the poet's realization of his hopes is one of those symbols which resist translation into abstract language. It appears to be an exteriorized image of a part of the self—like the objective "Esprit" the poet talks with in *Une Saison en enfer.* The choice of such an image—perhaps a romantic version of Prometheus' torment—makes the poet's incapacity remain obscure, on the material and psychological plane, but as we have seen in connection with "Le Bateau ivre" and "Mémoire," such uncertain causality is almost inevitable in poems couched in a highly symbolic mode.

The syntax of "Angoisse" provides another demonstration of how varied the prose of the *Illuminations* is. The statement of the poet's aspirations consists of one long, complex period divided into four paragraphs; the concluding paragraph abandons sentence form for a development of parallel and repetitive phrases. This shift in grammar and rhythm corresponds to the movement of despair with which the poem terminates: the poet's inability inspires a longing for self-destruction, which takes the inarticulate form of a cry.

The poems we have examined so far deal with a crisis of aspiration and incapacity. Other *Illuminations,* however, deal with the future transformation of life as imminent and realizable, and recall the closing chapters of *Une Saison en enfer* by their repetition of the word "new." "A une raison" is particularly relevant in this connection since, like "Matin," it also contains the image of mankind "en marche":

> Un coup de ton doigt sur le tambour décharge tous les sons et commence la nouvelle harmonie.
> Un pas de toi c'est la levée des nouveaux hommes et leur en marche.

Ta tête se détourne : le nouvel amour! Ta tête se
retourne : — le nouvel amour.

"Change nos lots, crible les fléaux, à commencer
par le temps," te chantent ces enfants. "Elève n'im-
porte où la substance de nos fortunes et de nos voeux,"
on t'en prie.

Arrivée de toujours, qui t'en iras partout.

[A tap of your finger on the drum releases all sounds
and initiates the new harmony. A step of yours is the
rise of new men and their forward march. You glance
aside: new love! You look back: new love. "Change
our lots, make our plagues vanish, beginning with
Time," the children sing to you. "Raise to any heights
the substance of our fortunes and wishes," they beg
you. Come from always, going everywhere.]

The title and the pronoun reference demand some observations: on several occasions in his later work Rimbaud
uses the word "raison" in a way which does not seem to
fit any dictionary sense but which does apparently imply
a force in the creation of a new order of things. The term
certainly does not designate the favorite faculty of eighteenth-century rationalists, for Rimbaud places the indefinite article before it, suggesting some cryptic class of powers. Those who have studied most closely the influence
of occultist literature on Rimbaud have not uncovered
any source for this use of "raison," although hermetic
philosophy might seem to be its most likely place of origin,
and we must provisionally conclude that it is of his invention.[5] The personification of "raison" is also significant: like the mysterious "Elle" in "Angoisse" Rimbaud
seems here to be creating a kind of elusive force that is
half-visible, half-abstract. One is reminded of the curious

5. Miss Starkie (*Rimbaud*, p. 171) equates "raison" with *logos* and
God, which is a suggestive interpretation, if perhaps too specific.

way in which the names of classical deities are also common nouns in Latin and Greek (cf. Ouranos, Venus). The stylistic effect is subtle and cannot be equated with ordinary allegory, which eschews such obscure conceptions as Rimbaud's "raison."

The "new harmony" and "new men" are analogous to expressions we have already encountered (cf. "Jeunesse"), but "new love" requires perhaps some interpretation. At first the word seems merely to have the romantic humanitarian sense, common in Hugo and Lamartine, of a future state of fraternity and mutual benevolence, but we should recall the erotic note associated with the life of the future in "Jeunesse" and "Angoisse." The ambiguous notion of "l'amour réinventé" is essential to Rimbaud's myth of life transformed. It hints at both a new spiritual state and new bodily pleasures. The abolishment of time demanded by children (who, as in other poems of Rimbaud's, seem especially associated with the future or the magical) likewise requires comparison with other poems: in "Jeunesse" IV as in "Soir historique," which we shall next examine, the men of the future have at their disposal all events present and past, and therefore Rimbaud seems to imply here something more than merely an atemporal state. All time is simultaneous in this conception. Finally, the last line with its play on words between "toujours" and "partout"—time compared with space—has an uncertain tone: it could refer to the necessity of coming change but could also ironically suggest that the poet is speaking of an eternally renewed hope that has little chance of fulfillment. Like "Jeunesse" and many other *Illuminations,* "A une raison" ends in ambiguity and a kind of retreat from affirmation on the part of the speaker.

"A une raison" invokes a change in the world in somewhat schematic terms like the concluding chapters of *Une Saison en enfer,* but elsewhere Rimbaud portrays its delights more concretely. "Soir historique," for example, describes in detail the "future nocturnal luxury" alluded to in "Vagabonds":

> En quelque soir, par exemple, que se trouve le touriste naïf, retiré de nos horreurs économiques, la main d'un maître anime le clavecin des prés; on joue aux cartes au fond de l'étang, miroir évocateur des reines et des mignonnes . . .
>
> A sa vision esclave, l'Allemagne s'échafaude vers des lunes; les déserts tartares s'éclairent; les révoltes anciennes grouillent dans le centre du Céleste Empire . . .
>
> La même magie bourgeoise à tous les points où la malle nous déposera! Le plus élémentaire physicien sent qu'il n'est plus possible de se soumettre à cette atmosphère personnelle, brume de remords physiques, dont la constatation est déjà une affliction. . . .

> [For example, in whatever evening the simple tourist happens to be, in retreat from our economic horrors, a master's hand enlivens the meadows' harpsichord; there are card games going on at the bottom of the lake, a mirror summoning up queens and favorites . . . Enslaved to his vision Germany rises up on scaffolds toward moons; the Tartar deserts light up; the ancient revolts swarm in the heart of the Celestial Empire . . . The same bourgeois magic wherever our trunk sets us down! The most elementary physicist senses it is no longer possible to put up with this personal atmosphere, this fog of physical remorse, the mere realization of which is already a torment. . . .]

Magical diversions in which all time and space—real or imaginary—become present are promised by this poem, which has something of the tone of a prospectus or advertisement. "Soir historique" is one of the best examples of Rimbaud's fondness for qualifying his visions with the language of commerce and science. He was free of the disdain, common among late nineteenth-century writers, for the marvels of contemporary civilization and, like Balzac, found something poetic in the sciences and modern economy. This unwillingness to restrict poetry to the pre-contemporary world is one of Rimbaud's great strengths: it prevents his mythopoeic bent from becoming archaizing and remote. At the same time his playing with the language of the practical world while evoking mythic realms provides him with a fundamental strain of irony. There is a self-conscious disparity between the imaginary domains evoked and the narrator's matter-of-fact tone. One is always aware of the virtuosity which holds together the oddly assorted elements of a poem like "Soir historique" and of the precariousness of the equilibrium.

The personal fog of physical remorse, as the poet calls present life, is a fairly complex image, suggesting isolation from the surrounding world, a guilty absorption in the self, and a kind of moral malaise provoked by matter. What he would escape from is our ethical morass, which would seem to be an emanation from our familiar landscape. The "changing of life" is a release from our conscience as well as from ordinary sights and sensations. This is expressed more overtly in "Solde," the *Illumination* in which Rimbaud carries farthest his fondness for commercial metaphor:

A vendre ce que les Juifs n'ont pas vendu, ce que noblesse ni crime n'ont goûté, ce qu'ignorent l'amour maudit et la probité infernale des masses; ce que le temps ni la science n'ont pas à reconnaître;

[SALE on what the Jews haven't sold, what nobility and crime haven't enjoyed, what cursed love and the infernal integrity of the masses don't know, what time and knowledge can't claim.]

On the pretext of a liquidation sale, the poet offers treasures beyond good and evil, time and knowledge. We recognize familiar kinds of images:

> Les Voix reconstituées; l'éveil fraternel de toutes les énergies chorales et orchestrales et leurs applications instantanées; l'occasion, unique, de dégager nos sens!

> [The Voices reconstituted, the fraternal awakening of all choral and orchestral energies and their instantaneous application; the sole opportunity to release our senses!]

Music is appropriately the first symbol for the release of the senses and the transformation of the material world, for it alone of physical pleasures has no relation to present nature. A new eroticism accompanies it, likewise divorced from known experiences:

> A vendre les Corps sans prix, hors de toute race, de tout monde, de tout sexe, de toute descendance! Les richesses jaillissant à chaque démarche! Solde de diamants sans contrôle!

> [SALE on priceless Bodies, removed from any race, any world, any sex, any heredity! Treasures bursting forth at every step! SALE on smuggled diamonds!]

"Smuggled diamonds"—we have previously seen the gem associated with eroticism (cf. "Angoisse"), and here the image sustains the theme of an impossibly advantageous bargain. The next items offered make us more aware that it is essential fulfillment which is being sold with no ethical considerations involved:

> A vendre l'anarchie pour les masses; la satisfaction irrépressible pour les amateurs supérieurs; la mort atroce pour les fidèles et les amants!

> [SALE on anarchy for the masses; on irrepressible

satisfaction for fine connoisseurs; on atrocious deaths for lovers and true hearts!]

The poet offers perfect consummation to all, whether it be pleasureful or not; thus lovers will achieve the death their state tends toward. The material possibilities of modern life, such as the nineteenth century could foresee them, are also thrown in; comfort, amusement, and freedom from work have economic implications which sustain the basic metaphor of the poem:

> A vendre les habitations et les migrations, sports, féeries et comforts parfaits, et le bruit, le mouvement et l'avenir qu'ils font!

> [SALE on habitations and migrations, sports, magic shows and modern installations, and the noise, movement, and future they create!]

Finally for the intellect the poet offers the ultimate transfiguration of mathematics and language:

> A vendre les applications de calcul et les sauts d'harmonie inouïs. Les trouvailles et les termes non soupçonnés, possession immédiate,

> [SALE on applications of calculus and unheard-of harmonic leaps, on rare finds in language—immediate delivery—]

The sequence of rather general conceptions which are detailed in "Solde" culminates in a burst of abstract words whose enthusiastic raid on the unintelligible is made more energetic by a jangling repetition of sounds:

> Elan insensé et infini aux splendeurs invisibles, aux délices insensibles, — et ses secrets affolants pour chaque vice — et sa gaîté effrayante pour la foule.

> [Insane and infinite urge toward invisible splendors
> and insensible delights—and its maddening secrets
> for each vice—and its frightening gaiety for the
> crowd.]

With the last sentences, however, we are left in doubt as
to the good faith of the sale:

> A vendre les Corps, les voix, l'immense opulence
> inquestionable, ce qu'on ne vendra jamais. Les ven-
> deurs ne sont pas à bout de solde! Les voyageurs n'ont
> pas à rendre leur commission de si tôt!

> [SALE on Bodies, voices, vast unquestionable wealth,
> on what can never be sold! The sale is not yet over!
> The representatives do not have to settle their ac-
> counts so soon!]

The treasures can have no price, and the merchant is not
willing to let them go so easily. The crafty final change
of direction is Rimbaud's characteristic signature. Those
who attempt to read this poem as another farewell to literature fail, in their single-mindedness, to appreciate the
duplicity of intention and the ironic resources of its author. "Solde" is a tentative revelation of what mankind's
fulfillment of its amoral nature would be. At the same
time, it hints at the incapacity of man to realize himself
and at the poet's exclusive possession of true power.

All these visions of life transfigured bear some relation
to *Une Saison en enfer,* but they remain apocalyptic without theological reference. Their epiphanies are assimilated to magic in a vague way and are largely purged of
religious meaning except insofar as one senses in them
a rejection of the Christian metaphysic of good and evil.
At least one *Illumination,* however, brings us back into
the climate of thought of *Une Saison en enfer* with its
exploration of history and religious philosophy. "Génie"
is a capital text, both in its stylistic distinction and in its

drawing together of motifs to be found explicit or implied
in other *Illuminations:*

> Il est l'affection et le présent puisqu'il a fait la
> maison ouverte à l'hiver écumeux et à la rumeur de
> l'été, lui qui a purifié les boissons et les aliments, lui
> qui est le charme des lieux fuyants et le délice sur-
> humain des stations. Il est l'affection et l'avenir, la
> force et l'amour que nous, debout dans les rages et
> les ennuis, nous voyons passer dans le ciel de tempête
> et les drapeaux d'extase.
>
> Il est l'amour, mesure parfaite et réinventée, raison
> merveilleuse et imprévue, et l'éternité : machine
> aimée des qualités fatales. Nous avons tous eu l'épou-
> vante de sa concession et de la nôtre : ô jouissance de
> notre santé, élan de nos facultés, affection égoïste et
> passion pour lui, lui qui nous aime pour sa vie
> infinie...

> [He is affection and the present, since he has made
> our house open to the foam of winter and summer's
> drone, he who has purified our food and drink, he
> who is the charm of fugitive spots and the super-
> human delight of resting places. He is affection and
> the future, strength and love, that we, erect in fury
> and troubles, see pass through the stormy sky and
> flags of ecstasy. He is love, a perfect, re-invented
> measure, a marvelous, unforeseen reason, and eter-
> nity: a machine beloved of fate's forces. We have all
> had the terror of his yielding and our own: oh enjoy-
> ment of our health, bursting of our faculties, egoistic
> affection and passion for him, he who loves us for his
> infinite life . . .]

In "Génie" as in "A une raison" the poet's aspirations are
associated not with his own *œuvre* but with an external
force. Even more clearly than in "A une raison," however,

this force is a deity, and the first two paragraphs detail his epithets and attributes. These flowing sentences have the hypnotic character of invocatory prayer with their monotonous repetition of words, notions, and the conjunctive formula A-and-B. The *génie* is connected with the spectacle of the natural world but in a particular way: his influence is always from above like that of the sun or moon, and thus this conception is not pantheistic but rather comparable to that of God in the Psalms. He is *almost* nature, but not quite. Among his promises and attributes are terms by now familiar: strength, health, and love re-invented; reason (with the special and somewhat cryptic sense Rimbaud gives the word), and eternity. Some of this language—especially phrases like "lui qui nous aime pour sa vie infinie"—resembles Christian devotional expression, but one must note on the other hand the particular physical and sensual emphasis in the passage: words like "concession," "affection égoïste," "passion" have a decidedly erotic character. The Oriental connotations of the word genie (which derives, in this sense, from the Arabic *jinn* rather than Latin *genius*) contribute further toward the voluptuary suggestion of the poem. Suddenly the cult of the genie is contrasted with Christianity:

> Et nous nous le rappelons et il voyage... Et si l'Adoration s'en va, sonne, sa promesse sonne : "Arrière ces superstitions, ces anciens corps, ces ménages et ces âges. C'est cette époque-ci qui a sombré!"
>
> Il ne s'en ira pas, il ne redescendra pas d'un ciel, il n'accomplira pas la rédemption des colères de femmes et des gaîtés des hommes et de tout ce péché : car c'est fait, lui étant, et étant aimé.

[And we call him back and he goes onward . . . And if Adoration disappears, let it ring, his promise ring:

"Away with these superstitions, these old bodies, these couples, and these ages. This epoch has foundered!" He will not go away, he will not come back down so much as one heaven, he will not accomplish the redemption of women's anger and men's gaiety and all this sin: for it is done, he being, and being loved.]

"Adoration" (the word has stronger religious associations in French than in English) is Christian worship, and with it are associated outmoded forms of love and eroticism. The genie's refusal to retreat from his pre-eminence or to descend and redeem man is in obvious contrast with Christ's mission, but a delicate ambiguity is suggested by the declaration that redemption is already accomplished by his very existence. There is a curious play on the notion of time and the point of epiphany in this poem: the genie is both present and future, promise and fulfillment. I believe the correct inference is that, unlike Christ, he need not manifest himself vulgarly and that the burden of realizing transfiguration lies on mankind alone. The syntax of the poem suddenly changes to a series of exalted exclamations, as the genie's attributes and powers are again proclaimed and in fuller detail:

O ses souffles, ses têtes, ses courses; la terrible célérité de la perfection des formes et de l'action.
O fécondité de l'esprit et immensité de l'univers!
Son corps! Le dégagement rêvé, le brisement de la grâce croisée de violence nouvelle!
Sa vue, sa vue! tous les agenouillages anciens et les peines *relevées* à sa suite.
Son jour! l'abolition de toutes souffrances sonores et mouvantes dans la musique plus intense.
Son pas! les migrations plus énormes que les anciennes invasions.

O lui et nous! l'orgueil plus bienveillant que les
charités perdues.

O monde! et le chant clair des malheurs nouveaux!

[Oh his respiration, his heads, his flights: the terrible
celerity of the perfection of forms and action. Oh
fecundity of the spirit and immensity of the universe!
His body! The dreamed-of release, the broken line of
grace crossed with new violence! His sight, his sight!
All the old kneelings and burdens raised up in his
wake. His light! The dissolving of all sonorous and
moving pains into the intenser music! His step! More
enormous migrations than the old invasions. Oh him
and us! Pride more benevolent than the lost charities.
Oh world! And the bright song of new sufferings!]

The kneelings and charities—symbols of Christianity—
are replaced by a new pride (the primordial Christian
sin) and a rejoicing in the body's form released from its
previous bondage. The physical attributes of the genie
are even further associated with the universe in this passage; his body is somehow an image of the world transfigured, perfect form and action. Thus his pace and the
possible migrations of mankind correspond; the light of
his eye is our new atmosphere. The conclusion of the
poem returns to harmonious periodic sentence structure
and repeats the key words of the preceding section in a
formal coda:

Il nous a connus tous et nous a tous aimés. Sachons,
cette nuit d'hiver, de cap en cap, du pôle tumultueux
au château, de la foule à la plage, de regards en regards, forces et sentiments las, le héler et le voir, et le
renvoyer, et sous les marées et au haut des déserts de
neige, suivre ses vues, ses souffles, son corps, son jour.

[He has known us all and loved us all. Let us, this

winter night, from cape to cape, from the tumultuous
pole to the castle, from the crowd to the shore, from
glance to glance, exhausted of strength and feelings,
hail him and see him, and send him on, and, under
the tides and at the top of the deserts of snow, follow
his sight, his respiration, his body, his light.]

These last lines intensify the most persistent image of the
poem, that of the globe embraced by the revolving spectacle of the atmosphere and the genie, whose position is
suggestive of that of some great celestial body. From the
image of the house in the opening lines through to the
end the earth is felt as something surrounded and the
genie as a moving but ever-present force: he goes away,
he is action and speed, yet still he remains. Though not
part of the earth, he is contiguous with it and influential
upon it.

There are two significant phrases in "Génie" which we
have avoided commenting on until this point: "la grâce
croisée de violence nouvelle" and "le chant clair des malheurs nouveaux." Violence and suffering have been implied in the evocation of life transformed in "Solde," but
not exalted as here. Both terms seem perhaps curious in
a poem which envisages the redemption of humanity, but
they are actually congruent with Rimbaud's imaginative
processes: the fraternity and salvation of mankind does
not, in his poetry, have the sentimental connotations it
often has elsewhere, no more than does the future *amour
réinventé* resemble chastity. Since he speaks of states beyond good and evil determined solely by considerations
of esthetics and satisfaction, they can include violence,
suffering, and cataclysms like the cosmic upheaval with
which "Soir historique" ends. No ethical values such as
we know them are present. Thus in reading a poem like
"Matinée d'ivresse" we must recall that its rather demonic
vocabulary is free of Christian-Satanic connotations:

O *mon* Bien! O *mon* Beau! Fanfare atroce où je ne trébuche point! Chevalet féerique! Hourra pour l'oeuvre inouïe et pour le corps merveilleux, pour la première fois! Cela commença sous les rires des enfants, cela finira par eux. Ce poison va rester dans toutes nos veines même quand, la fanfare tournant, nous serons rendus à l'ancienne inharmonie. O maintenant, nous si digne de ces tortures! rassemblons fervemment cette promesse surhumaine faite à notre corps et à notre âme créés : cette promesse, cette démence! L'élégance, la science, la violence! On nous a promis d'enterrer dans l'ombre l'arbre du bien et du mal, de déporter les honnêtetés tyranniques, afin que nous amenions notre très pur amour. Cela commença par quelques dégoûts, et cela finit, — ne pouvant nous saisir sur-le-champ de cette éternité, — cela finit par une débandade de parfums.

[O *my* Good! O *my* Beautiful! Atrocious fanfare in which I do not stagger! Magic rack! Hurrah for the undreamed-of work and the body's marvels, for the first time! It began under the laughter of children, it will end with them. This poison will remain in all our veins, even when, as the fanfare turns, we shall be given back to our old discord. Oh now, us so worthy of these tortures, let us gather up with fervor this superhuman promise made to our created souls and bodies: this promise, this madness! Elegance, science, violence! We were promised the burial in shadow of the tree of good and evil, the deportation of tyrannic decencies in order to bring forth our very pure love. It began with a few feelings of revulsion and it ends—not being able to capture this eternity on the spot—it ends with a rout of perfumes.]

This is one of the best examples of the elaborate webs of words and images which Rimbaud weaves together in almost inextricable fashion. At first it is difficult to decide which terms are the principal ones and which are merely complementary or analogous, whether death by poison is the actual subject of the poem or merely a metaphoric reflection of another theme. I think it preferable to take the erotic vocabulary as basic: the distinction of *je* and *nous,* the ironic conception of a "pure" love which is opposed to decency and ethics, the insistence on the body, and the concluding wry remark, which would best seem to refer to orgasm ("cette éternité"), establish fairly well a kind of sexual situation—the somewhat vague forms of *l'amour réinventé.* The use of musical terms is not surprising, nor the mention of the poet's *œuvre,* for already in "Jeunesse" we have seen them occur in erotic contexts. Torture and poison, however, are more unusual accompanying images, but they must be taken for their dramatic, sensory value rather than in a moral sense, just as violence and misfortune stand among the splendid promises of the genie. There is a satisfaction to be found in pain as well as in pleasure, and it should not be deprecated; in "Matinée d'ivresse" and "Génie," no distinction is made between them based on the traditional categories of desirable and undesirable. The "rire des enfants" is again a passing, associated image which can best be understood by comparison with other poems: children and adolescents (Rimbaud usually does not distinguish the two clearly) sometimes appear in Rimbaud's work in almost the guise of presiding spirits present at actions of a magical, mythic, and even erotic character. Thus it is children who in "A une raison" cry for transformation of the world, and in another *Illumination,* "H," they supervise sexuality.[6]

"Matinée d'ivresse" continues with rather formal repetitions and the evocation of an almost Oriental setting appropriate to eroticism:

6. Cf. also "Mémoire" and the first two sonnets in "Les Stupra."

Rire des enfants, discrétion des esclaves, austérité des vierges, horreur des figures et des objets d'ici, sacrés soyez-vous par le souvenir de cette veille. Cela commençait par toute la rustrerie, voici que cela finit par des anges de flamme et de glace.

Petite veille d'ivresse, sainte! quand ce ne serait que pour le masque dont tu nous as gratifié. Nous t'affirmons, méthode! Nous n'oublions pas que tu as glorifié hier chacun de nos âges. Nous avons foi au poison. Nous savons donner notre vie tout entière tous les jours.

Voici le temps des *Assassins*.

[Children's laughter, slaves' discretion, virgins' austerity, horror of the faces and objects here, hallowed be by the memory of this vigil. It started with complete brutishness, now it is ending with angels of flame and ice. Little drunken vigil—holy! if only for the mask you have bestowed upon us. We affirm you, method! We shall not forget that you glorified yesterday each one of our ages. We trust in poison. We shall give our whole life every day. This is the time of the *Assassins*.]

A sudden surge of religious vocabulary marks the second half of the poem. The sentence "Nous n'oublions pas que . . ." sounds like a pastiche of devotional language, and "Nous savons donner . . ." evokes ironic recollection of pious texts. The justification for this tone, as well as for the symbols of poison and torture, is found in the last word of the poem: Assassins. It seems fairly certain that Rimbaud drew, for his imagery in "Matinée d'ivresse," on Michelet's account of the medieval Moslem sect of the Assassins or hashish eaters, who by skillful political murder terrorized Islam during the middle ages.[7] The roman-

7. *Histoire de France*, 2 (Paris, 1833), 216–20.

tic historian does not fail to describe in his luxurious style the ideals of perverted religion, recondite knowledge, and esthetic refinement that prevailed among this cult, which supposedly owed some of its peculiar character to the use of drugs. All these themes are associated by Rimbaud with an erotic subject, which they qualify, color, and shade. The result is an exceptionally subtle interplay of images from which it is difficult to pick out the dominant subject.

Different as "Matinée d'ivresse" is in tone from other *Illuminations* we have examined, the poem is nonetheless constructed around themes present elsewhere: the *œuvre,* music, new knowledge, aspirations toward the atemporal, and love re-invented. If the sexual motif is preponderant, the essential nucleus of key terms remains unchanged. The better we understand that many of the *Illuminations,* while distinct in mood and technique, share certain basic imaginative elements, the more easily we can read them without recourse to arbitrary hypotheses of one sort or another. The anticipation of future men of violence which we encounter in "Génie" and "Matinée d'ivresse" thus clarifies "Parade":

> Des drôles très solides. Plusieurs ont exploité vos mondes. Sans besoins, et peu pressés de mettre en oeuvre leurs brillantes facultés et leur expérience de vos consciences. Quels hommes mûrs! Des yeux hébétés à la façon de la nuit d'été, rouges et noirs, tricolores, d'acier piqué d'étoiles d'or; des facies déformés, plombés, blêmis, incendiés; des enrouements folâtres! La démarche cruelle des oripeaux! — Il y a quelques jeunes, — comment regarderaient-ils Chérubin? — pourvus de voix effrayantes et de quelques ressources dangereuses. On les envoie prendre du dos en ville, affublés d'un *luxe* dégoûtant.

[Very tough types. Several have exploited your worlds. Without needs and hardly eager to put to use their brilliant faculties and their experience with your consciences. What mature men! Eyes lethargic as a summer night, red and black, tricolored, of steel studded with golden stars. Deformed features, leaden, livid, burnt out; joking hoarse voices! The cruel gait of spangles! There are some young ones—what would they think of Cherubino?—gifted with frightening voices and a few dangerous skills. They are sent to strut around town, got up with disgusting luxury.]

The *vous* to whom the poem is addressed is clearly what Rimbaud calls elsewhere "les êtres actuels," whereas the invaders belong to a superior race sufficiently detached from moral concerns as to be able to understand and manipulate the mechanism of conscience in ordinary men. Totally independent of normal needs, their lives consist of one long mythic spectacle of dangerous power. In their ravaged faces can be read the depths of their experience, which cannot but surpass that of their audience. Since the organizing metaphor of "Parade" is that of a band of itinerant entertainers, the second paragraph puts them on stage:

O le plus violent Paradis de la grimace enragée! Pas de comparaison avec vos Fakirs et les autres bouffonneries scéniques. Dans des costumes improvisés avec le goût du mauvais rêve ils jouent des complaintes, des tragédies de malandrins et de demidieux spirituels comme l'histoire ou les religions ne l'ont jamais été. Chinois, Hottentots, bohémiens, niais, hyènes, Molochs, vieilles démences, démons sinistres, ils mêlent les tours populaires, maternels, avec les poses et les tendresses bestiales. Ils interpréteraient des pièces nouvelles et des chansons "bonnes filles." Maîtres jongleurs, ils transforment le lieu et

les personnes et usent de la comédie magnétique. Les
yeux flambent, le sang chante, les os s'élargissent, les
larmes et des filets rouges ruissellent. Leur raillerie
ou leur terreur dure une minute, ou des mois entiers.

[Oh the most violent Paradise of furious grimaces!
No comparison with your Fakirs and other stage buf-
foonery. In costumes improvised in the style of bad
dreams they play sad ballads, tragedies about ma-
rauders and demigods wittier than history or religions
have ever been. Chinese, Hottentots, gypsies, fools,
hyenas, Molochs, old lunatics, sinister demons, they
mingle popular, maternal ways with bestial postures
and caresses. They might interpret new plays and
Nice-Nelly songs. Master jugglers, they transform the
surroundings and people and use magnetic comedy.
Their eyes flame, their blood sings, their bones
broaden, tears stream from their blood-shot eyes.
Their jeers or their terror last a minute or whole
months.]

A fabulous theater where all time and place can come
together is one of Rimbaud's favorite conceptions in the
Illuminations; "Soir historique" promised for the future
one such interminable spectacle, and "Parade" pursues
this vision. Here, however, it is the actors who retain our
attention as much as the play: they have a curiously self-
sufficient, narcissistic, or hermaphroditic character, and
in retrospect we realize how much of the eroticism in the
poems we have already read seems solitary or at least un-
directed toward a clear object. The poet of "Jeunesse"
and "Angoisse," the genie, the bodies of "Solde," even the
narrator of "Matinée d'ivresse" seek or have attained a
state of sensual satisfaction which is subjective in character and either does not take account of or does not imply
a partner. The more we study the eroticism in the *Illumi-*

nations, the more *l'amour réinventé* comes to resemble an
actual biological change, whose analogue can only be
found in the ancient myths of hermaphroditic or sexually
self-contained beings. These actors with their protean
shifts from motherliness to bestiality, from sentiment to
savagery, are complete in themselves.

"J'ai seul la clef de cette parade sauvage." "I *alone . . . ,*"
exclaims the narrator at the climax of the spectacle, where
the actors fix their magnetic stare on the audience and
make time and place shift and vanish. The exasperated
tension between the poet and the present world, which
has been implicit in many of the poems we have examined,
assumes a particular intensity in "Parade." Here the poet's
œuvre does not "rise in the masses" as in "Jeunesse," and
there is no exterior objective force arousing revelation as
in "Génie." The emphasis shifts in "Parade" toward the
poet's *private* initiation into a transformed world. The
introduction of this conflict between resistant reality and
personal vision gives a peculiar mordant character to certain *Illuminations.* "Vies," for example, does not look
forward to a future, like most of the poems we have considered, but back to the past. The changing of life is no
longer in question: the breach between the poet and mankind is too wide. "Vies" is too long to quote in entirety,
but the conclusion gives some taste of its rich implicit
ironies:

> Dans un grenier où je fus enfermé à douze ans j'ai
> connu le monde, j'ai illustré la comédie humaine. . . .
> A quelque fête de nuit dans une cité du Nord, j'ai
> rencontré toutes les femmes des anciens peintres. Dans
> un vieux passage à Paris on m'a enseigné les sciences
> classiques. Dans une magnifique demeure cernée par
> l'Orient entier j'ai accompli mon immense oeuvre et
> passé mon illustre retraite. J'ai brassé mon sang. Mon
> devoir m'est remis. Il ne faut même plus songer à

cela. Je suis réellement d'outre-tombe, et pas de commissions.

[In an attic where I was shut up at the age of twelve I came to know the world, I illustrated the human comedy. . . . At some nighttime celebration in a northern city I met all the women in the old masters. In an old passageway in Paris I was taught the classical sciences. In a magnificent dwelling surrounded by the entire Orient I accomplished my vast work and spent my illustrious retirement. I grew restive. I have been charged with another task. I mustn't think any more of all that. I am really from beyond the tomb, and no messages transmitted.]

There are striking parallels here with the closing chapter of *Une Saison en enfer:* the summing up of past triumphs and the anticipation of a new *devoir.* But these resemblances are merely superficial: "Vies" is not philosophical and dialectic; its force comes solely from the dramatic situation and the particular character of the speaker. The contrast between his world and "yours" creates an implicit criticism of the latter, which is qualified however by our realization that the speaker's magic is vain: it has remained subjective, incapable of leaving any trace in the world and has only served to cut him off from reality. "J'attends de devenir un très méchant fou," he remarks earlier.

The boastful tone of "Vies" is another form of that irony which Rimbaud usually employs in his poems on magic and the supernatural and which lends so distinctive a tone to the *Illuminations.* One constantly senses in the poems we have examined a certain self-consciousness of the speaker about his subject. Odd, ambiguous closing sentences are a frequent sign of it. It is as if the very way Rimbaud's imagination worked, with its tendency toward the mythic and enormous, inspired diffidence in him and an urge toward a sardonic redress of the balance between reality and imagination. This autocritical process constitutes a kind of arraignment of poetry as Rimbaud understood it, for he was nurtured on romantic conceptions of the primacy of the imagination and the Word as forces in life. As he pushed these notions to an extreme and became absorbed above all in visionary modes of poetry, the tension he felt between the Word and the world, between the domains of imagination and real possibilities, seems to have become more acute and to have produced a tart, ironic undercurrent seldom completely absent from his verse. More than other poets, he apparently felt the conflict between the power of poetry and the crushing presence of ordinary experience to be a problem which could not be ignored even in the very texture of poems. Certain other late nineteenth-century writers happily embraced forms of philosophical idealism which affirmed the sole reality of art, but such was not Rimbaud's case, and he devoted one of his most finished poems to the subject of the inaccessibility of the essential, imagery realm.

"Conte" is the only fable among the *Illuminations,* and its style is unique; "Conte" describes, from a detached, third-person point of view, an attempt to achieve a higher state of love and knowledge, the changing of life:

> Un Prince était vexé de ne s'être employé jamais qu'à la perfection des générosités vulgaires. Il prévoyait d'étonnantes révolutions de l'amour, et soupçonnait ses femmes de pouvoir mieux que cette complaisance agrémentée de ciel et de luxe. Il voulait voir la vérité, l'heure du désir et de la satisfaction essentiels. Que ce fût ou non une aberration de piété, il voulut. Il possédait au moins un assez large pouvoir humain.
>
> Toutes les femmes qui l'avaient connu furent assassinées. Quel saccage du jardin de la beauté! Sous

le sabre, elles le bénirent. Il n'en commanda point de
nouvelles. — Les femmes réapparurent. . . .

   Il s'amusa à égorger les bêtes de luxe. Il fit flamber
les palais. Il se ruait sur les gens et les taillait en
pièces. — La foule, les toits d'or, les belles bêtes
existaient encore.

[A Prince was vexed that he had never exerted himself save toward the furthering of vulgar benevolence.
He anticipated remarkable revolutions in love, and
suspected his wives of being capable of more than
mere willingness enhanced with paradise and luxury.
He wanted to see Truth, the hour of essential desire
and assuagement. Whether or not this was aberrant
piety, he remained adamant. He did enjoy at least
rather broad terrestrial powers. All the women who
had known him were assassinated. What rapine in
the garden of Beauty! Under the sword they blessed
him. He did not order any new ones. The women
reappeared. . . . He amused himself by slaughtering
expensive pets. He burnt down palaces. He rushed
on people and sliced them into pieces. The populace,
the golden roofs, the pure-bred animals still existed.]

The urbanity of the prose with its elegant expressions,
incisive rhythms, and concision of statement contrasts
drolly with the violent subject. The chronicler's attitude
resembles that of some sophisticated and skeptical eighteenth-century *philosophe* who has chosen to discourse
upon human folly. He notes with laconic amusement and
satisfaction the inability of the prince to destroy the world
by himself—the resistance of reality to metaphysics. The
conclusion of the poem maintains the same *distinction*
of tone, while indulging, after the fashion of Voltaire, in
lurid sexual innuendoes and witty misuse of the language
of causality:

Un soir il galopait fièrement. Un Génie apparut, d'une beauté ineffable, inavouable même. De sa physionomie et de son maintien ressortait la promesse d'un amour multiple et complexe! d'un bonheur indicible, insupportable même! Le Prince et le Génie s'anéantirent probablement dans la santé essentielle. Comment n'auraient-ils pas pu en mourir? Ensemble donc ils moururent.

Mais ce Prince décéda, dans son palais, à un âge ordinaire. Le Prince était le Génie. Le Génie était le Prince.

La musique savante manque à notre désir.

[One evening he was haughtily riding. A Genie appeared whose beauty was indescribable, unmentionable even. His features and bearing gave promise of a manifold, complex love! Of an unspeakable happiness, an unbearable one even! The Prince and the Genie were doubtless annihilated in an act of essential salubrity. How could they not have died of it? Together therefore they died. But the Prince passed away in his palace at an ordinary age. The Prince was the Genie. The Genie was the Prince. The sweetest music is not up to our desires.]

The prevalence of narcissistic eroticism in the *Illuminations* has already been remarked: here, the relation between the prince and the genie becomes the symbol of the imagination attempting to transform life and succeeding only in turning in on itself. "Conte" is a remarkable example of how Rimbaud manipulates his recurrent themes in the *Illuminations,* shifting their modality and obtaining new resonances from them. *L'amour réinventé,* the ecstatic revelation of "Génie" and "Matinée d'ivresse," here becomes the vehicle of his most melancholy irony. By a change of perspective from lyrical solipsism to the narrative conventions of the apologue, the exalted figments of the imagination come to serve as a criticism of that faculty: the inherent fallaciousness of *l'amour réinventé,* its irrelevance to biological reality, is made clear. "Conte" is a perfect embodiment of Rimbaud's simultaneous tendencies toward lyrical creation and the destruction of all elevated feeling. As such it illuminates the often cryptic thrusts of irony elsewhere in the *Illuminations.* Finally the mocking return of a musical metaphor —the usual accompaniment to visions of the changing of life—further emphasizes the relation of "Conte" to the poems we have previously considered.

The *Illuminations,* like all of Rimbaud's later work, are built of mythic, poetic conceptions, and it is not really profitable to grope for the "transpositions of reality" or sources, which have so often been sought in them. The most useful way in which to analyze such symbolic poems is through a consideration of their shape, their dominant terms, and the analogies they offer with similar pieces of writing. Thus, in examining these eleven poems, we have attempted to point out certain words and conceptions which, in various combinations and with varying degrees of emphasis, relate a group of *Illuminations.* We have explored the different resonances which the word love bears: idealistic and fraternal, tranquilly voluptuous, or violent and bestial. Likewise Rimbaud's vision of a future race ranges from the exalted one common in humanitarian myth to a more sinister conception of a superman. The term which we have borrowed from *Une Saison en enfer* to describe the common thematic impetus of these poems is "changing life," which is another ambivalent idea with suggestions in turn of building and renewal or of destruction and extinction. *Œuvre,* with its connotation of all manner of work from the poet's to the mason's, is again a key word whose meaning shifts delicately according to context and which resists any univocal interpretation.

Magic can be called the means toward the changing of life, but the concept of magic for Rimbaud is so rich as to include both apocalyptics and mere spectacle. Finally, we have observed the peculiar character of the irony present in these poems. They are not concerned, like *Une Saison en enfer,* with the dialectic of the spirit trapped in a certain moment of history, but with the processes of the poetic, visionary faculty. Their irony is not that of the soul and body condemned to annihilation despite itself, but the drama of the gratuitous life which is that of the imagination when it must be confronted with material realities. Whereas the narrator of *Une Saison en enfer* contemplates actual death, the poet of the *Illuminations* is beset by intimations of failing powers of vision and the insentient existence to which he must return. The nervous, acid mood we have so often encountered derives from this sense of impending impotence, of the ebbing away of poetry.

Rimbaud's imagination is not systematic, and even the related poems we have studied do not "mean" anything as a collection. His repeated use of certain terms is an aid in clarifying many passages, but we must not pretend that his vocabulary always has a constant value or that one poem specifically refers to something in another, as if they constituted a story or even a proper cycle. They only complement one another in a limited fashion, and even the transformation of the world around which we have organized our discussion is merely a convenient expression which lacks nuance and should not be taken as an indication of a clear plan or project on Rimbaud's part. The order in which we have examined these *Illuminations* is, of course, merely a critical expedient, and we have purposely omitted certain relevant poems which would have demanded excessive tangential commentary. Thus in "Barbare" there is a passage about assassins which brings to mind "Matinée d'ivresse" but which did not suit the needs of our analysis. Another poem, "Mouvement," develops the imagery of great migrations found in "Solde," "Génie," and elsewhere. Again, "Ouvriers," despite its realistic narrative convention, has a certain correspondence with "Angoisse." It is not our purpose, however, to exhaust the *Illuminations,* but simply to indicate a way of reading them. It would be unwieldy to pursue further the interrelations, echoes, and analogies which connect various *Illuminations.* The nature of this poetry should by now be evident, and one need only approach the problem with method and discretion. Since the *Illuminations* are also important as individual experiments in the form of the prose poem, we must now turn our attention to Rimbaud's contribution to the development of this genre and his place in the history of it.

7. *Illuminations* II: The Form of the Prose Poem

IN French literature, the origins of the prose poem and the concomitant debate over "poetic prose" can be traced back at least as far as the end of the seventeenth century and Fénelon's *Télémaque,* but the genre as such is a product of the romantic period.[1] Several factors contributed to its rise: on the theoretical level, the notion of poetry had become divorced somewhat from that of verse form, and poetry was not considered to be an objective quality so much as a range of emotions evoked in the reader. Chateaubriand, the greatest literary figure of the opening years of the nineteenth century, had shown by his practice that a high order of lyricism could be created with the materials of mere prose, and to his example was added that of prose translations of ancient or foreign poems. The romantic period saw the publication of numerous translations of unfamiliar German, English, and Spanish works, and prose renderings were accepted as perfectly valid; Chateaubriand's *Paradise Lost* (1835) and Gérard de Nerval's *Faust* (1828) are characteristic prose versions. However it was not until 1842 that there appeared Aloysius

1. The best account of the history of the prose poem is S. Bernard, *Le Poème en prose de Baudelaire jusqu'à nos jours* (Paris, 1959).

Bertrand's *Gaspard de la nuit,* which is usually recognized as the first real collection of prose poems, and it had no significant successor before Baudelaire's *Spleen de Paris* (1869).

The form of the prose poem presented a problem which both Bertrand and Baudelaire were obliged to face and solve. Bertrand wanted his short accounts of medieval life to be something other than mere prose fragments like notes or jottings, and so divided them into "stanzas" with occasional refrains and other repetitions as unifying elements. This pattern is apparently derived from prose translations of foreign ballads or other stanzaic poems; "L'Alchimiste" will serve as an example of it:

> Rien encore! — Et vainement ai-je feuilleté pendant trois jours et trois nuits, aux blafardes lueurs de la lampe, les livres hermétiques de Raymond Lulle.
>
> Non, rien, si ce n'est, avec le sifflement de la cornue étincelante, les rires moqueurs d'une salamandre qui se fait un jeu de troubler mes méditations.
>
> .   .   .   .
>
> Et la cornue toujours plus étincelante siffle le même air que le diable, quand Saint Eloi lui tenaille le nez dans sa forge.
>
> Mais rien encore! — Et pendant trois autres jours et trois autres nuits, je feuilletterai, aux blafardes lueurs de la lampe, les livres hermétiques de Raymond Lulle!

Bertrand's book was sufficiently original to attract the admiration of Baudelaire and others, but it is not difficult to perceive how limited his conception of the prose poem is. The stanzaic divisions are imposed from without and have no correspondence to the poem's meaning; whereas in verse, stanzas hold together the poem by virtue of meter and rime, here they serve no function other than to distinguish the lines for the eye from ordinary prose. Likewise the framing line is a purely mechanical device which, in the absence of rime, loses much of its melodic value.

Though Baudelaire expressed the desire to emulate Bertrand in *Le Spleen de Paris,* he actually modified the nature of the prose poem by including in his work a number of pieces whose form owes nothing to the earlier poet's "ballads." "L'Etranger" suggests the character of Baudelaire's innovations:

> — Qu'aimes-tu le mieux, homme énigmatique, dis? ton père, ta mère, ta soeur ou ton frère?
> — Je n'ai ni père, ni mère, ni soeur, ni frère.
> — Tes amis?
> — Vous vous servez là d'une parole dont le sens m'est resté jusqu'à ce jour inconnu.
> — Ta patrie?
> — J'ignore sous quelle latitude elle est située.
> — La Beauté?
> — Je l'aimerais volontiers, déesse et immortelle.
> — L'or?
> — Je le hais comme vous haïssez Dieu.
> — Eh! qu'aimes-tu donc, extraordinaire étranger?
> — J'aime les nuages... les nuages qui passent... là-bas... les merveilleux nuages!

No artificial divisions borrowed from verse occur here: the form of the poem is shaped by its content, like that of any well-constructed paragraph. The strength of "L'Etranger," as of many of Baudelaire's prose poems, comes from its density, ellipsis, and implications. Baudelaire exploits the gift for dramatic situation evident in his verse and has no need to embellish his writing with factitious indications that it is different from normal prose. It may seem idle and unfair to compare so great a writer with a minor one, but the contrast between genuine dramatic conceptions and mere descriptiveness dominates the history of the prose poem in the nineteenth century.

The prose poem thus had two distinct tendencies by 1869, when Rimbaud began his poetic career. *Le Spleen de Paris* had just been revealed in its posthumous entirety, and some of the literary men whom Rimbaud was to come to know in Paris—Verlaine, Cros, Forain—began soon after to imitate it.[2] We cannot be certain precisely when or how Rimbaud got the notion of working in this form, but he had certainly tried it by the spring of 1872.[3] However, aside from *Une Saison en enfer* and the *Illuminations,* only six prose works remain: an odd fantasy entitled "Prologue," which was evidently written in childhood; a speech of Charles d'Orléans in favor of clemency for the imprisoned François Villon, which was a school exercise in spring 1870; a first-person story of schooldays, "Un Coeur sous une soutane"; a political satire relative to events of spring 1871, the "Lettre du baron de Petde-chèvre," whose attribution is not absolutely confirmed; some fragments called "Déserts de l'amour"; and the passages imitated from the Gospel, which we have mentioned in connection with *Une Saison en enfer.* The form and structure of these works does not demand any particular consideration, but their texture does: most of them are parodies, pastiches, or otherwise allusive in style. Furthermore they are cast for the most part in the first person. It is evident that from the beginning Rimbaud's gift for prose was to a large extent a dramatic one: characters in situation interest him. Even in the Gospel narratives, the implicit contrast in language between Rimbaud's version and the ancient text puts the speaker's

2. Bernard, p. 350.
3. See Chapter 5, note 1.

attitude and view of the world in distinct relief. A particularly fine example of Rimbaud's sensitivity to levels and areas of linguistic usage is "Un Coeur sous une soutane." The narrator is both a romantic poet and a pustular seminarian, mystically devout and chastely in love with a certain Thimothina Labinette, to whom he composes litanies full of *stellae maris* and *turres Davidicae*. The density of allusion to nineteenth-century manners and middle-class, provincial, pious milieus makes it impossible to quote adequately from these "intimités d'un séminariste" in the course of our discussion, but the text can be studied with great profit; in it Rimbaud reveals himself the equal of Flaubert in singling out the right *idée reçue* or cliché to characterize each speaker.

The style of *Une Saison en enfer* again reflects a narrator's voice, but so complex a one in its mythic and ironic modulations that this poem cannot really be compared with the earlier prose works. What we should note here about the language of *Une Saison en enfer* is its clear break with the traditional measures and sentence patterns of French prose; for this long monologue Rimbaud devised a new flow of speech in which sentences and fragmentary expressions are bound together in an idiosyncratic punctuation of dashes, suspension points, semicolons, and so forth. Exclamations, questions, and imperative expressions abound;[4] endless repetitions of *je* and *et* violate the consecrated rhetorical principles of French prose, and occasional rime adds a note of cacophony which was specifically condemned by stylists. When we compare the rough drafts of *Une Saison en enfer* which have been preserved with the finished version, we see that Rimbaud did not even plot his prose in sentences but

4. For the imperative in *Une Saison en enfer* see F. Scarfe, "A Stylistic Interpretation of Rimbaud," *Archivum Linguisticum*, 3, fasc. 2 (1951), 186–92.

rather in clusters of key words, with little syntactic *liaison.*[5]

This brief account of Rimbaud's early prose and *Une Saison en enfer* together with our previous occasional remarks on stylistic variety in the *Illuminations* should make one thing clear: we cannot properly speak of Rimbaud's style (in the singular) any more than we can of Joyce's. His conception of style was an entirely new one and has no analogue in the great French prose writers before him. For Rimbaud a style is a system suited to a specific poetic conception, and not an author's characteristic mode of expression. Though we know that the language varies among the novels of Stendhal or Flaubert, we can still talk without much difficulty of abstractions which we call their styles. In the case of Rimbaud, however, we are obliged, if we wish to be accurate, to speak of the style of this or that specific poem. While we readily recognize certain words or kinds of images for which he shows great predilection, it is impossible to reduce the grammatical and prosodic patterns of his poems to any system, and therein lies the key to his conception of the prose poem. The latter is free not only of all customary rhetorical principles but also from any systematic peculiarities of the poet, and in this way it differentiates itself from ordinary prose. Even when, as in "Conte" or "Vagabonds," Rimbaud follows the accepted canons of French style, one senses that he is doing so in order to achieve an unusual effect: the normalcy of this prose becomes an experiment and a distinctive device.

Although we cannot establish a general pattern in the styles of the *Illuminations,* we can point out certain aspects of style on which Rimbaud's attention frequently focussed, and which are considerably exploited in this or

5. See Bernard, pp. 167–70, and J. Rivière, *Rimbaud* (Paris, 1930), p. 209.

that poem. Paragraphing, isolation of words, repetition, inspissation of imagery, and allusive forms are among the most important of them and will constitute the principal topics of our analysis. "Barbare" illustrates the possibilities of separating phrases on the space of the page, a device which Bertrand had already used, though probably without realizing the significance of it. The title seems to have its original sense of strange and foreign rather than that of cruel, and the poem evokes, in terms which recall other *Illuminations,* a timeless state in a symbolically remote spot:

> Bien après les jours et les saisons, et les êtres et les pays,
>
> Le pavillon en viande saignante sur la soie des mers et des fleurs arctiques; (elles n'existent pas.)
>
> Remis des vieilles fanfares d'héroïsme — qui nous attaquent encore le coeur et la tête — loin des anciens assassins —
>
> Oh! Le pavillon en viande saignante sur la soie des mers et des fleurs arctiques; (elles n'existent pas.)
>
> Douceurs!
>
> Les brasiers, pleuvant aux rafales de givre, — Douceurs! — les feux à la pluie du vent de diamants jetée par le coeur terrestre éternellement carbonisé pour nous. — O monde! —
>
> (Loin des vieilles retraites et des vieilles flammes, qu'on entend, qu'on sent,)
>
> Les brasiers et les écumes. La musique, virement des gouffres et choc des glaçons aux astres.
>
> O Douceurs, ô monde, ô musique! Et là, les formes, les sueurs, les chevelures et les yeux, flottant. Et

les larmes blanches, bouillantes, — ô douceurs! — et la
voix féminine arrivée au fond des volcans et des grottes
arctiques.

Le pavillon...

[Long after the days and seasons, and the creatures
and countries, the pavilion of bloody meat on the
silk of seas and arctic flowers. (They don't exist.)
Recovered from the old fanfares of heroism—which
still attack our heart and head—far from the old
assassins—Oh! the pavilion of bloody meat on the
silk of seas and arctic flowers. (They don't exist.)
Sweetness! Embers raining in blasts of frost—Sweetness!—Flames in the rain of diamond-wind, cast by
our terrestrial heart, eternally charred.—Oh world!—
(Far from old haunts and old loves, which we hear
and feel.) The embers and foam. Music, the revolution of abysses and the impact of ice-drifts on stars.
Oh Sweetness, oh world, oh music! And there: forms,
exudations, hair, and eyes floating. And boiling white
tears—oh sweetness—and the feminine voice in the
depths of volcanoes and arctic caves. The pavilion . . .]

The odder images are not too difficult to justify: the pavilion or tent of red meat, besides its exotic splendor,
suggests warmth and softness (*douceur*) and comfortable
isolation. The seascape and sky, to which words like
"brasiers," "chevelures," "formes," "larmes," and so forth
apply, are described in terms of a play of light and forms
rather than as static contours—one suspects some in-
debtedness for the marine setting to Baudelaire's "Vie
antérieure." The diamond into which the poet's heart
has been incinerated recalls the association of love and
gems in "Angoisse," and eyes in the sea is an image already
found in "Le Bateau ivre." The choice of the arctic setting
(which Rimbaud with characteristic irony calls nonex-

istent) is important insofar as it is symbolic of spiritual elevation. The pole is the top of the world and, in a naïve cosmology, the part of the globe most exposed to the heavens and light. The poet has abandoned the life of the assassin and old loves (one senses the contrasting relation between "Barbare" and "Matinée d'ivresse") and receives the revelation of one of those deity-like presences in which the *Illuminations* are rich: the feminine voice he hears has not erotic connotations so much as epiphanic ones.

Our principal concern, however, is the shape of "Barbare." Rimbaud was one of the first writers (Flaubert and Mallarmé were others) to realize the importance of typographical disposition as an indication of rhythm: the movement of "Barbare" has nothing to do with sentences, for there is not a main verb in the whole poem, but depends on the blanks, the space which isolates these floating phrases. This arrangement is not really comparable in effect to the mechanical "stanza" divisions of Bertrand and his imitators, for the latter are so regular as to fail to emphasize. Rimbaud, on the other hand, manages to suggest a pattern of emotive and vocal stresses by his paragraphing. (His peculiar punctuation also contributes towards this: as in *Une Saison en enfer,* he gives back to the too familiar signs their proper value as phonetic indications.) One of Bertrand's techniques is preserved: repetition, which seems to be an almost inevitable formal recourse in the absence of verse or the sentence structure of prose, and Rimbaud exploits it fully. "Barbare" even takes on a cyclical character, like many poems with refrain: the final repetition of "Le pavillon" with its suspension periods suggests a *da capo* movement.

Although "Barbare" is an exceptionally beautiful poem, one cannot help but realize the limitations of its form: if Rimbaud's techniques are far more sophisticated than Bertrand's, his materials are nevertheless similar in the end. However, with the sole structural devices of spacing and repetition Rimbaud created some truly astonishing poems, whose essential sameness is by no means obvious. The middle sections of "Enfance" in particular are most virtuoso examples of what can be done with patterns of repetition and variation. First a family in the country is evoked, all of whose members are dead, departing, or absent:

II

C'est elle, la petite morte, derrière les rosiers. — La jeune maman trépassée descend le perron. — La calèche du cousin crie sur le sable. — Le petit frère (il est aux Indes!) là, devant le couchant, sur le pré d'oeillets. — Les vieux qu'on a enterrés tout droits dans le rempart aux giroflées.

[It's she, the little dead girl, behind the rosebushes. The deceased young mother comes down the steps. The cousin's carriage screeches on the sand. The little brother (he's in the Indies!) there, against the sunset, in the carnation field. The old people who were buried upright in the bank of gillyflowers.]

The poem continues developing images of absence, which, paradoxically and by its oppressiveness, becomes a presence, a force. As before, short, simple sentences contribute a note of naïveté and quietness to the style and allow us to focus our entire attention on what is *not happening:*

L'essaim des feuilles d'or entoure la maison du général. Ils sont dans le midi. — On suit la route rouge pour arriver à l'auberge vide. Le château est à vendre; les persiennes sont détachées. — Le curé aura emporté la clef de l'église. — Autour du parc, les loges des gardes sont inhabitées. Les palissades sont si hautes qu'on ne voit que les cimes bruissantes. D'ailleurs il n'y a rien à voir là-dedans.

Les prés remontent aux hameaux sans coqs, sans enclumes. L'écluse est levée. O les calvaires et les moulins du désert, les îles et les meules!

[The swarm of golden leaves surrounds the general's house. They are in the South. You follow the red road to get to the empty inn. The manor house is for sale; the shutters are removed. The parish priest must have taken away the church key. Around the park the gamekeepers' lodges are uninhabited. The fences are so high you can only see the rustling tree tops. Anyway, there's nothing to see inside. The meadows stretch up to hamlets without roosters or anvils. The sluice-gate is raised. Oh the crosses and mills in the wilderness, the islands and haystacks!]

These lines are an exercise in the manifold ways of expressing negation, from implication to grammatical form. With repetitions of elementary sentence patterns and images which, though brilliantly varied, all express vacancy, the haunting sense of solitude reaches the dimensions of a kind of expectation. The tension is relieved in the final paragraph, where, with a daring shift of tense, absence is replaced by presence, as if the vacuum created by the disappearance of man automatically filled itself with a new kind of being:

Des fleurs magiques bourdonnaient. Les talus le berçaient. Des bêtes d'une élégance fabuleuse circulaient. Les nuées s'amassaient sur la haute mer faite d'une éternité de chaudes larmes.

[Magic flowers were droning. The slopes lulled him. Fabulously elegant animals moved about. Heavy clouds piled up on the high sea made of an eternity of warm tears.]

The bold switch to the imperfect tense has the effect of intensifying the presence and duration of the flowers and animals. The preceding present tenses have, by and large, a neutral, vague aspect with which the protracting imperfect vividly contrasts, for the latter, alone among French tenses, can indicate unmistakably the extended presence of an action. However, since the imperfect has, besides its peculiar aspect of prolongation, a reference to past time, Rimbaud also shifts the narration to the third person. In the previous paragraphs, although no *je* occurs, the point of view is first-person; with the introduction of the pronoun *le* the narrator suddenly becomes objective. By changing persons as well as time-reference and verbal aspect, Rimbaud makes the continuity of the poem clearer: we see that the narrative has simply altered in mode but not in subject. It is difficult to imagine a more elegant manipulation of grammar.

The repetitions of "Enfance" II concern mainly sentence form and type of imagery. In the third section of the poem, a justly famous one, verbal parallels occur of the sort classical rhetoric called anaphora:

III

Au bois il y a un oiseau, son chant vous arrête et vous fait rougir.

Il y a une horloge qui ne sonne pas.

Il y a une fondrière avec un nid de bêtes blanches.

Il y a une cathédrale qui descend et un lac qui monte.

Il y a une petite voiture abandonnée dans le taillis, ou qui descend le sentier en courant, enrubannée.

Il y a une troupe de petits comédiens en costumes, aperçus sur la route à travers la lisière du bois.

Il y a enfin, quand l'on a faim et soif, quelqu'un qui vous chasse.

[In the wood there is a bird. Its song stops you and makes you blush. There is a clock that does not strike. There is a crevice with a nest of white animals. There is a cathedral that goes down and a lake that goes up. There is a little carriage abandoned in the thicket or running down the path with ribbons on it. There is a troop of tiny comedians in costumes you glimpse through the edge of the wood on the road. Finally, when you are hungry and thirsty, there is someone to chase you away.]

The landscape is similar to that of "Enfance" ii and the theme is again that of the child's relation to being, but even more than in the preceding section the animate and inanimate fuse together into sheer presence. Here the hallucination of human absence yields to the feeling of ubiquitous consciousness. But in contrast to the foregoing section "Enfance" iii ends with the intrusion of a hostile reality: the world of men.

The three middle sections of "Enfance" contain an exceptionally subtle modulation of pronouns: although the point of view is, with the exception noted above, that of the first person, *on* and *vous* are substituted for *je* until the fourth part, giving the usual pronoun a very dramatic character when it finally appears after so much postponement:

IV

Je suis le saint, en prière sur la terrasse, — comme les bêtes pacifiques paissent jusqu'à la mer de Palestine.

Je suis le savant au fauteuil sombre. Les branches et la pluie se jettent à la croisée de la bibliothèque.

Je suis le piéton de la grand'route par les bois nains; la rumeur des écluses couvre mes pas. Je vois longtemps la mélancolique lessive d'or du couchant.

Je serais bien l'enfant abandonné sur la jetée partie
à la haute mer, le petit valet suivant l'allée dont le
front touche le ciel.

Les sentiers sont âpres. Les monticules se couvrent
de genêts. L'air est immobile. Que les oiseaux et les
sources sont loin! Ce ne peut être que la fin du monde,
en avançant.

[I am the saint praying on the terrace, as the peaceful herds graze as far as the sea of Palestine. I am
the savant in a dark armchair. Branches and rain
flail the window of my library. I am the wayfarer on
the highway through the dwarf woods. The roar of
sluice-gates drowns out my step. I see for a long time
the melancholy gold wetwash in the west. I could
be the child forgotten on the pier drifting toward
the high sea, the little page going along the tree-
lined walk whose top touches the sky. The paths are
rough. Broom is covering the hills. The air is motionless. How far away the birds and springs are! It can
only be the end of the world ahead.]

The first two lines stress, besides aloneness, the privileged
character of the poet's experience and establish a relation
between prayer and knowledge, which are journeys into
intangible realms, and the walk which is the subject of
the rest of the passage. The fantasy of reaching the end
of the world is one of those mythic cosmological notions
of which we have already seen an example in "Barbare"
and to which Rimbaud's imagination was especially sensi-
tive. To render it he chooses images of the sun setting in
the west, the sky slanting down like the ceiling of an attic,
and stunted plant life. "Enfance" IV carries farther than
the preceding sections the movement of isolation: here
the narrator perceives real nothingness about him, which
Rimbaud manages to convey by images that imply dimi-
nution. The constant mention of water, which we associ-

ate with expanses so vast as to seem empty and with
ceaseless movement toward unknown endpoints, contributes also to the feeling of ebbing reality and imminent
vacuity.

In "Villes," which we shall now turn to, the device of
repetition is again used, but the movement of the poem
is entirely different from that of "Enfance" by reason of
its lack of paragraphing and spacing. "Ce sont des villes,"
cries the poet, and proceeds to describe them in terms
reminiscent of the "future nocturnal luxury" we mentioned in the previous chapter. The following extract is
characteristic:

> C'est un peuple pour qui se sont montés ces Alle-
> ghanys et ces Libans de rêve! Des chalets de cristal
> et de bois qui se meuvent sur des rails et des poulies
> invisibles. Les vieux cratères ceints de colosses et
> de palmiers de cuivre rugissent mélodieusement dans
> les feux. Des fêtes amoureuses sonnent sur les canaux
> pendus derrière les chalets. La chasse des carillons
> crie dans les gorges. Des corporations de chanteurs
> géants accourent dans des vêtements et des oriflammes
> éclatants comme la lumière des cimes.
>
> .   .   .   .
>
> Quels bons bras, quelle belle heure me rendront
> cette région d'où viennent mes sommeils et mes
> moindres mouvements?
>
> [For a people these dream Alleghenies and Lebanons
> were built! Crystal and wood chalets moving on rails
> and invisible pulleys. Old craters bordered by colossi
> and copper palm trees roar melodiously in the fire.
> Love celebrations sound on the canals hung behind
> the chalets. The carillons' hunting party screams in
> the gorges. Corporations of giant singers rush up in
> garments and oriflammes as brilliant as the light on

the peaks. . . . What warm arms, what fine hour will
bring me back to this place, which provides me with
my dreams and slightest movements?]

The devices holding together this cascade of images, which
in themselves have been sufficiently accounted for in our
discussion of "Soir historique," are not difficult to analyze:
virtually every sentence contains words indicating place
and movement or sound. Furthermore, simple sentence
structures predominate. The sequence has so much sameness and lack of development or direction that Rimbaud
is obliged to stop it by the blank alexandrine distich of
the final sentence (most mute *e*'s should be dropped). The
formal and orotund movement of the latter has a closed
character, even though rime is lacking, and effectively
halts the relentless preceding rhythm. However, in contrast to the elements of regularity in sentence form, there
is a certain discontinuity of sense: these lines do not build
up any picture that conforms to real space. Some commentators, inspired by the term *Illuminations,* have analyzed "Ville" and similar poems in terms of visual perception and have tried to ascertain how Rimbaud arrived at
a result so remote from ordinary descriptive writing.[6]
The relation of poetry to the pictorial is an exceedingly
delicate matter, like the relation of a writer's experience
to his work, and I do not believe it is a very fruitful topic
of inquiry in regard to Rimbaud. The contradictions and
inconsistencies of the spatial imagery of "Villes" stem,
to my mind, from Rimbaud's attempt to create density,
a more complicated weight of meanings than prose
normally bears. However, the impression of complexity
risks being counterbalanced by one of mannerism.
"Ponts," "Métropolitain," the second "Villes," "Promontoire," and "Scènes" all have the same accumulation of
conflicting visual indications as "Villes," though with

6. See especially Bernard, pp. 177–211.

less systematic sentence structure, and a reading of them in close succession leaves one with a feeling of mechanicalness. Indeed Rimbaud's crowding of images into massive blocks seems to me one of his less successful experiments, and there are poems (among them "Jeunesse" II, which we have examined) where the striving for density degenerates into chaos and nonsense.

The effect of congestion and accumulation in "Villes" is intensified by the lack of paragraphing or spacing, the devices which give lightness and radiance to poems like "Barbare" or "Enfance." The eye influences one's sense of rhythm, and one has the impression that the prose of "Villes" is exceedingly heavy—a feeling that is increased by the difficulty with which one takes in all the chaotic imagery. As a matter of fact, however, "Villes" is not rhythmically sluggish, but some of Rimbaud's other urban descriptions are. The verb often disappears and the resultant predominance of nouns is ponderous; sentences become freighted with endless subordinate elements (cf. "Promontoire") or else vanish in an underbrush of verbiage (cf. "Métropolitain"). Striking phrases here and there redeem these poems—which further suffer from sameness of imagery—but it is impossible to count them among Rimbaud's finest achievements. We must beware as much of thinking of the *Illuminations* as a collection of even quality as we must take care not to assume they all derive from a common inspiration.

The new tendencies we have observed in Rimbaud's handling of the prose poem—the isolation of images in detached lines or short irregular paragraphs and the creation of abnormally dense blocks of prose—account in a general way for his innovations, but at least three poems demand special comment. In the last chapter we remarked in passing on the peculiarities of "Conte," which is a fable, and "Solde," which is patterned on a sale announcement. One other *Illumination,* "Dévotion," uses an allusive form that deserves attention. The echoes which this curious and difficult text evokes in the reader's mind are from Villon's *Lais* and *Testament,* works Rimbaud had studied at school in 1870:

A ma soeur Louise Vanaen de Voringhem : — Sa cornette bleue tournée à la mer du Nord. — Pour les naufragés.

A ma soeur Léonie Aubois d'Ashby. Baou — l'herbe d'été bourdonnante et puante. — Pour la fièvre des mères et des enfants.

A Lulu, — démon — qui a conservé un goût pour les oratoires du temps des Amies et de son éducation incomplète. Pour les hommes! A madame***.

A l'adolescent que je fus. A ce saint vieillard, ermitage ou mission.

A l'esprit des pauvres. Et à un très haut clergé.

Aussi bien à tout culte en telle place de culte mémoriale et parmi tels événements qu'il faille se rendre, suivant les aspirations du moment ou bien notre propre vice sérieux.

Ce soir à Circeto des hautes glaces, grasse comme le poisson, et enluminée comme les dix mois de la nuit rouge, — (son coeur ambre et skunks), — pour ma seule prière muette comme ces régions de nuit et précédant des bravoures plus violentes que ce chaos polaire.

A tout prix et avec tous les airs, même dans des voyages métaphysiques. — Mais plus *alors.*[7]

[To my sister Louise Vanaen de Voringhem: her blue cornet turned toward the North Sea.—For the ship-wrecked. To my sister Léonie Aubois d'Ashby. Bow! —humming, stinking summer grass. For mothers' and

7. I have amended "spunk" to "skunks," which is a common furrier's term in French and which the editors of the Pléiade edition prefer. The other reading, however, is quite as defensible.

children's fevers. To Lulu—a demon—who has kept a taste for private chapels from the period of The Friends and her imperfect education. For men! To Madame X. To the adolescent I was. To this holy elder, a hermitage or mission. To the spirit of the poor. And to a very high clergy. As well, to any worship in so memorial a place of worship and amid such events that one must accept it, following the aspirations of the moment or else our own serious weakness. This evening at Circeto of the high ice, oily as fish, illuminated like the ten months of the red night (its heart amber and skunk fur) as my sole prayer silent as these night regions and preceding a burst of intrepidness more violent than this polar chaos. At any cost and with any accompaniment, even in metaphysical flights—but no more, *afterwards*.]

Villon's poems consist of a series of bequests, frequently ironic or cryptic, and include, after the fashion of wills, an indication of the place and time of signing. They are a summing up of his moral experience of the world by one about to depart in death or travels. Rimbaud adopts Villon's scheme of listing inheritors with certain remarks about the use the bequest is to be put to (the formula *à—pour—*, the bequest itself being usually omitted), but at the same time he assimilates the form to a kind of elliptic prayer: the title "Dévotion" has almost exclusively a religious sense in French, though the word does not lack ironic and pejorative connotations. The general subject of this act of devotion is worship itself and the poet's experience of it. The first two bequests are obscure, like so many of Villon's, and the odd ring of the ladies' names may be an imitation of the medieval poet's quaintness. Both women are "sisters"—the ecclesiastical meaning is doubtless the correct one here, since Louise Vanaen wears the cornet of the Sisters of Charity—and both seem engaged in some kind of succor. The "humming, stinking grass" recalls a phrase of "La Chanson de la plus haute tour," a poem dealing with spiritual aspirations, but I do not think we should insist that Rimbaud is referring precisely to his own earlier work. In contrast to the good-working sisters, the third legatee, with her demonic love of religiosity, is clearly a representative of the Christian-Satanic sensibility so lengthily portrayed in *Une Saison en enfer*. Her education is incomplete because she remains in a backward stage of spiritual development. "Amies" suggests the lay associations prevalent in Roman Catholic countries, and "pour les hommes" hardly needs comment.

With the fourth paragraph we become more sharply aware of the dividing time point in which the poet writes: the old man appears to be his future self in contrast to the adolescent. This mention of himself is clarified as the poem proceeds: he is doing homage to his own religious experience as well as to that of others—to any cult, as a matter of fact, which suits the circumstances, however durable or valid it may be. The irony of the poem emerges here more clearly, as we realize that all spiritual aspirations, benevolent, demonic, and otherwise, receive equal tribute.

A passage which I take to be the dating of the will follows. Circeto seems to me to designate a place, with *à* changing in sense, as it also does somewhat punningly in the last line. The North Pole is evoked; amber, which comes from northern shores, and skunk fur, which Rimbaud probably associated with cold climates, are joined with the mention of a lengthy night like that of the polar circle, in which odd light—the aurora borealis—is seen. The significance of this arctic imagery is, as I have earlier indicated, that the pole is a supreme vantage-point from which to survey the world lying beneath one's feet, a symbolically proper spot for one about to take leave of the life he has known.

The time point is again emphasized: this moment of prayer will yield to some ominous and violent change in the poet. He concedes in the last paragraph his readiness for the metaphysical flights of religion at the present, but "no more *afterwards.*" This insistence on a time point between now and transformation is, of course, characteristic of the *Illuminations,* and "Dévotion" is connected with the cycle of metamorphosis poems in the tangential way the latter relate to one another.

From this short survey of formal elements in the *Illuminations* it should be apparent that Rimbaud went very far toward investigating all the possible devices by which short prose poems could distinguish themselves from fragments of ordinary prose. Both in typographical disposition and in more strictly linguistic invention, the *Illuminations* anticipate the great flowering of the prose poem in twentieth-century French literature without, for that, being merely archaic prototypes. Indeed, one may legitimately question whether the prose poem since Rimbaud has, save on rare occasions, ever approached his mastery of the form. Too often it has been treated as a vehicle for vague impressions or meditations phrased in undistinguished language or lacking structural coherence. Proust's youthful prose poems in *Les Plaisirs et les jours* are typical in this respect: they are the production of a writer with a taste for languorous prose but who does not yet know how to subordinate it to a design, to a total effect. In a somewhat different way, the many fine phrases and richly textured passages that Gide would publish when he had no more serious project betoken the same unsuccessful striving after a short but finished poem in prose. And one has only to glance at French literary reviews of today to realize how strong the obsession with the prose poem still is. Rimbaud's example remains a dangerous and provocative one.

The historical importance of Rimbaud, however, does not lie primarily in his influence on later writers: his ties with Claudel, with surrealism, and with other movements are much-touted but largely factitious, or at least sufficiently limited as not to overimpress the impartial observer.[8] Lesser writers do not hesitate to place themselves under his aegis, but one senses that they are usually acting more under the spell of that "myth of Rimbaud" which M. Etiemble so denounces than from any technical concern with his poetry. For Rimbaud was a nineteenth-century romantic poet, and the initial significance of his work is not to be grasped without reference to a specific historical context.

To begin with, Rimbaud's poetry is, from the formal standpoint, a kind of microcosm of nineteenth-century verse. From Hugo to the *vers-libristes* and the prose poets, the history of French poetry is closely tied up with problems of prosody: there was a prolonged, perhaps submerged, but nevertheless present crisis over the inadequacy and narrow range of the instrument inherited from the neo-classical period.[9] The peculiar rapidity with which Rimbaud's talent evolved allows us to appreciate in the work of one poet many of the stages—rhetorical verse, colloquial language, stanzaic forms, *vers libérés*, prose poem—through which French poetry passed during this period, as well as to sense the real urgency of the question of versification for a late nineteenth-century poet. From the standpoint of prosodic variety Rimbaud's work is probably more interesting than that of any other French poet, and for this reason it offers numerous basic

8. An interesting essay on this problem is F. Petralia, *Le Rimbaud de Claudel*, Langues Vivantes, No. 49 (Brussels, 1956).

9. The malaise provoked by the linguistic archaism and rigidity of French versification is reflected in a vast number of somewhat bizarre nineteenth-century theories of prosody. See Y. Le Hir, *Esthétique et structure du vers français* (Paris, 1956), pp. 109–75.

lessons in esthetics which are essential to understanding the history of French verse.

Skill at prosody however is not in itself enough to raise a poet's work to the first rank; even more than as a technician of French verse, Rimbaud occupies one of the most significant places in nineteenth-century literature for the degree to which his work sums up vital spiritual preoccupations of the period. By virtue again of his eclecticism and the accelerated development of his thought, Rimbaud's poetry encompasses the most widely divergent non-orthodox religious philosophies of his time; from Satanism to the spiritual evolution of humanity, from pantheism to the redemption of the individual, from occultist notions of language to Paganism, much of the farrago of contemporary reactions against Christianity marked his writing. But more important than the facts of influence on him is the synthesis which Rimbaud achieved of such disparate elements in the last verse poems, *Une Saison en enfer,* or the *Illuminations.* From the beginning of the nineteenth century, poets had aspired to create works of vast philosophical implications, but insufficiency of means continually doomed them to failure. The usual problem was a hopelessly expository approach to language, an inability to bridge the gap between idea and symbol, abstract conception and poetic embodiment. The heritage of neo-classicism weighed heavy despite theoretical refusals of it. The first French poet who succeeded in overcoming this problem was Hugo, but unfortunately the poems in which he went farthest in achieving a new metaphysical vision, symbolically rendered and unmediated by discursive language, were never finished. *Dieu* and *La Fin de Satan* remained unpublished until after his death. Rimbaud was working in a much-attempted area of poetry when he composed his poems of 1872 and after, but his success is perhaps unique. In Rimbaud's later work there is no conceptual framework that protrudes, even in the case of *Une Saison en enfer,* where a genuine dialectic pattern can be abstracted from the poem; there is no tension between idea and expression. From "Le Bateau ivre" to the *Illuminations* we have observed that Rimbaud's poetry does not need keys or make reference to things outside itself; it can only be interpreted by exploring the relations among its parts. This harmonious mode of imagination is what we have called Rimbaud's mythopoeia, his ability to conceive poems as symbolic structures, whose meaning is one with their shape and detail, and it is this achievement which determines his essentiality to French literature.

Index

Works cited, except Rimbaud's own, are entered under the name of the author.